Letting God

Create Your Day

Volume 6
Paul A. Bartz

CREATION MOMENTS

Letting God Create Your Day: Volume 6
By Paul A. Bartz

Copyright © 2010 Creation Moments, Inc.

Creation Moments, Inc.
P.O. Box 839 Foley, Minnesota 56329
www.creationmoments.com
800-422-4253

ISBN 1-882510-19-4

Printed in the United States of America
Printing and production costs for this book were underwritten by supporters of Creation Moments.

Foreword

No one needs to be reminded that science and technology are moving forward with dizzying speed. There are even new scientific disciplines and technologies that didn't exist a couple of decades ago. With all of this growth, many disciplines have even subdivided themselves into specialty niches. This is often because knowledge is growing so fast that it becomes more difficult to stay on top of what was once accepted as a single scientific discipline.

Who, a generation ago, talked about plant defenses or plant behavior? Or intelligent-seeming behavior by bacteria? Did you know that there are still twenty million cave people living in the world today? Or have you heard about the moths that try to outsmart bats? Did you know that there is a hummingbird that flies faster than a reentering Space Shuttle, relative to body length?

Yet, every one of these glorifies our Creator as they show forth His handiwork or dispel some evolutionary myth.

Then there are so many things that people "know" that simply aren't so. Primary among these, of course, is evolution. But there are many other things that people "know" that aren't so that piggyback on evolution. The first that comes to mind is that we can understand the creation in which we live without including God in our thinking. Another is that if there is a God, He is not intimately involved in His creation in an ongoing sense. Or that when it comes to our future, we are on our own.

What we know about these things must be informed by Scripture. And that knowledge will influence how we deal with still more issues ... such as climate change. How that knowledge influences what we believe will color how we look at such issues as whether it's possible that a giant asteroid will wipe out all life on Earth. In short, when you stare into a universe without God, it becomes a terrifying place. Looking at eternity without God is even more terrifying.

That's why we want to go beyond intelligent design. The fact that God is Creator and involved in His creation naturally

3

leads to some additional questions. What is His mind toward the creation? What is His mind toward us? Answers to such questions – and many more – are ultimately found in the Bible. God's power and might are seen in the stars and in volcanoes. But that He is merciful can only be learned from God's Word. God's wisdom can be seen in the design of the hand. But His victory over sin, death and the devil are seen in the pierced hands of His Son, Jesus Christ. We must go to His Word to learn how this victory is ours.

We rejoice to commend this book for your edification and for the glory of God.

Paul A. Bartz
Author, Creation Moments™

Gecko Physics

Hebrews 3:4
"For every house is built by someone, but He who built all things is God."

For 75 years, scientists have been trying to figure out how the gecko can walk across a ceiling. Scientists ruled out suction or glue. Then it was thought that perhaps the tiny hairs on its feet were able to grasp microscopic imperfections in the surface on which it walks. However, the gecko can not only walk across a polished glass ceiling, it can even hang by just one toe.

Geckos have tiny hairs on their feet called setae. From these tiny hairs grow even tinier hairs called spatulae. These spatulae are so tiny that there are about a billion of them on each foot. Researchers have found that these tiniest hairs are so small that they contact the molecules of a surface so closely that they actually use the very forces that hold the molecules together! Scientists have tested the strength of these forces, called van der Waals forces, for the first time. They found that these forces are much more powerful than first thought. As the gecko walks across a surface, it unrolls its toes, bringing the spatulae into contact with the surface. Then it gives a tiny tug that aligns the spatulae parallel to the surface, increasing their hold by 10 times. As the gecko lifts its foot for the next step, it levers the spatulae off the surface, breaking the bond. Based on this research on the gecko's trick, scientists are working to develop glues based on the same principle.

While geckos and chance evolution know nothing about van der Waals bonds, the Creator Who made them both has left His signature in this unique and elegant design.

Prayer: Lord, help me to bear witness to Your wisdom and love. Amen.

Ref: *Science News*, 7/15/00, p. 47, "Gecko toes tap intermolecular bonds."

Attentive Parents Give a Lasting Gift

Titus 2:4
"...that they admonish the young women to love their husbands, to love their children...."

It should be obvious that attentive parents are a blessing to their children. However, as we look around us, we see too many examples of inattentive parenting. Now scientists in Canada have experimentally demonstrated one of the benefits of attentive parenting.

Researchers divided 32 female rats into two groups. One group was made up of naturally attentive mothers who paid a great deal of attention to their newborns. The other group was made up of mothers that were careless and inattentive to their newborns' needs. Once the young rats were grown, they were tested for memory and intelligence. They were placed in a swimming maze that required them to find a submerged platform in the tank. On the first day, all the rats did about the same. But on the second day, and for the rest of their lives, the rats whose mothers had paid attention to them scored much higher. Researchers found that the rats who were carefully nurtured had extra connections in the part of their brains called the hippocampus and had more receptors for a neurotransmitter important for learning. These features of the brain form during the first days after birth. In short, a caring mother spurs brain development that benefits the child for the rest of its life. Researchers say that since human development is similar, attentive human mothers give their children a lifelong gift.

Children are a great gift and trust we receive from God. Now science has shown us one of the ways parents can bless their children for life.

Prayer: Dear Father in heaven, give us loving, attentive parents. Amen.

Ref: *Minneapolis Star Tribune*, 7/23/00, p. E5, "Nurturing, intelligence linked."

Was Noah a Brain Surgeon?

Genesis 50:2
"And Joseph commanded his servants the physicians to embalm his father. So the physicians embalmed Israel."

Most of us were amazed when we first learned that physicians in ancient Egypt did brain surgery. Even more amazing is that the skulls of their patients showed *healing*; they accomplished such complicated surgery without killing their patients. That physicians had the knowledge to do such delicate operations thousands of years ago challenges the modern, evolutionary view that humans began as primitives.

Where did such knowledge come from? How did man learn that relieving fluid pressure on an injured brain prevented further damage and promoted healing? Obviously, according to the modern view, the first would-be physician to try brain surgery had no idea what he was doing. However, history paints a very different picture. Recently, archaeologists in west central China discovered a skull of someone who had brain surgery over 4,000 years ago. A large hole in the center of a series of cracks had been made by scraping through the bone. The skull shows that healing took place after the surgery, indicating some degree of success. Even older examples of successful brain surgery have also been found in eastern Europe. Creationist dating would place these examples to within several centuries after the Flood.

That the knowledge and skill to do successful brain surgery was so widespread so long ago suggests that man had such knowledge and skill even before the Flood. Noah may even have passed on knowledge that had been passed down to him from Adam himself!

Prayer: Thank You, Lord, for the blessings of medical knowledge. Amen.

Ref: Discovering Archaeology (online), 3-4/00, "Cranial Surgery in Neolithic China."

Those Clever Siberian Chipmunks

Psalm 7:10
"My defense is of God, Who saves the upright in heart."

Siberian chipmunks are pretty low on the food chain. Everything from snakes to foxes seek out a chipmunk meal. However, Siberian chipmunks are very clever at using one of their enemies to defend themselves. If a Siberian chipmunk discovers a dead snake, it will be understandably careful in making sure that it is dead. Once it is certain, the chipmunk will chew on the dead snake's skin. Then, in behavior naturalists call "self-anointing," the chipmunk applies the chewed snake skin to its coat. The chipmunks will also self-anoint with snake urine and feces. Field studies showed that while the chipmunks ignore the carcasses of frogs, birds or lizards, they will self-anoint in this way from four species of snake.

Further field observations explained the reason for this strange behavior. Snakes are less likely to eat an anointed chipmunk. The snake odor on the chipmunk may also deter other animals that feed on the chipmunks. The chipmunks' defense strategy raises some difficult questions for those who believe that the living world is a product of chance. How could these chipmunks figure out that coating themselves with the skin of their mortal enemy would protect them from that enemy?

The task of developing this strategy and then overcoming its natural fear to approach that enemy, albeit dead, seems far too large for a chipmunk's mind. However, it is a small and simple task for the Creator Who made all things and taught the chipmunks to protect themselves. That same God protects us from that old serpent, the devil, through His Son, Jesus Christ.

Prayer: Dear Father, help me to daily put on Christ to have Your protection. Amen.

Ref: *Bombardier Beetles and Fever Trees*, p. 51.

Eating Your Way to a Better Mood

Psalm 27:1
"The LORD is my light and my salvation; whom shall I fear? The LORD is the strength of my life; Of whom shall I be afraid?"

Dutch researchers have concluded that you can indeed eat your way to a better mood. It's not how much you eat, and in some cases the secret is what you don't eat. But if you are easily frustrated and stressed, you may be able to avoid these moods.

Dutch researchers were investigating tryptophan, which the brain uses to make serotonin, a neurotransmitter that improves your mood. They prepared two chocolate drinks, one that contained a milk protein rich in tryptophan and another with casein, another milk protein. Volunteers who had been pre-evaluated for their susceptibility for stress drank one or the other of these with breakfast and again later in the morning. At mid-day, the volunteers spent 20 minutes at a computer doing math problems as loud industrial noise blared in the background. Researchers then evaluated each subject's mood, pulse rate, stress hormones and brain serotonin levels. None of the subjects who had the tryptophan-rich chocolate drink showed any stress factor, no matter how prone to stress they naturally were. Other research has shown that sugar or starch-rich foods also raise serotonin in the brain. Researchers concluded that simple diet modifications that include tryptophan prior to expected times of stress can help the average person respond to stress. They also warn that meat protein blocks the brain's absorption of tryptophan.

While we can cast all our fears and frustrations on the Lord, it is good to know that He has provided us with a way to better cope with nagging, daily stress.

Prayer: Lord, I cast all my cares on You for You care for me. Amen.

Ref: *Science News*, 7/8/00, p. 23, "Stress-prone? Altering the diet may help."

How to Set a Scientist Humming

Genesis 2:20a
*"So Adam gave names to all cattle, to the birds of the air,
and to every beast of the field."*

For over a century, textbooks have used the Galapagos Island finches as an example of evolution in action. The facts are that the differences between these finches are less than the differences in the human population – and nobody claims that we are evolving!

A lesser-known example of evolution in action was recently challenged in the scientific literature concerning certain hummingbirds found on the island of St. Lucia in the Caribbean. For a long time it was claimed that one species of hummingbird was diverging and becoming another species. However, it now turns out that the birds were nothing more than the male and the female of the same species! The male of the species has a relatively straight bill perfectly designed to allow efficient feeding of the nectar from the red and orange blooms of a flower related to the bird of paradise. The female bird, on the other hand, has a longer, sharply curved bill that is perfect for feeding on the green flowers of a different plant, also related to the bird of paradise.

Those who believe in evolution point to such differences and argue that it is the environment that has caused these differences to develop. The creationist would certainly agree but point out that those variations are strictly limited. Giving one of these variations another species name does not make it a different species and thus cannot be used as evidence for evolution in action. Again, to use the human example, humans come in different colors but no one now applies different names or claims that we are evolving.

Prayer: Lord, help me understand how Your hand is revealed in Your creation. Amen.

Ref: *Science News*, 7/22/00, pp. 52-53, "Flowers, not flirting, makes sexes differ."

Don't Be Fooled by the Illusions of the Sinful World

Jeremiah 7:24
*"Yet they did not obey or incline their ear, but walked in
the counsels and in the imagination of their evil heart, and
went backward and not forward."*

Everyone knows the answer to the old question: Which is
heavier, a pound of feathers or a pound of lead? Yet the first time
most of us were asked, we wanted to answer that it was the pound
of lead. Researchers may have discovered why we naturally think
the pound of lead is heavier.

Canadian researchers used a size-weight illusion that has
been fooling people for over a century. It uses two boxes of
identical weight, even though one is twice the size of the other.
Subjects usually expect the larger box to be heavier, so they apply
more effort to lift it. After lifting each box five or ten times,
subjects learn to lift each box with the same effort. Nevertheless,
they now believe that the smaller box is heavier. Researchers
found that the knowledge of how hard to grip something and how
much force is needed to lift it is processed in one part of the brain.
But the estimation of an object's weight is processed in a different
part of the brain. That part of the brain processes thoughts based
on our expectations. While these two parts of the brain
communicate, it appears they don't share everything. The result is
the illusion that the smaller box is heavier.

Our expectations color how we interpret the world around
us. This is why scientists who believe in evolution often cannot see
the clear evidence of the Creator. Because our perceptions are
tainted by sin, we need the additional corrective of God's revealed
Word.

*Prayer: Lord, do not let me be misled by the illusions of
the sinful world. Amen.*

Ref: *Science News*, 6/24/00, p. 407, "Hands, not eyes, hold clue to illusion."

Another Cost of Divorce

Matthew 19:6
"So then, they are no longer two but one flesh. Therefore what God has joined together, let not man separate."

The Bible teaches that marriage is one man and one woman, united into one flesh for life. Traditional morality has reflected this view. However, modern Western culture has viewed divorce as a freedom that should be available to everyone. The popular term "no-fault divorce" attempts to give the impression that divorce has few consequences. Two recent studies, however, clearly show the real cost of divorce.

Researchers with the Oregon Social Learning Center studied the effects of divorce on adolescents. They examined the behavior of junior high and high school males. They found that boys from families where there had been a divorce were much more likely to experiment early with sex than boys whose parents had never divorced. Another study by a sociologist at the University of Wisconsin in Madison looked at the effects divorce has on young women. The study tracked the behavior of nearly 4,000 young women. He found that young women from divorced marriages were much more likely to have babies out of wedlock than those from families untouched by divorce. Both studies show that one cost of divorce is a casual attitude toward sex on the part of children of divorced parents.

When God gave us marriage in the Garden of Eden, He intended it to be a lifelong union. While divorce brings heartbreak to the adults involved, God also knew that children of a divorce would follow the example of their parents in taking the gift of sex too lightly.

Prayer: Lord, thank You for the gift of marriage. Help me always honor it. Amen.

Ref: *Minnesota Christian Chronicle*, 7/6/00, p. 19, "Stable, two-parent families produce the healthiest kids."

Cicada Racket Is Designed

Psalm 19:1a, 4a
"The heavens declare the glory of God.... Their line has gone out through all the earth, and their words to the end of the world."

While the call of the cicada sounds like raucous chaos to us, researchers have only just learned that these amazing creatures have a complicated system of communication. Cicada beetles live underground for 13 to 17 years before emerging to live a few brief weeks to sing and mate before they die.

Immature cicadas feed off the fluids flowing through tree roots. One acre of ground can have as many as 400 pounds of immature cicadas beneath its surface. Once out of the ground, cicadas molt into their final adult form and, after a few days, are ready to begin mating. At this point they have only four to six weeks to mate before they die. Males begin their call to find a suitable female. The males rasping call ends by slurring into a lower pitch. Then he listens. If a female is interested she will make a click with her wings. The male responds and after several successful conversations, the male changes his style. If the female responds to this change with more clicks, the female will allow him to mate. Eggs are laid in the twigs. After they hatch, the hatchlings fall to the ground and begin burrowing to start the life cycle again.

While the racket made by cicadas sounds like random noise to us, it is a complex communication system that follows set rules. Complex systems of communication can only be the product of an intelligent Designer, the very Creator God that is revealed in the Bible.

Prayer: Thank You, dear Father, for the gift of communication. Amen.

Ref: *Science News*, 6/24/00, pp. 408-410, "Cicada Subtleties."

Scientists Admit Bankruptcy of Big Bang Theory

Genesis 1:1
"In the beginning God created the heavens and the earth."

A young student once asked Martin Luther what God was doing before He made the creation. Luther is said to have responded by telling the young man, "He was making switches to use on children who ask foolish questions." Now some evolutionary physicists are asking what the universe was like before the big bang.

Traditional big bang theorists have always said that there was nothing before the big bang. However, all evolutionary physicists know that the big bang theory has some major problems. For instance, in the earliest moments of the big bang, theory says that the universe would have had an infinite density and temperature. Another problem is that no known physics applies to these earliest moments of the universe. A physicist with the European Laboratory for Particle Physics has proposed that the universe did exist a long time before the big bang. He theorizes that it was just large enough so that it was not infinite in temperature or density and about one sixteenth of an inch across. He further theorizes that the universe existed for a long time in this condition. He describes the pre-big bang universe as being in the simplest state that you could imagine, a condition he calls "the state of triviality." Traditional physicists point out, however, that this new theory is also filled with unprovable assumptions.

The real lesson here is that neither the big bang theory nor any other theory that we can conceive can account for the universe. Only God's hand can explain the universe we see.

Prayer: I praise You, Lord, for Your Word is always trustworthy. Amen.

Ref: *New Scientist,* 6/3/00, pp. 24-27, "Before the Big Bang."

Human Lie Detectors

Exodus 20:16
"You shall not bear false witness against your neighbor."

Many people have wondered at the abilities of savants. These are people who have very low intelligence, yet they can do seemingly impossible mental tasks. Some savants have been able to instantly name the day of the week when given any date within the last 6,000 years. Others have been able to instantly give a correct solution to tedious mathematical calculations. Could such abilities reflect a throwback to the mental abilities the human race once had?

New research suggests another ability that man may have been created with, but most of us have lost: the ability to detect when we are being lied to. Researchers suspect that people with brain damage that limits their ability to understand speech might be superior at detecting lies. Such people, who have damage to the left hemisphere of their brain, are called aphasics. The study included aphasics who could understand individual words, but not sentences. The study group also included undergraduate students. They were all shown a videotape of 10 people, each appearing in two segments. In one segment, each person lied, while in another, the person told the truth. The undergraduates did no better than chance would allow at detecting lies. However, the aphasics could accurately detect a lie almost two-thirds of the time!

Were we created with the ability to detect when we are being lied to? Such ability surely doesn't arise by chance but is rather a God-given gift for our protection.

Prayer: Lord, help me to always honor the truth in my speech. Amen.

Ref: *Nature*, 5/11/00, p. 139, "Lie detection and language comprehension."

Cyanide for Breakfast?

Acts 8:23
"For I see that you are poisoned by bitterness and bound by iniquity."

Tropical passion vines have a unique defense against insects that would nibble on their leaves. Its leaves contain sealed packets of cyanide that are made inactive by being linked with sugar molecules. There are other sealed packets with an enzyme that releases the sugar molecules, activating the cyanide. When an insect chews on the leaves, both packets are broken, the cyanide is activated and another predator is gone.

However, the caterpillar of the tropical butterfly Heliconius sara can munch away happily on the leaves, oblivious to the cyanide, apparently immune to the powerful poison. Scientists wondered why these caterpillars didn't die. They found out that the caterpillar has an enzyme that prevents the release of the cyanide. This enzyme changes the cyanide to a harmless sulfur-based chemical before the leaf's enzyme can cause the cyanide to be released. However, the caterpillar still has to be careful because some vines grow special defensive hairs that can impale an unwary caterpillar.

Evolutionists would have us believe that these caterpillars, by trial and error, evolved the ability to neutralize the cyanide. Even if we were to grant the ridiculous idea that caterpillars are smart enough to do this, this explanation still doesn't work. Any caterpillar that would munch the passion leaves would face instant death without a chance to experiment or reproduce. However, the Creator of all chemistry has once again demonstrated His existence by this obvious and clever relationship.

Prayer: Dear Father, remove any poison of bitterness from my heart. Amen.

Ref: *Science News*, 7/22/00, p. 59, "How butterflies can eat cyanide."

The Oracle of Delphi Was More than a Legend

Jeremiah 29:9
"For they prophesy falsely to you in My name; I have not sent them, says the LORD."

New archaeological evidence supports the factuality of the Greek legend about the prophet or oracle of Delphi.

According to legend, the site where the oracle would prophesy was discovered thousands of years ago by a goat herder. He found that his goats acted strangely at a crack or fissure in the rock. As he investigated the fissure, he breathed some of the fumes coming from it and was said to enter a prophetic state. Around 140 B.C. a temple was built over the fissure. Its centerpiece was a platform built over the fissure where, for nearly 2,000 years, the oracle would speak forth. Modern researchers considered the legend nothing more than a myth. However, now geologists have found that two geological faults pass right beneath the temple site. They analyzed a calcium-rich rock called travertine deposited on the temple walls by a natural spring. Tiny bubbles in the travertine were filled with methane and ethane gas that can have small narcotic effects. Further, ethylene, which can bring about a dreamlike state, is still released by a nearby spring.

The idea that the ancients were gullible simpletons who easily accepted fantastic stories stems from evolution. Evolution claims that man has evolved upwards, eradicating the myths of his ancestors through science. The fact is the theory of evolution is the worst of all possible myths and stands in the way of truth.

Prayer: Lord, never let me be misled from Your truth by false prophets. Amen.

Ref: *National Post Online*, "The oracle of Delphi - high on ethylene?"

Why Creation Science Is Science

Exodus 20:11a
"For in six days the LORD made the heavens and the earth, the sea, and all that is in them, and rested the seventh day...."

Two of the most basic requirements of the scientific method are that scientific theories must be testable and able to predict future discoveries. Evolutionary scientists say that creationism is not scientific because it fails these requirements.

Their claims, however, are without merit. For example, creation scientist Dr. Russell Humphries made several predictions about future findings in a paper published in a scientific journal in 1984. He began with the biblical description of the Earth and the planets having been created roughly six thousand years ago and that in the beginning all the planets had a magnetic field. Based on the rate that the Earth's magnetic field is decaying, small planets like Mercury and Mars should have no magnetic field left. However, the strong fields they had at their creation should be recorded in their rocks. He also predicted the strengths of the magnetic fields of Uranus and Neptune. Later, Voyager II confirmed his predictions. Now, the Mars Global Surveyor has confirmed that the rocks of Mars do record a strong magnetic field in the past, just as predicted.

While these findings support the Bible's repeated insistence that the creation is young, they provide us with another lesson. As in the past, there are still scientists who believe in creation, who publish scientific papers and even live to see their theoretical predictions confirmed.

Prayer: Dear Father, continue to bless the work of creation scientists. Amen.

Ref: *Creation Matters* (CRS), 5-6/99, p. 8, "Mars Global Surveyor Confirms Creation!"

How Big Is the Largest Living Organism?

Psalm 77:14
*"You are the God who does wonders; You have declared
Your strength among the peoples."*

How big is the largest living organism on Earth? We all
know that the giant Redwoods of California grow larger than any
whale. However, there are other living organisms that dwarf even
the Redwoods.

The mushrooms that spring up in your yard or the forest
are actually only the fruit-bearing part of a larger fungus. The main
part of the fungus exists as a mass of filaments that grow
underground. In 1992 scientists discovered such a fungal growth in
the state of Washington and declared it to be the largest living
thing known. It covered 1,500 acres. The only sign of the fungus
were the golden mushrooms that popped up each fall. Despite their
common name – the honey mushroom – researchers say that while
they are edible, they don't really taste all that good. Despite its
immense size, researchers have now discovered an even larger
fungus of the same species. It extends three feet deep beneath the
Malheur National Forest in eastern Oregon. This monster,
estimated at 2,400 years old, is three-and-a-half miles across and
covers 2,200 acres! No one has taken on the hopeless job of
estimating its weight. The problem with this fungus is that as it
spreads, it kills trees. That's why the United States Forest Service
is trying to learn how to control it.

The huge dinosaurs and whales of today reflect the power
and creativity of the Creator. Likewise, this huge fungus that
produces the honey mushroom reflects the Creator's unlimited
imagination as He formed all living things.

*Prayer: Help me, dear Father, to also bear witness to
Your power and love. Amen.*

Ref: *Minneapolis Star Tribune*, 8/5/00, p. A17, "2,400-year-old Oregon fungus is largest living
organism."

"The Fountains of the Deep" Discovered!

Proverbs 8:27-28
*"When He prepared the heavens, I was there, when He
drew a circle on the face of the deep, when He established
the clouds above, when He strengthened the fountains of
the deep...."*

The Bible mentions "the fountains of the deep" several
times. We are told that God opened the fountains of the deep
during the Flood, suggesting seismic activity. When God ended the
flooding, we are told that God closed the fountains of the deep,
suggesting that they continue to exist, albeit with less water than at
creation. Now scientists say that they may have found an
astonishing reservoir of water deep in the earth.

The water they believe they have found does not exist in
huge underground oceans. The water is tied up in minerals, held
there by the tremendous pressures and temperatures deep in the
earth. Researchers have shown, for example, that a mineral called
wadslyite, which exists only at temperatures above 1800° (F) as
deep as 400 miles below the earth, can still hold water. Scientists
have figured that if 60 percent of this layer is wadslyite, as seismic
data indicate, it could contain enough water to fill 10 oceans.
Researchers have also analyzed the amount of this water that is
brought to the surface during volcanic eruptions and concluded
from their findings that there could be enough water deep in the
earth to fill 30 oceans! Because of the way the water is stored,
scientists don't expect it to all be released at once.

There are many more wonders in the creation than we
know about. That's why it is a mistake for anyone to dismiss any
of the Bible's statements about any of these wonders, all of which
testify to our Creator.

*Prayer: Thank You, Lord, for Your promise not to send
another great flood. Amen.*

Ref: *New Scientist*, 8/30/97, pp. 22-26, "Deep Waters."

Seals Show Super-Human Recognition Skills

John 10:3-5
"He calls His own sheep by name...and His sheep follow
Him because they know His voice, but they will never
follow a stranger."

Evolutionary scientists are often hard-pressed to explain human or even superhuman-like intelligence in animals. For example, let's say that you last saw your child when she was four months old. It is now four years later. Are you certain you could pick out your child in a room full of 100 four-year-old little girls?

A researcher with the National Zoological Park in Washington, D.C. has been studying the northern fur seal's amazing ability to recognize family members. Nursing mothers are the only mothers among mammals that leave their nursing pups for as long as two weeks. They return after they have fed, having no problem finding their own young among the crowded colony. When the young reach the age of four months, they begin their migration south for the winter. The next spring, the young seals migrate back to their place of birth and easily recognize their mothers. After recording the voices of more than two dozen seals, the researcher wanted to prove that recognition was taking place through the sound of an individual seal's voice. Seals who heard the playback of their mother or child's voice paid attention to the speakers, while others did not. After a year of not hearing a mother or child's voice, each seal still paid attention to the recording of its mother or child. Even after four years, mother and child recognized each others' voices.

Such memory and intelligence can only have intelligence as its source. That source is a loving Creator Who knows us even after our parents are gone.

Prayer: Thank You, dear Father, for loving to hear my voice in prayer. Amen.

Ref: *Science News*, 7/29/00, p. 69, "Mom, is that you? Seals show family recall."

Luciferin Could Lead to Glowingly Young Skin

John 8:12
"Then Jesus spoke to them again, saying, 'I am the light of the world. He who follows Me shall not walk in darkness, but have the light of life.'"

The ocean is filled with animals that can generate their own light. Even Charles Darwin admitted that his theory of evolution could not explain how this bioluminescence might have evolved. As modern evolutionists try to explain how it might have evolved, they are making some interesting practical discoveries.

Bioluminescent creatures use a variety of luciferin molecules that produce light when combined with oxygen. The result can be blue, green, bright red or violet light. Today we want to look at the most common form of luciferin. Though most bioluminescent animals use this luciferin, most of them can't make it for themselves. It apparently enters their system through their diet. However, no one knows which creature produces it. Researchers are primarily interested in its ability to combine so efficiently with oxygen. This ability allows the luciferin to deactivate free radicals. Each of us produces free radicals in the process of living. In low doses these oxidants produce aging. In large quantities they produce death. So researchers exposed cultured human cells to a fatal dose of free radicals. Then they added common luciferin. They found that even low doses cleaned up the free radicals and saved the cells. Based on what they learned, researchers hope to produce true anti-aging skin creams and cure Alzheimer's disease.

No light, including bioluminescence, has evolved. All light originates with God, including the spiritual light of His Truth.

Prayer: Lord, help me never to be led away from the light of Your Truth. Amen.

Ref: *New Scientist*, 7/22/00, pp. 34-35, "First Light."

Good Tasting Facts

Psalm 34:8
"Oh, taste and see that the LORD is good; blessed is the man Who trusts in Him!"

New research is showing that we can forget just about everything we ever learned about how we taste food. To begin with, we don't taste with our tongues, but with our brains. Remember those tongue maps that we all learned in school? They show that we taste sweet on the tips of our tongues, salt and sour flavors on the sides, and bitter tastes at the back of our tongues. In truth, research shows that we taste each of these flavors all over our tongue. And, no, those little bumps on your tongue are not taste buds. Rather, each of those bumps contains *many* taste buds. Further, the right half of your tongue does not communicate with the left half of your tongue. Each half has its own nerve that runs to the brain that interprets signals from the tongue as taste. These nerves pass right under your eardrum. That's why a virus infecting your ear can cause you to lose some ability to taste. Dental Novocaine is often administered very close to these nerves, which is why some people experience phantom tastes when the dentist gives them a shot.

Most amazing is the part that touch plays in taste. If the right half of your tongue is numbed and you drag a flavor from the right half of your tongue to the left, only the left half will taste it. However, if you drag the flavor from the left half of your tongue to the right, your brain concludes that the left half of your tongue should experience the flavor, and it does, despite being numbed.

The ability to taste flavors is a blessing from our Creator. He even invites us to Himself by urging us to taste and see that He is good.

Prayer: Thank You, Lord, for the gift of taste, for You are good. Amen.

REF.: *Discover*, 7/00, pp. 70-75, "Tourist is a taste lab."

Crustacean Invasion!

Ephesians 3:17
"That Christ may dwell on your hearts through faith; that you, being rooted and grounded in love..."

The relationships between two or more creatures are sometimes so well-designed and complex that there is no conceivable way that they could have evolved. Sacculina carcini is a microscopic crustacean that begins life as a free-swimming larva. The female first seeks out a crab for a host, then she searches for a tiny hole in the crab's leg joint. Finding one, she inserts a hollow tube through the hole and squirts a few cells that are herself into the crab, leaving most of her body behind. As she grows as a large bulge on the underside of the crab, she is also sending tendrils throughout the crab's body.

When Sacculina is ready to mate, she offers one or two pinhole openings to any available male. If a male finds her, it molts off most of itself, enters the tiny hole and fuses with the female. There they continuously fertilize eggs, producing thousands of new larvae every two weeks. At this point Sacculina is in complete control of the crab which is now unable to produce, grow or do anything other than eat. The crab even grooms its reproductive pouch that now scatters Sacculina larvae. Most amazingly, infected male crabs grow female features as well as female behaviors to help scatter Sacculina larvae even more effectively.

The complexity of this relationship surely requires a Creator that is much greater than any crustacean.

Prayer: Lord, let there be room in my life only for You and Your Word. Amen.

REF.: *Discover*, 8/00, pp. 80-85, "Do Parasites Rule the World?"

God Knows Best About Families

Exodus 20:12
"Honour thy father and thy mother: that thy days may be long upon the land which the LORD thy God giveth thee."

Traditionally, families have been considered the foundation of a culture. After God gave man marriage, He next created families – not cities – so that parents are clearly important. However, in the past few years it has become fashionable among psychologists to produce studies that supposedly show that parents are largely irrelevant to children's development.

Now a painstaking study on the Caribbean island of Dominica has documented the importance of the family. Researchers checked the cortisol levels in the saliva of the island's children for more than a decade. Cortisol levels in the saliva rise when people are under stress. High cortisol levels disable the immune system, slow growth and disrupt other healthy body functions. Not only did the researchers check the cortisol levels several times a day, but they also conversed with the children about what was going on in their lives. Even when children got into fights with one another, there was little if any rise in cortisol levels. However, even slight disruptions within the family raised cortisol levels. Based on the events that led to such rises, researchers concluded that there is nothing more important to children than a healthy two-parent family. These studies conclude that nothing is more important to children than pleasing their parents.

While this study contradicts studies that declared parents irrelevant, it does support the Bible's view of the importance of the family.

Prayer: Lord, strengthen our families so they may raise godly children. Amen.

Ref: *Discover*, 8/00, pp. 66-69, "Family Matters."

Mystery in the Highest Layer of the Sky

Amos 9:6
"It is he that buildeth his stories in the heaven...The
LORD is his name."

When the popular media announce the findings of
scientists, their conclusions generally sound quite certain. The
general public is thereby given the impression that science has the
answer to every question. The fact is, there are still many
mysteries that continue to resist scientific explanation.

When meteors hit the Earth's atmosphere, they generate
friction, get hot and normally begin to glow at an altitude of about
62 miles. Incoming meteors above a certain size can be tracked
and their speed checked by radar. When reports of meteors
beginning to glow as high as 124 miles – twice the height they
should – began coming in, scientists at first dismissed them. It is
true that the atmosphere can expand when the sun is active, but it
never expands that much. Then Russian cosmonauts and later
astronauts began reporting the too-high glow surrounding their
reentering spacecraft. During reentry one night, astronauts reported
that the glow that shouldn't have been there at all reached the
intensity of daylight! Scientists are stumped over the cause of the
glow. Some have suggested that it might have something to do
with magnetic disturbances in the ionosphere.

The Bible is our only source of absolutely certain
knowledge. Thousands of years before man learned that the
atmosphere had different layers, the Bible not only mentioned
those layers, but taught that God had designed the atmosphere to
have layers.

Prayer: Lord, help me to learn more about what Your
Word says. Amen.

Ref: www.geocities.com/CapeCanaveral/Cockpit/3240/ meteors.htm, A. Ol'khovatov.

The Wasp that Conforms a Spider to Its Will

Romans 12:2a
"And be not conformed to this world: but be ye transformed by the renewing of your mind...."

While a particular species of tropical spider is spinning its web, the female of a species of tropical wasp swoops in and paralyzes the spider with her sting. She then lays a single egg on the spider's abdomen. The spider eventually wakes up, apparently none the worse, and continues spinning her web normally for the next week or so. That's when the wasp egg hatches and the wasp larva begin to suck juices from the spider. The larva continues to grow until it is ready to spin its cocoon. At this point, the larva causes the spider to spin a twisted tent-like web instead of its normal web. When the protective tent is completed, the larva kills the spider and eats it. Then it spins its own cocoon under the protection of the tent.

Researchers wanted to find out if the wasp larva was actually causing the abnormal spider behavior. When freshly hatched larva were removed from the spider, the spider continued spinning normal webs. Researchers also removed the larva after the spider was induced to spin a tent. It spun tents for several days before going back to its regular web style.

How would a wasp evolve the ability to reprogram the spider's natural behavior to its needs? This relationship was designed by our Creator Who wishes to transform us into the image of His Son, Jesus Christ.

Prayer: Lord, help me to be conformed to Your image rather than the world's. Amen.

Ref: *Science News*, 8/12/00, p. 109, "Wasp redesigns web of doomed spider."

We Don't Know More than We Know About Dinosaurs

Matthew 14:35
"And when the men of that place had knowledge of him, they sent out into all that country round about, and brought unto him all that were diseased...."

What did dinosaurs look like? That and more are things we don't know about dinosaurs. We know so little about dinosaurs because we have so few of their fossilized bones. Professional dinosaur artists joke: "If all we knew about elephants were their bones, they would probably be reconstructed to look like giant hamsters!" Neither the trunk nor the ears have any bones.

Scientists rarely find a complete dinosaur skeleton. One recent reconstruction was based on only 40 percent of the skeleton. Then there is the question of how some species walked. They may have walked with crouched legs like an alligator or with straight legs like an elephant. We have no idea whether dinosaurs had eyes with slit pupils as do reptiles or round pupils as do birds. Nor do we know whether they could see color. If they could, it's quite possible that some dinosaurs had coloration that helped camouflage them. There are very few fossilized imprints of dinosaur skin, so we have little idea how they would appear to the eye. All this uncertainty has resulted in three very different reconstructions of the Velociraptor.

What we look like on the outside is not as important as what we are inside. When we recognize Jesus Christ as our Lord and Savior, He cleanses us from all sin and gives us eternal life.

Prayer: Dear Lord, help me to lead others to recognize You as their Savior. Amen.

Ref: *Discover*, 9/00, pp. 74-80, "What Did Dinosaurs Really Look Like...And Will We Ever Know."

What Should Science Do with Mysteries?

Colossians 1:27
"To whom God would make known what is the riches of the glory of this mystery among the Gentiles; which is Christ in you, the hope of glory...."

You're standing in a crowded room when you feel something, turn around and discover someone staring at the back of your head. Studies show that some dogs can detect when their master leaves for home and go to watch for him with 80 percent accuracy. A cat is separated from its vacationing family 800 miles from home. It turns up on its home doorstep weeks later. Unconnected fungal threads in the soil find each other and form a mushroom. These events are all mysteries investigated by researcher Rupert Sheldrake.

Doctor Sheldrake has been a research fellow with the Royal Society and has a very impressive scientific background. He says that undetectable fields may link the master and his dog or the cat and her family. He calls this phenomenon "morphic resonance." Some scientists applaud his search for answers while others scorn his suggestion of undetectable fields. He compares these fields to an effect in physics that Einstein called "spooky action at a distance." It is known that two photons or two electrons emitted by the same atom are somehow linked, even when miles apart. Theoretically, what happens to one affects the other even at the other side of the universe. Dr. Sheldrake says that science should look into these mysteries, not fear them.

There are still many mysteries, the greatest of which is God's love for us.

Prayer: I thank You, dear Father, for the mystery of Your love for me. Amen.

Ref: *Discover*, 8/00, pp. 60-65, "Heresy."

Wise Raider Ants

Proverbs 2:6
"For the LORD giveth wisdom: out of his mouth cometh knowledge and understanding."

There are more than 20 species of slavemaker ants. These ants raid the colonies of other species and carry off larvae and pupae to raise as workers in their own colonies. Some slavemaker ants kill all the adults in the raided colony, while others simply steal a few immature individuals. Researchers wanted to know what the effect slavemaker ants had on surrounding colonies of the victim species.

Scientists began with a species of slavemaker ant that is so tiny that a complete colony can live inside an acorn. They raid the colonies of even smaller species for their slaves. Some post guards at the entrance of colonies during a raid to keep the adults in the colony, some do not. These species do not kill the adults, nor do they take all the young. Scientists compared the effects of these more "humane" slavemaker ants with the more ruthless species that simply take over another colony, killing the adults and eating all the larvae. They found that the more "humane" species had little effect on surrounding colonies while ruthless species decimated surrounding colonies by 30 percent. The more "humane" slavemakers were actually being wise stewards of their potential victims.

Such wisdom did not originate in an ant's brain. Nor does wisdom arise from chance. Rather, it was programmed in these ants by an all-wise Creator.

Prayer: Fill me, Lord, with the wisdom of Your saving truth. Amen.

Ref: *Science News*, 8/19/00, p. 116, "Slavemaker Ants: Misunderstood Farmers?"

Grazing Crocodile Discovered!

Genesis 1:30
"And to every beast of the earth, and to every fowl of the air, and to every thing that creepeth upon the earth, wherein there is life, I have given every green herb for meat: and it was so."

Paleontologists recently made a totally unexpected discovery. While excavating fossils in Madagascar, they found a strange-looking, pug-nosed crocodile. Its multi-cusped teeth, similar to vegetarian ankylosaurs' and stegosaurs' teeth, show that this crocodile was also a vegetarian!

Researchers positively identified the creature as a crocodile because it had the bony plates in its skin. These plates, called osteoderms, distinguish crocodiles from dinosaurs. Scientists named the unusual new species Simosuchus. It appears that a fully-grown Simosuchus was about three feet long. It had a thicker head and neck than most crocodiles, possibly for burrowing. It resembles another extinct species discovered in Uruguay. Researchers speculated that this resemblance suggests that there was once a land bridge across the Atlantic extending from Madagascar to Uruguay.

Those who believe what the Bible says should not be surprised at this seemingly amazing discovery. The Bible teaches that before sin entered the world, all creatures were vegetarians. Once Adam and Eve sinned, death became a reality for all creatures. Some creatures obviously began adapting to eating meat, but is seems not all crocodiles became meat-eaters, as evidenced by Simosuchus. Creationists also believe that the fossils resulted from the worldwide Genesis Flood that would have mixed the remains of animals from all continents so they did not necessarily migrate to where their fossils are found.

Prayer: Lord, even though marred by sin, Your creation is wondrous. Amen.

Ref: *Discover*, 9/00, p. 16, "A Broccoli-Eating Croc?"

Sentinels from the Crypts

2 Thessalonians 3:3
"But the Lord is faithful, who shall stablish you, and keep you from evil."

Your digestive system is a marvel of design. The average adult's small intestine has a surface area the size of a football field. Its lining is constantly eroded by digestive juices, so it must be completely replaced every few days. This means that your small intestine must grow enough tissue to cover two football fields every week!

The lining is replaced every few days by the stem cells just below the lining itself. Though the small intestine provides a nice warm environment in which bacteria can thrive, the amount of bacteria in the small intestine is far less than expected. Researchers have long suspected that this intestine has some way of controlling bacterial growth. Now they have discovered that the secret lies in the tiny pits in the lining called crypts. In these crypts, under the layer of stem cells are cells called Paneth cells. These Paneth cells produce lysozyme, an enzyme that breaks down bacterial cell walls. In addition, they discovered that the Paneth cells also produce defensins, a class of proteins that have antimicrobial powers. Defensins are powerful enough to kill even the bacteria that cause food poisoning.

Our Creator has provided us with many sources of protection to make life possible. However, we must go to Jesus Christ to find spiritual protection from the devil and the eternal consequences of our sin.

Prayer: Dear Father, fill me with unfailing trust in Your promises. Amen.

Ref: *Science News*, 8/26/00, p. 135. "Tales from the crypts: Cells battle germs."

The Structure of DNA Has Not Been Left to Chance

Psalm 104:24
"O LORD, how manifold are thy works! in wisdom hast thou made them all: the earth is full of thy riches."

The DNA molecule is a marvelously designed information storage system. All the information necessary to make you is packed into a microscopic space. Even our most sophisticated methods of storing information cannot approach the efficiency of DNA. However, there is much more to appreciate about the structure of DNA.

Physicists used a computer to create virtual models of molecules. The molecules were depicted as beads connected to each other by tubes. Researchers were trying to find out the most efficient shape necessary to get as much molecule as possible into the smallest space. They then confined these virtual molecules within variously-shaped electronic containers. Researchers then had the computer wiggle and slither the molecules into different shapes within each container. They were looking for the most efficient way for the molecules to fill a given space. They discovered that the most efficient shape for a molecule is the specific helix shape found in protein molecules. Other research has shown that the double helix shape that DNA uses is likewise the most efficient way to pack as much molecule into the smallest space.

As an information storage system, DNA was clearly designed by a very wise Creator. Now we learn that DNA molecules, along with proteins, were also designed to have the most efficient shape possible – another fingerprint of our wise Creator, not a product of chance.

Prayer: Dear Father, make me wise with Your wisdom. In Jesus' Name. Amen.

Ref: *Science News*, 8/19/00, p. 125, "To pack a strand tight, make it a helix."

Spider Spit Can Be Good for You

Proverbs 17:22
"A merry heart doeth good like a medicine: but a broken spirit drieth the bones."

While extract of spider might seem like something you would find in a spooky cartoon, such compounds have a long history in medicine. Now researchers at several universities are establishing that spider venom from several species can offer mankind benefits.

Researchers at the State University of New York at Buffalo found that during a heart attack, chemical signals are released that often results in heart fibrillation that can kill the patient. These researchers then found a protein in the venom of the Chili Rose Tarantula that blocks the channels that release the chemical signals that can lead to fibrillation.

Another group of researchers at the University of Connecticut are studying the venom of the Australian funnel web spider. A compound in this venom is deadly to crickets, fruit flies and cockroaches, yet harmless to rats. Researchers are exploring the possibility of engineering a virus that would make its own version of the compound so that it infected only specific pests. The goal is to develop a form of pest control that left no pesticide residue in the environment.

In His love for mankind and His perfect knowledge of biochemistry, God not only designed a perfect creation but also provided resources to counter the effects of sin. We can be even more thankful that He sent His Son to counter the *eternal* effects of sin in our lives.

Prayer: Dear Father, I thank You for Your mercy to sinful human beings. Amen.

Ref: *Discover*, 9/00, p. 2, "Elixir of Spider Spit.."

You *Do* Have Rocks in Your Head!

Psalm 94:9
"He that planted the ear, shall he not hear? he that formed the eye, shall he not see?"

Some biological structures are so complex that evolutionary scientists say they took many millions of years to evolve. At the same time, and usually unsaid, is the fact that these structures only work in their finished form – the evolving forms would have no survival value.

In the hearing organs of your ear is the complex system that helps you keep your balance. This system is made up of fluid-filled cavities and semicircular canals that are also filled with fluid. These organs provide a constant stream of information to your brain, along with what you see and touch, to tell you where you are in space. The key to this system are calcium crystals called otoliths that literally means "ear rocks." These otoliths are held inside a gelatin-like membrane. Tilt your head to the right and gravity causes the otoliths to bump into tiny hairs that send chemical signals to your brain. If these ear rocks break loose, they bump into the wrong hairs. This results in the brain receiving signals that don't agree with what you are seeing. These conflicting signals produce vertigo.

Our elegant and precise balance system is useless to us except in its finished form. That simple fact rules out any evolutionary origin. The obvious alternative is that our balance system, along with everything else that exists, has an all-wise Creator.

Prayer: Lord, I praise You for placing Your fingerprints all over the creation. Amen.

Ref: *Minneapolis Star Tribune*, 9/24/00, p. E3, "How to stop the world from spinning."

Songs of the Sky, Sea and Mountains

Psalm 46:10
"Be still, and know that I am God: I will be exalted among the heathen, I will be exalted in the earth."

Those who live near the polar regions of the Earth are familiar with the colorful auroras that dance across the night sky. Sometimes these night shows become so intense that viewers report hearing an unearthly type of eerie music during the colorful displays. Sometimes people just report feeling something during the displays. Now, researchers using highly sensitive instruments have confirmed that these light shows can set up pressure waves in the lower atmosphere. They measured infrasound waves that begin at the very lowest level of human hearing – about 20 hertz.

Modern, sensitive equipment has been able to hear other strange sounds in the atmosphere. One example, inaudible to the human ear, is called "mountain music." Researchers using sensitive equipment have confirmed that such sounds are generated as winds blow through mountain ranges. Researchers report an increase in suicides when warm downslope winds blow. The sea, too, sings as winds pass over its surface. The "song of the sea" is sung at far lower notes than humans can hear. Since such low frequencies can carry for thousands of miles, scientists speculate that the "song of the sea" could be a blending of all the storms in the world, each storm providing its unique tones to a symphony as long as the Earth has been here.

Could these strange songs be the creation's way of praising its Creator?

Prayer: Lord, help me to praise You with my every thought, word and action. Amen.

Ref: *Science Frontiers,* Sept.-Oct., 2000, p. 4, "Listening for the Unhearable."

Cat-Loving Rats

2 John 1:7a
"For many deceivers are entered into the world, who confess not that Jesus Christ is come in the flesh."

According to evolution, given enough time protozoans can become people. Researchers have been studying a protozoan that almost seems intelligent enough to be human.

The protozoan, Toxoplasma gondii, can infect humans, but it cannot reproduce in humans. It can only reproduce in cats. However, the protozoan's strangest ability comes into play when it infects rats. Because they cannot reproduce in rats, a protozoan in a rat needs to get to a cat if it hopes to continue its kind. Rats normally avoid cats and even places that have a cat's scent. However, rats infected with this parasite not only lose their fear of cat scent, they seem to prefer the scent of cats. When a careless and infected rat is captured by a cat, the protozoan is finally in a friendly environment where it can finally reproduce.

Here we have an instance where a protozoan apparently knows the difference between cats and rats. It also knows how to change the rat's natural fear of the cat into a preference to be around cats. Evolutionists would have us believe that blind chance evolution was able to give this protozoan these amazing abilities. It takes a lot of faith to believe that. Why not simply believe that our wise Creator built this seemingly intelligent behavior into the protozoan and dismiss evolution as the lie of the greatest deceiver of all?

Prayer: Help me, Lord, never to be deceived by the devil. Amen.

Ref: *Science News*, 8/12/00, p. 109, "Parasite deludes rats into liking cats."

Mechanical Crocodiles?

Job 10:10-11
"Hast thou not poured me out as milk, and curdled me like cheese? Thou hast clothed me with skin and flesh, and hast fenced me with bones and sinews."

According to evolutionary theory, crocodiles are the most primitive creatures, predating even the dinosaur; yet scientists admit they have the most complex heart plumbing of any creature.

The heart valves of most vertebrates are opened by surging blood, and once the blood has passed, the valve closes. Crocodiles, alligators, gavials and caimans, have active heart valves consisting of cogged teeth made of connective tissue. Located just inside the valve in the right ventricle, these cogged teeth allow the valve to open or remain closed, depending on conditions. Researchers wanted to know why the crocodile's heart is designed this way, so they monitored the heart of a living animal. They treated the creature with a compound that mimics the blood chemistry of a relaxed animal. In response, the cogged teeth locked the valve closed, returning the blood to another circuit of the body, rather than to the lungs. When researchers gave the crocodile another compound to reverse the relaxed state, the cogs opened up so that the blood could get to the lungs. Scientists are not certain why the crocodile's heart can do this and have suggested it helps them stretch their oxygen supply on long dives.

The fact that the supposedly primitive crocodilians have the most complex heart of any animal does serve one known purpose. It shows the folly of placing living things in a progression from the simplest to the most complex.

Prayer: Dear Father, I thank You for Your wisdom which I see all around me. Amen.

Ref: *Science News*, 8/26/00, p. 133, "Toothy valves control crocodile hearts."

Vegetarian Piranhas?

Genesis 1:30
"And to every beast of the earth, and to every fowl of the air, and to every thing that creepeth upon the earth, wherein there is life, I have given every green herb for meat: and it was so."

The originally perfect world that God gave to us had no death. Death was introduced when man sinned. This leaves us with the question: What did the first carnivores eat before there was death?

The piranha is one of today's most ferocious carnivores. They hunt in schools of 30 or more fish, sporting teeth so sharp that they are often used as razors by South American Indians. If they lose a tooth, a complete new set of teeth quickly emerges from the gum. So what would piranhas eat in a perfect world where there was no death? The answer may be found in the pacu that looks so much like a piranha that misidentification is common. While piranhas are known as basically carnivorous, pacus are primarily vegetarian. They are satisfied with eating aquatic plants and fruit that have fallen in the water. It would appear from the genetic evidence that piranhas and pacus belong to the same created kind and that pacus are closer to the original, vegetarian type. After man's fall into sin, genetic mutations became a reality. Mutations in the original piranha kind, coupled with a shortage of vegetation to eat, may have led some of the original created kind to begin scavenging carcasses. Eventually, some of the kind became the piranha we know today. Not because of upward evolution, but because of degeneration of the original kind.

Prayer: I praise You, Lord, for so wisely providing for all Your creatures. Amen.

Ref: *Creation*, 9-11/00, pp. 20-22, "Piranha."

There's a Lot of Neither Animal, Vegetable Nor Mineral

Psalm 89:5
"And the heavens shall praise thy wonders, O LORD: thy faithfulness also in the congregation of the saints."

The United States alone has 3,800 species of lichens. Lichens are neither plants nor animals; they are living composites of two and sometimes three organisms. Commonly, these are a fungus and an alga: some lichens include the blue-green algae. These living things combine to form the familiar lichen.

Besides serving as reindeer food, lichens break up rocky soil. Scientists studying the DNA of the various fungi and algae that form different lichens report that they are unable to arrive at a single evolutionary tree for either lichens or the fungi or algae. It seems that the "simple lichen" is a very complex living thing. Fungi and algae reproduce in different ways, but when they combine to form a lichen, reproduction can be very difficult. Apparently, one species found reproduction so difficult that it doesn't reproduce! Aside from just growing, it seems to spread only when parts are broken off and root elsewhere. Some lichens reproduce by producing spores that contain only the fungal component of the lichen. Unless these spores end up where the appropriate alga can be found, no new lichen will grow. Still other lichens reproduce by growing ready-made packets that contain bits of both the fungus and the alga.

Lichens not only defy man's attempt to classify living organisms but remain as complex wonders of God's creating hand.

Prayer: I stand in awe, O Lord, of Your wonders, especially my salvation. Amen.

Ref: *Science News*, 8/26/00, pp. 140-142, "Yikes! The Lichens Went Flying."

Not Just Six Numbers

Isaiah 40:28a

"Hast thou not known? hast thou not heard, that the everlasting God, the LORD, the Creator of the ends of the earth, fainteth not, neither is weary?"

Even astronomers and cosmologists who believe in evolution recognize that conditions have to be exactly right throughout the universe for any life to be possible. For example, the Earth must be just the right distance from the sun. They call this the anthropic principle.

In his book, *Just Six Numbers*, Britain's Astronomer Royal, Martin Rees, suggests that six physical values are crucial to a universe that will support life. If, when a universe is formed, any one of these six numbers is not precisely right, life will be impossible in that universe. For example, when helium is formed from hydrogen in the sun, seven thousandths of its mass is turned into energy, warming the Earth. If a universe formed where only six thousandths of the mass would be converted to energy, no bonding could take place and there would be no stars. That universe would have only hydrogen. Raise that value to eight thousandths and hydrogen would fuse into helium too rapidly, and all its stars would have burned out by now. Likewise, if the values of the other five factors Rees lists were not precisely what they are in our universe, life itself would be impossible.

One physicist, awed at such precise order, suggested that these facts must finally drive us to a divine Creator. That divine Creator is not merely numbers, but one all-wise, loving God Who sent His only Son to save us from our sins.

Prayer: Awed at Your creation, Lord, I am humbled by Your salvation. Amen.

Ref: *Discover*, 11/00, pp. 64-69, "Why Is There Life?"

God Demonstrates Rapid Canyon Formation

Genesis 7:19
"And the waters prevailed exceedingly upon the earth; and all the high hills, that were under the whole heaven, were covered."

Many people find that large canyons carved into the earth lend credibility to evolution's claims that the Earth is millions of years old. But how long does it *really* take water to carve a large canyon through solid rock?

Providence Canyon, also called Georgia's Little Grand Canyon, in southwest Georgia, is 160 feet deep, 600 feet wide and 1,300 feet long. However, just 150 years ago what is now a beautiful wooded canyon was flat farmland. Both local accounts as well as scientific study indicate that the canyon began with some minor erosion about 1850. By 1859 a local church had to be moved so that it didn't fall into the canyon. As the year went by, local farmers lost farm animals and equipment as the canyon continued to grow. Pretty soon, roads and fences also had to be moved. A 10-year study that ended in 1994 found that canyon growth is continuing. The growth of Providence Canyon is caused by the heavy rainfalls and the soft rock in that part of Georgia.

Geologists who believe that the biblical Flood was worldwide also believe that the Grand Canyon was formed as we see it today in just a few months or weeks. The evidence indicates that an inland lake left by the Flood drained through a massive crack in the up-lifted plateau. No, millions of years are not necessary.

Prayer: Thank You, Lord, for the beauty that remains on this sinful earth. Amen.

Ref: *Creation*, 9-11/00, pp. 46-48, "Canyon Creation."

Warm, Cuddly Dinosaurs?

I Corinthians 15:39
"All flesh is not the same flesh: but there is one kind of flesh of men, another flesh of beasts, another of fishes, and another of birds."

Discovered in southern Germany in 1861, the fossil was of a bird-like creature having feathers as well as certain reptile characteristics such as teeth. Named Archaeopyteryx, meaning "Early wing," it has long since become the textbook evidence for evolution; in this case, the transition from the dinosaurs to the birds. As unlikely as this may seem, the facts are that some theropod dinosaurs, such as the compsognathus, were never much bigger than a chicken. The T. rex is a very large theropod.

In 1986, published evidence suggested that Archaeopteryx was a fake and since that time there has been a concerted effort to establish that the birds did evolve from the dinosaurs. However, not all scientists are convinced, since there are some daunting problems. For example, dinosaurs were always considered to be cold-blooded like reptiles today, whereas birds are warm-blooded. An evolutionary transition from cold-blooded to warm-blooded involves dozens of changes that must all take place at the same time and work together perfectly. To overcome this problem and make the transition easier, the leading paleontologists then claimed that dinosaurs were warm-blooded. The film *Jurassic Park*, released shortly after this time, promoted the Velociraptor as the warm-blooded dinosaur.

It is possible that some dinosaurs were warm-blooded, but evolutionary assumptions in this ongoing debate are clearly being placed ahead of convincing evidence. Objective science would reveal the Creator.

Prayer: I thank You, Lord, that though You are all-powerful, You are loving. Amen.

Ref: *Discover*, 12/00, pp. 38-40, "Were Dinosaurs Warm-Blooded?"

A Fly with Ears Like an Owl

Isaiah 7:18a
"And it shall come to pass in that day, that the LORD shall hiss for the fly that is in the uttermost part of the rivers of Egypt...."

Most flies have no hearing system whatsoever, yet in Scripture God speaks as if flies could hear Him. Now scientists have discovered a fly that has a remarkable sense of hearing, and this fly is just the type of fly God might call upon to execute His judgment.

Scientists report a parasitic fly that not only can hear, but can hear directionally. You and I have several thousand sensory cells in each ear, but this parasitic fly has only about 100 such cells in each ear. We hear directionally because our ears are spaced far enough apart, but clearly the fly's ears are not. An elegant design solves this problem. The fly's eardrums are connected so that when one eardrum picks up a sound, a vibration is transferred to the other eardrum. The fly's nervous system is able to tell which ear heard the stronger vibration and on that basis determine which eardrum is closer to the sound's source. This allows the fly to locate the sound's source as good as any owl or cat!

As electronic devices become smaller, we regard them as more sophisticated than earlier models. By this standard, this parasitic fly is much more sophisticated than supposedly more-evolved creatures. A much better answer is that this fly was created to follow the orders of its Creator.

Prayer: Lord, help me to do Your will and glorify You. Amen.

Ref: *Science News*, 11/11/00, p. 308 "Psst. This fly's ears can rival a cat's."

Grading Biology Textbooks

Proverbs 22:6
"Train up a child in the way he should go: and when he is old, he will not depart from it."

Public educators maintain that creationism should be rejected as "unscientific" and not to be taught in the classroom. Now the tables have been turned on this argument by a researcher who graded the scientific content of 10 biology textbooks.

Dr. Jonathan Wells of the Discovery Institute evaluated 10 textbooks published between 1998 and 2000 on the basis of scientific accuracy. With two earned Ph.Ds, Dr. Wells fully recognized that, like any other scientific theory, evolution would have to be revised or discarded if it is not supported by the facts. Each textbook was graded on how it dealt with seven evidences offered for evolution. He found that not one has stood the test of time. His "F" grading outnumbered all other grades, except for two that earned a grade of "D." He found that the "F"-graded books dogmatically treated evolution as unquestionable fact and uncritically relied on logical fallacies. For example, in all the textbooks, Darwin's tree of life – supposedly showing common ancestry for all living things – was presented as fact. None of the "F" textbooks mentioned the "Cambrian explosion" of complex life forms that preceded simple life forms. The discovery was made in 1909 and fully reported in the 1970s. It completely devastates Darwin's idea of common ancestry.

Dr. Wells has documented creationist claims that science textbooks tend to misrepresent the evidence for evolution and present the theory in a dogmatic manner.

Prayer: I thank You, Father, that Your Book is true, for it tells me of salvation. Amen.

Ref: Discovery Institute online, "An Evaluation of Ten Recent Biology Textbooks."

Is the Elephant an Overgrown Shrew?

Romans 1:22
"Professing themselves to be wise, they became fools...."

As our knowledge of DNA continues to grow, the traditional claims about which creatures evolved from a common ancestor are looking even less likely.

For centuries, scientists have classified animals based on their appearance and lifestyle. As a result, for example, mice and shrews were considered more closely related to one another than to, say, elephants. Now, scientists have found unique markers in three proteins in widely diverse groups of animals. They have concluded that since all the order of mammals called Afrotheria have these markers, they must all have descended from the same ancestor in the distant past. Statistical analysis shows that the unique markers could not have evolved several times; thus, all the animals in this order came from a single mating pair of ancestors. The problem is, these unique markers tie together everything from elephants to aardvarks and shrews. Aside from being all mammals, many of these animals have no obvious similarities. So different from one another are many of these creatures that some biologists actually reject the proposition that they all have a common ancestor. Others insist that this genetic analysis proves a common ancestor.

We have a suggestion for those who know of no mechanism that could randomly produce the same marker proteins in such diverse animals. Consider the possibility that each of these creatures have the same Creator.

Prayer: I thank You, Lord, for the wisdom You give to us in Your Word. Amen.

Ref: *Science News*, 1/6/01, p. 4, "Genes Seem to Link Unlikely Relatives."

If You Build It, Thank God

Genesis 1:28a
"And God blessed them, and God said unto them, 'Be fruitful, and multiply, and replenish the earth, and subdue it....'"

After God finished the creation, He turned it over to mankind, commanding us to subdue it. This is our science commission, but to do this wisely and productively requires that we actively seek to learn more about His creation.

Some ways to do this – such as harvesting and preserving fruits, berries and grains – were immediately obvious. Now, modern science is leading us to an even deeper appreciation of the raw materials God gave us. Carbon has always been amazing because of its versatility. For example, it can take the form of graphite or a diamond. Now, scientists are finding that carbon is even far more talented than this. Carbon is the only element that at atomic level can act like a metal. Recently, however, an even more amazing property has been discovered. Carbon atoms can be formed into long, hollow tubes called nanotubes containing millions of atoms. These structures can conduct electricity and, depending on how they are structured, can behave as semiconductors, transistors and even switches. Scientists are still investigating the possibilities nanotubes might offer. But in theory, a computer made of nanotubes could store the entire contents of the Library of Congress in a computer the size of a sugar cube!

God's command to subdue the creation was His invitation to learn about the amazing properties He has hidden in what He has made.

Prayer: Help us, dear Lord, to use all You have given us to spread the Gospel. Amen.

Ref: *Discover*, 2/01, pp. 20-21, "Molecular Beauty."

Real Firebugs

Psalm 77:11
"I will remember the works of the LORD: surely I will remember thy wonders of old."

Modern science has invented some fairly sensitive infrared detectors. Unfortunately, really sensitive infrared detectors need to be cooled below normal environmental temperatures. However, to hear those who believe in evolution tell it, mindless chance has managed to design and build several different types of extremely sensitive infrared detectors several different times, all of which work at normal environmental temperatures.

Both pit vipers and rattlesnakes can detect infrared radiation. However, there are also dozens of insects for whom infrared detectors are an important part of their life cycle. For example, when the siricid wasp senses the heat of a forest fire, it will fly for miles toward the fire. It is looking for hot spots where the fire has pretty much burned out. Then the female will lay about 100 eggs in the bark of a fire-weakened tree. Those eggs will not hatch for years. But when they do, the young insects will begin searching for forest fires where they can find non-sibling mates to begin the cycle again. The beetle, Melanophila, uses a different method to sense fires miles away. Such insects are found all over the world, with some 20 species alone identified in North America's Pacific Northwest.

The ability to detect infrared radiation at environmental temperatures, which our best science has yet to accomplish, is clearly the product of the intelligent design of our Creator God.

Prayer: With all You have made, dear Lord, I glorify You. Amen.

Ref: *Science News*, 3/3/01, pp. 140-141, "Why Fly into a Forest Fire?"

Advice for Teachers and Students

Proverbs 23:24
"The father of the righteous shall greatly rejoice: and he that begetteth a wise child shall have joy of him."

In a recent issue of *Physics Today*, professor Mano Singham makes the refreshing confession that students are under tremendous pressure to accept the theories taught by their professors. However, he more insightfully points out that the pressure is not so much intellectual as ideological. Professor Mano Singham teaches physics at Case Western Reserve University.

Singham admits, professors prefer that their students accept what they teach on their professorial authority. However, he also admits that when students do this, the result is that they hold the same views as their teacher, and this amounts to little more than brainwashing. As a result, students trained in this way are unlikely to shake up the world with new ideas.

Signham advocates helping students think critically. He goes so far as to use the example of origins. While he would prefer that students uncritically accept on his authority that evolution is true, he notes that this kind of training would lead students to uncritically accept anyone's propaganda in any area of life. So he urges students to carefully examine the arguments for and against any issue, including what is taught in the classroom. They should not accept anything just because some authority says it is true. Students should stand up for what they believe.

For the past 50 years, creationists have been saying this very thing about modern education.

Prayer: Lord, prosper all godly learning among Your people. Amen.

Ref: *Physics Today*, 6/00, pp. 54-55, Mano Singham, "Teaching and Propaganda."

Survival of the Least Fit?

Matthew 5:5
"Blessed are the meek: for they shall inherit the earth."

If evolution offers one message to modern man, it is: "Blessed are those who are aggressive." And while nature is often used to illustrate the value of this principle, it can also be used to illustrate the opposite of this principle.

Male Tanzanian cockroaches compete with each other for status among the population through rough wrestling matches. When one of those wrestling matches break out, those males with the lowest status scamper off. Evolution would argue that the highest-status males would be the most popular with the females, but quite the opposite is true. High-status males communicate using primarily the scents of two pheromones, but the lowest-status males use three. And the females prefer the third pheromone that is almost lacking in the high-status males. To further contradict evolutionary thinking, the female's preference for low-status males also leads to fewer males being born in the next generation, and fewer overall offspring.

Evolutionary scientists admit that this arrangement goes against all evolutionary ideas about sexual selection. Nor can they find any evolutionary advantage that would favor this development.

True science seeks to simply describe nature without trying to fit it into any ideological system. This is a good example of the creation not fitting into the evolutionary interpretation. It can also be used as an example of God's principle that the meek shall inherit the earth.

Prayer: Dear Father, help me to be Your humble servant. In Jesus' name. Amen.

Ref: *Science News*, 3/3/01, p. 135, "Roach females pick loser with good scents."

Fat That's Good for You

Genesis 1:31
"And God saw every thing that he had made, and, behold, it was very good. And the evening and the morning were the sixth day."

After God finished the creation, He looked at all He had made and declared it very good. By God's standards, that means perfect. Once man sinned, decay entered the creation. The question is, how could things that were once good become bad?

As we all know, too much fat in your diet is not good for you. It increases your chances of disease, including cancer and diabetes. However, in 1984 scientists identified a substance in hamburger that reduced the chance of cancer in mice. This substance was finally identified as a type of fat called CLA, which is molecularly very similar to the "bad" fat. Further research has shown that when CLA is added to the diet, those who are dieting are more likely to add muscle mass as they lose fat. Further, CLA added to the diet of type II diabetes patients significantly lowered their blood sugar as well as blood levels of another fat that causes heart disease.

The difference between fat that promotes health and fat that can ruin health is nothing more than the position of a few atoms in a molecule. Is it possible that, as a result of sin, a few mutations, which are part of sin's effect on the creation, changed our cells' ability to produce good fat so that they produce bad fat? We can rejoice that one day Jesus Christ will return to reverse all the effects of sin.

Prayer: Come, Lord Jesus. Amen.

Ref: *Science News*, 3/3/01, pp. 136-138, "The Good Trans Fat."

Hezekiah's Tunnel Really Was Hezekiah's

2 Chronicles 32:30a
"This same Hezekiah also stopped the upper watercourse of Gihon, and brought it straight down to the west side of the city of David."

The Old Testament mentions that King Hezekiah ordered a tunnel to be dug from the spring of Gihon in order to divert water into the city, to the pool of Siloam. This was a defensive measure taken to provide Jerusalem with water as Sennacherib's army approached to lay siege to the city.

Biblical critics couldn't deny that the tunnel had been dug; it's still there. But they pointed out the tunneling was too advanced for Hezekiah's day. Back then – 2,700 years ago – tunnels were dug by digging vertical shafts, then interconnecting them underground. Hezekiah's tunnel is a marvel because it was started at both ends, it is not straight but "S" shaped and cuts through sold rock. Despite an inscription where the diggers met dating it to Hezekiah's time, critics argued that the tunnel was dug 500 years later. Now, using two different types of radiometric dating, scientists from Hebrew University have confirmed that the tunnel does indeed date to Hezekiah's time. Moreover, studies on the weathering of the rock also date it to 2,700 years ago.

Christians believe that the Bible is God's Word, and therefore without error, because the Holy Spirit has worked faith in Jesus Christ in our hearts. However, it is always good to see its accuracy demonstrated to those who may not know Jesus Christ as their Lord and Savior.

Prayer: We give You thanks, O Lord, because Your saving Word, which tells us of our Savior, is trustworthy. Amen.

Ref: *Minneapolis Star Tribune*, 9/14/03, "Science backs up Bible's age for tunnel."

No Brain, All Eyes

Ecclesiastes 6:9
*"Better is the sight of the eyes than the wandering of the
desire: this is also vanity and vexation of spirit."*

We generally associate eyes with our brain because they
are two closely working parts of our nervous system. Our brain is
necessary to interpret what our eyes see. However, the brittlestar, a
relative of the starfish, has thousands of eyes and no brain.

The brittlestar's body is covered with a pliable crystalline
material. Inserted in this material are literally thousands of
perfectly shaped lenses that collect light. Each of these lenses is
about half the diameter of a human hair. Researchers commented
that these lenses are much finer than anything we can engineer.
Studies show that all of these lenses work together to act as one
giant eye. They seem to work rather like the compound eye of the
fly. The lenses focus incoming light on photoreceptors.
Researchers believe that this arrangement allows the brittlestar to
form a rough image of its surroundings and tell what time of day it
is. If the light becomes too bright, the brittlestar can darken its
skin, in effect, putting on sunglasses. Even more amazing is that
the brittlestar does all of this despite the fact that it doesn't have a
brain! As one researcher put it, "This is very clever engineering."

The wonders that have come from God's creative hand can
lead even evolutionists to use the language of creation. Yet, God's
greatest wonder is His plan for our salvation.

**Prayer: I give You thanks, dear Lord, for the beauty and
the wonder Your hand has placed into the creation.
Amen.**

Ref: *Discover*, 11/01, p. 16, Maia Weinstock, "A Thousand Eyes Without a Face."

The Animal Robot Chimera

Proverbs 1:5
"A wise man will hear, and will increase learning; and a man of understanding shall attain unto wise counsels."

The two-wheeled robot scoots around the top of a workbench. Depending on how it is hooked up, it goes toward or away from the light. This reaction is entirely controlled by a real, living, animal brain.

The brain, as well as part of the spinal cord, was taken from a lamprey. It can be kept alive in chilled saline solution for weeks. Scientists used a lamprey's brain because it has large, easily identified neurons and easily recovers from any damage it might inadvertently suffer during surgery. The lamprey's brain is connected to the robot that is fitted with light-detecting sensors. Another set of wires ran from a portion of the brain that controls the animal's muscles to the motors that control the little robot's wheels. Depending on which part of the brain the wires from the light sensors were attached to, the little robot would move toward or away from the light, and even go in circles or spirals. Scientists hope that this amazing research will lead to implants and prostheses that can be controlled directly by the brain.

That a living brain can control designed, manmade devices indicates that the brain, itself, is designed and not a result of random evolution. God, Who is the ultimate designer, has, in His love, also designed our salvation, worked for us by Jesus Christ.

Prayer: Thank You, dear Lord, for productive research which can be used to help those in need. Amen.

Ref: *Science News*, v. 158, p. 309, S. Perkins, "Lamprey cyborg sees the light and responds."

The Tsunami and the Animals

Job 12:7
"But now ask the beasts, and they will teach you; And the birds of the air, and they will tell you;"

Almost everyone in the world today knows of the terrible disaster that struck the coasts of Southeast Asia. The North American news media have given daily body counts, reported human tragedy and damage. Yet, as far as is known, none have mentioned the animals.

However, Asian reports from the damaged areas comment not only on the ability of trees to withstand the devastating waves but the almost total absence of animal deaths. It appears that the animals – from flamingos to elephants – took off for the hills long before the humans. The Chinese have done extensive investigations on animals and earthquake detection, but they are at a loss to explain it. Chinese scientists simply conclude that animals have far greater sensitivity than the best of scientific instruments.

Reuters reported from Thailand that the elephants used in the tourist business at Khao Lak began to "cry" at 9 am, about the time of the quake. Some elephants broke their hefty chains and raced away toward the jungle-clad hills, taking their surprised tourists and guides with them. Some people were even picked up by the elephants, using their trunks. They all came to a point on high ground where the waves stopped just short of where they stood. Three thousand, eight hundred people died in that area. God is merciful to those sensitive enough to His warnings.

Prayer: We thank you, Father, for teaching us by this example of our insensitivity to Your warning signs and Your mercy to the animals. Amen.

Ref: Reuters, January 3, 2005, Mark Bendeich, "Jumbos Save Tourists from Tsunami."

The Best Swimming Wing

Genesis 1:21a
"And God created great whales, and every living creature that moveth, which the waters brought forth abundantly, after their kind...."

An unusual example of a design in nature that runs counter to human common sense is found in the pectoral flippers of the humpback whale. The leading edge of these flippers, which one would intuitively expect to be smooth, actually sport evenly spaced bumps.

After all, airplanes, as well as birds, have sleek leading edges on their wings. These smooth edges would seem to be the most efficient at cutting through the air, which is a fluid, just like water. Puzzled about this, scientists recently made two models of the humpback's pectoral fins. One had a smooth edge, while the other had the bumps that appear on real fins. These models were taken for testing in a wind tunnel. Not surprisingly, the smooth-edged fins performed like a standard wing. However, the humpback model did much better! It generated 8 percent more lift and a third less drag than the standard design. What's more, the bumpy wing could angle 40 percent more steeply into the air than the sleek model before it stalled. Since water, like air, is a fluid, these principles would apply to a real humpback fin, enabling humpbacks to be more nimble in the water.

This unusual design comes in handy for the humpback because they feed on fast-moving schools of nimble herring and sardines. Obviously, God gave them a special design to help them do this.

Prayer: Father, I thank You that Your thoughts are not our thoughts. Help me to think more like You. Amen.

Ref: *Scientific American*, 8: 2004, pp. 18-19, "Bumpy Flying."

Living Fossils, Evolution's Oops

Psalm 104:30
"Thou sendest forth thy spirit, they are created: and thou renewest the face of the earth."

Living fossils are creatures believed to be extinct and known only through the fossil record. The most famous living fossil is the Coelacanth. It is a fish that textbooks claim has been extinct for 70 million years, according to the evolutionary timetable. Now we know that schools of them live in the Indian Ocean.

To make the claim that a creature is extinct is really only an opinion until the entire earth has been searched and no living specimen found. Another example based upon opinion is the trilobite, said to typify the Cambrian period. Textbooks regard it as an index fossil, indicating that any rocks in which its fossil is found must therefore be Cambrian. The index fossil system was placed in serious question again when living trilobites were found. Other living fossils used to date rock layers are the Graptolites. They supposedly lived 300 million years ago and have been considered a reliable indicator of that age. We know now that they are still with us.

The point is not just the discovery of creatures thought to be long extinct. The point is that opinions based upon their fossils are the foundation for the millions of years essential for the doctrine of evolution. As Scripture says, the foolishness of God, Who made all these creatures, is greater than the wisdom of man.

Prayer: Thank You, dear Father, for the truth of Your Word, for I cannot rely on the wisdom of man. Amen.

Ref: *Back to Genesis*, 11: 2000, "The Profusion of Living Fossils."

How Long Can Bacteria Sleep?

Luke 14:34
*"Salt is good: but if the salt have lost his savour,
wherewith shall it be seasoned?"*

For thousands of years salt has been considered valuable as a both a seasoning, a preservative and even as a means of payment. But could salt preserve bacteria alive for thousands or even millions of years?

In the year 2000, researchers claimed to have revived bacteria that were entombed within salt crystals from a New Mexico mine. Geologists dated the layer they were taken from at 250 million years. Scientists admit bacteria could not last, even dormant, for that long. Other research has shown that the random effects of molecular motion, even within a dormant bacterium, will cause the DNA to break down. After 100,000 years, there should be no DNA left. For this reason, other researchers said that the bacteria found must be a result of contamination and were therefore modern bacteria. After all, they said, an examination of the DNA of the salt bacteria is very similar to that of modern bacteria. After hundreds of millions of years of supposed evolution, it should be quite different.

If you forget evolution and its supposed long ages there is a more rational solution to this mystery. No one questions that DNA, even of bacteria, can survive for several thousand years. If the salt deposit from which the bacterium was taken was laid down as a result of Noah's Flood, the bacteria could well have survived.

Prayer: Lord, I thank You for the gift of faith and the evidences that support the truth of Your Word. Amen.

Ref: *Creation*, 9-11: 2001, p. 15, "Salty Saga."

Rube Goldberg Flukes

Genesis 3:17
"...cursed is the ground for thy sake; in sorrow shalt thou eat of it all the days of thy life...."

The lancet fluke is a parasite that accomplishes its life cycle in a most complicated, Rube Goldberg manner.

Mature lancet flukes live in cows and other grazing animals. Their eggs are spread in the manure left by the animal. Snails, which naturally eat the manure, eat the eggs. Once in the snail's intestines, the eggs hatch. The flukes make their way to the outside of the snail. Meanwhile, the irritated snail tries to get rid of the flukes by imprisoning them in balls of slime, which it leaves behind in the grass. A foraging ant is likely to find the ball, filled with hundreds of flukes. When the ant eats it, the flukes leave the ant's intestinal tract, finally settling as a cluster of nerves that control the ant's mandibles. The ant seems perfectly normal until the sun begins to set. Then the ant, under the control of the flukes, climbs a blade of grass, and the mandible clamps shut on the end. There the ant waits to be consumed by a grazer, where the lancet life cycle begins all over. Even stranger, if the ant isn't eaten by the time the sun returns, the ant returns to normal life, until the next sunset.

Although parasites are part of the curse of sin, the lancet fluke is still a testimony to God's incredible creativity.

Prayer: Father, thank You for sending Your Son to reverse the curse of our sin with His death and Resurrection. Amen.

Ref: *Discover*, 8: 2000, pp. 80-85, "Do Parasites Rule the World?"

Dinosaur Bones Not Always Fully Fossilized

Genesis 1:24
"And God said, Let the earth bring forth the living creature after his kind, cattle, and creeping thing, and beast of the earth after his kind: and it was so."

Most listeners to these programs will at some time have visited a museum to see the dinosaurs. Of course, the tangible remains consist of fossil skeletons, and if one is allowed to touch the bones, they are as hard as rock. Sometimes they are actually cement or plaster since they are copies. However, we are told that over millions of years the original bone had been replaced by minerals. Except for the millions of years, this is often true – but not always. Fence posts, for example, have been found mineralized at one end and plain wood at the other.

In 1993, *Science Research News* reported graduate student Mary Schweitzer's reaction when examining a slice of 65-million-year-old T. rex bone from Montana, using the electron microscope: "I got goose bumps ... it was exactly like looking at a slice of modern bone ... How could blood cells survive that long?" To compound the problem, strands of DNA were later identified within the blood.

What does this mean? Firstly, from the known rate at which the DNA structure breaks down under natural radioactivity, the cells were clearly less than 10,000 years old. Secondly, this is not an isolated case, and a major argument is now brewing behind the cloistered walls of academia.

This is further mounting evidence against the popular but godless doctrine of evolution.

Prayer: Lord, Your Word is truth. Preserve me in Your truth. Amen.

Ref: *Science Research News*, Sept. 7, 1993, Vol. 261.

Rejoice in God's Goodness

Proverbs 15:13
"A merry heart maketh a cheerful countenance: but by sorrow of the heart the spirit is broken."

There are countless scientific studies designed to find out how diet, environment and our habits influence our health. These studies urged us to eat this, not eat that and generally give up bad habits.

Now, a study of almost 3,000 people between the ages of 53 and 85 shows that depressed people in this age group are far more likely to die from heart disease than those who show no sign of depression. The study not only measured severe depression, which often requires its own medical care, but also people who reported feeling helpless, hopeless or apathetic. Study participants were also checked for any signs of coronary heart disease at the start of the study. Then they were tracked for four years. Those with even mild signs of depression died of coronary disease at a much higher rate than those who reported no signs of depression. This was even true for those who had no coronary disease at the beginning of the study. They also noted that the subject's weight, blood pressure, smoking and alcohol use had no bearing on the results.

Scripture reminds us to rejoice in the Lord and His salvation, but only a minority ever do. While severe depression may need medical care, that minority can attest to rarely feeling depressed when they remember what God has given us in His Son, Jesus Christ.

Prayer: *Father, fill me with the joy of the salvation I have through Your Son, Jesus Christ. Amen.*

Ref: *Science News,* 3. 31: 2001, p. 205, "Depression linked to heart deaths."

The Power of Faith

2 Timothy 3:13
"But evil men and seducers shall wax worse and worse, deceiving, and being deceived."

The history of science supposedly supporting evolution shows the power of expecting to find something, whether it exists or not.

Following the publication of Darwin's book in 1859, there was much speculation over the so-called primordial slime believed to be the origin of life. Ernst Haeckel predicted a whole family of creatures that would lead from the slime to the first one-celled organisms. It was thought that such creatures might exist at the bottom of the sea, so H.M.S. Challenger began taking samples of the sea bottom. Protoplasmic blobs were found in all the sample bottles. Scientists, eager to confirm Haeckel's prophetic words, proclaimed these as "life in the making," naming them Bathybius haeckeli. However, a few years later, a chemist pointed out that the preserving agent used in the sample bottles was alcohol and when sea water is added to alcohol, an amorphous precipitate of sulfate of lime is formed. It had nothing to do with life, but the embarrassment was never reported by the English press.

In truth, if you are convinced that there is no God, it will be very difficult for you to see any evidence of Him. And if you believe that witches can fly on brooms, you will find evidence for it. People did it for generations. Evolutionists continue today to find evidence for what they expect to be true.

Prayer: Father, let the teaching of Your Word keep me from being deceived by the devil, the world and my own flesh. Amen.

Ref: *Creation*, 12/00-2: 2001, pp. 36-41, "Life from life...or not?"

Loving Snakes

Job 26:13
"By his spirit he hath garnished the heavens; his hand hath formed the crooked serpent."

Mention snakes or other crawly reptiles and people usually shy away. Typically, snakes have a reputation for being dangerous, or at best, completely unable to show affection. New research shows us that in many cases this isn't true at all.

A number of studies have now shown that at least some snakes take care of their young, have friends and even prefer to hang around with relatives. Mother pythons will stay coiled around their eggs for the two months they take to hatch, not even leaving them for food. Though she is cold-blooded, should the temperatures drop too low, she can generate muscle heat by shivering. A black-rattler mother will stay with her hatchlings for nine days. During that time, she can protect them from predators. The young snakes can barely see at all until they shed their skin at nine days, after which they set off on their own. Cage studies involving non-sibling and sibling rattlesnakes showed that non-siblings distance themselves from each other. However, rattlesnakes that were siblings would touch each other frequently and often intertwined. Live-bearing skinks, found in Australia, are monogamous for life.

While evolution leads people to think of reptiles as primitive, here we see that their Creator, the God Who is love, blessed them with feelings for one another. This, too, is testimony of His loving nature.

Prayer: Father, I thank You for Your gift of love through Jesus Christ. Help me show that same love to others. Amen.

Ref: *Science News,* 3/27: 2004, pp. 200-201, Susan Milius, "The Social Lives of Snakes."

The Early Bug Gets the Water

Job 28:26
"To cause it to rain on the earth, where no man is; on the wilderness, wherein there is no man...."

How do you get the water you need in a desert in which it almost never rains? We have often looked here at how God's designs in nature show us practical designs we may never think of. The water-hoarding beetle provides us with one more such example.

This particular beetle is found in southwestern Africa in the Namibian Desert where it almost never rains. Early in the morning, a fog settles over the desert. Any water that might condense out of it is quickly evaporated by the sun and daily winds that come later in the day. But the beetles are up early to collect the water from the fog on their backs. Their back shell has tiny bumps about a half millimeter in diameter. The tops of the bumps are covered with a material that attracts water. The valleys between the bumps are coated with a waxy material that repels water. So, when large enough droplets of water collect on the bumps, they roll down into the waxy valleys, and down those valleys into the beetle's mouth. Researchers have duplicated the beetle's covering and found that such coverings will aid desert survival for man.

This design also teaches us that these beetles, and all the other myriad living things in creation, were not produced by mindless evolution, but by a loving, caring Creator.

Prayer: Lord, we thank You for all Your good gifts in season, even the rain, but most of all we thank You for Your love. Amen.

Ref: nytimes.com/2001/11/06/science/06OBSE.html

Fossil Inventory: Surprises for Some

Genesis 1:24
"And God said, Let the earth bring forth the living creature after his kind, cattle, and creeping thing, and beast of the earth after his kind: and it was so."

Everyone will remember those school textbook diagrams showing the ever-upward progression of living organisms, including man. We recall the horse series found in textbooks and the museum displays showing the evolution of the horse: the first stage as a small mammal, and after several transitions, the modern horse. The claim that fossils in the rock layers show a progression from simple life in the lowest layers to the most complex life at the top accompanies these diagrams.

Recently, the journal *Science*, reported that paleobiologists who study these fossils reevaluated all the fossil-bearing rocks that have been found in the last 180 years. What was their reaction to the meaning of the fossil record after their new inventory? "We may have been misled for twenty years," said one scientist. Another commented, "For the first time, a large group of people is saying paleobiology has been making a mistake." Why are they reacting this way? They have had to conclude, on the basis of the fossil evidence, that there never was an ever-upward progression of complexity of life forms as they had expected. The species that are represented in the fossil record show no evidence of the classic evolutionary development traditionally found in school textbooks.

In short, the fossil record supports the biblical claim that all the kinds of animals appeared about the same time.

Prayer: I thank You, Lord, for the great diversity and beauty You have created in the living world. Amen.

Ref: *Creation*, 9-11: 2001, p. 7, "Fossil re-count limits diversity."

Hornbills that Understand Monkey

Colossians 1:28
"Whom we preach, warning every man, and teaching every man in all wisdom; that we may present every man perfect in Christ Jesus...."

With the exception of basic messages such as aggression, communication between two entirely different species has seldom been observed among animals in the wild. We know that many animals among the same species give each other specific warnings about an impending danger. However, scientists have never noted one species recognizing the specific warning given by a second species.

Diana monkeys on the Ivory Coast of Africa face two primary threats: leopards and crowned eagles. When one of these threats appear, the spotter gives a very specific bark-like call depending on the type of threat. Of course, the monkeys need to respond differently to each threat – whether it comes from the leopard below or the eagle above. So it helps them to know what they are facing. On the other hand, a bird named the yellow hornbill is threatened only by the crowned eagles. Researchers noted that these birds ignored the monkeys' warning about the leopards. But when the monkeys signaled danger from the eagle, the yellow hornbill took defensive measures. Researchers confirmed their observations using tape-recorded monkey calls. The researchers were amazed that these birds understood the monkey warnings in an intelligent manner.

Such intelligence comes from the Creator, Who has given the gift of such intelligence to His creatures in a way that provides for their survival. This shows His loving care for His creation.

Prayer: Father, thank You for Your love, especially for Your forgiving love to me in Your Son, Jesus Christ. Amen.

Ref: *Science News*, 3/20: 2004, p. 188, "Hornbills know which monkey calls to heed."

Smart Leaves

Job 36:5
"Behold, God is mighty, and despiseth not any: he is mighty in strength and wisdom."

As science learns more about the universe, some are suggesting that they see basic mathematical principles that underlie everything. This principle – which one scientist has called "cellular automata" – might be at the root of everything from astronomy to zoology.

The leaves of plants have pores that let in carbon dioxide. However, if the pores open too far, or remain open too long, the plant may lose too much water. How does a plant that has no brain or nervous system keep these factors in balance? Researchers had always thought that the pores work independently. However, close study has shown that patches of pores in a leaf open and close together. In fact, over several minutes, opened and closed patches of pores move across a leaf in patterns.

As scientists studied these patterns, they realized that the pattern they were looking at was what they call "distributed, emergent computation" or "cellular automata." The individual cells of the leaves are working with each other to perform complex, large-scale computations. In short, the cells of plant leaves are working together as a computer, even though they lack a central processor.

While evolutionists would hope to explain this built-in intelligence by chance, it is difficult to get around the fact that intelligence is built into the creation. Such intelligence can only be ascribed to an intelligent source – our Creator.

Prayer: Dear Father, I thank You for Your wisdom, and I pray that I may grow in wisdom, guided by Your Word. Amen.

Ref: *Science News*, 2/21 2004, pp. 123-124, Erica Klarreich, "Computation's New Leaf."

Tickled Locusts

Proverbs 30:27
"The locusts have no king, yet go they forth all of them by bands...."

Normally, the desert locusts mentioned in the Bible are shy and reclusive and are green in color. What turns them into the multi-colored army that sweeps across the land, eating every leaf in sight?

Even the book of Proverbs marvels at how locusts, without any leaders, behave like a destructive army. Yet they live most or all of their lives as grasshoppers. However, there are seven species of these locusts that now and again can become a destructive swarm. It happens when their population spikes, usually due to an abundance of food. But what triggers the change? Researchers put a rolling ball in a cage to jostle a solitary locust. After a few hours, the locust was ready to jostle fellow locusts. Then, researchers took a small paintbrush and began to tickle various parts of the insect. After long, tedious hours of locust tickling, they found that simply touching a locust's hind leg made it ready to swarm. They concluded that when the locust population spikes, the insects begin to jostle each other, and that touching turns them into a destructive swarm.

One might conclude that when God wanted to punish people in Old Testament times with a plague of locusts, He simply blessed the locusts until they began to jostle against one another. Then they were ready to swarm at His bidding.

Prayer: Lord, do not let me be plagued by my sin, for I believe that You have earned my forgiveness on the cross. Amen

Ref: *Science News*, 3/31: 2001, p. 199, S. Milius, "Touching legs turns shy locusts gregarious."

Fast Water, Quick Canyons

Genesis 8:3a
"And the waters returned from off the earth continually...."

Visitors to the Grand Canyon will recall the Park Rangers saying that it took millions of years for water to carve out the Canyon. We have looked at examples of rapid canyon formation in previous programs, and today we have one more example.

Back in 1926, a canal in the desert of Walla Walla, near Washington, became clogged with tumbleweeds. When heavier than normal spring rains occurred, water began to back up. So workers diverted the water to a ditch leading to a nearby creek. The old ditch was not large – six feet wide and never more than 10 feet deep – but the large water flow of 80 cubic feet per second began to carve out the ditch. The fast-moving water soon created what many have called a miniature Grand Canyon. Over six days, the water moved five million cubic feet of dirt and rock. The result is a canyon over a quarter of a mile long, 120 feet deep and 120 feet wide.

Canyons throughout the world have undoubtedly been formed by large volumes of water moving a large amount of rock in a short time. While none of these canyons are as large as the Grand Canyon, the return of waters to the ocean after the Genesis Flood provides more than enough power to carve a feature as large as the Grand Canyon.

Prayer: I rejoice, dear Father, that You have judged my sins in Christ, but have given me forgiveness. Amen.

Ref: *Back to Genesis*, 12: 2001, p. d, John D. Morris, "How Long Does It Take for a Canyon to Form?"

Plants Have Immune Systems

Malachi 4:2a

"But unto you that fear my name shall the Sun of righteousness arise with healing in his wings...."

People and mammals have a multi-pronged immune system. When a bacterial infection is detected, cells begin to release nitric oxide, which kill bacteria and begin a cascade of other defense strategies. Ultimately, antibodies that directly attack any invader are produced.

In recent years, scientists have discovered that even in certain plants there are immune systems that respond to infectious agents. These researchers, working with mustard plants, subjected them to 15 proteins unique to infectious microbes. In response, the plants began producing nitric oxide. Measurable increases of this gas were noted within two minutes of exposure. And, just as in people and mammals, the nitric oxide began to kill real microbes. It also begins a chain of other strategies that would enable the plant to fight infection. In some cases, the entire plant – not just the plant cells exposed to the infectious agents – also joined in fighting the "infection." Further research has shown that a number of genes in the mustard plant are involved in defense against infectious agents.

While no plants have yet been found to produce antibodies, it appears that many plants have immune systems similar to our own. At creation, God said everything was "very good," so there were no diseases. But He gave us immune systems anyway because He knew we would fall, just as He already had our salvation worked out.

Prayer: I thank You, Lord, for the spiritual healing You have given to me through the forgiveness of sins. Amen.

Ref: *Science News*, 10/23: 2004, p. 260, S. Milius, "Green Red-Alert."

Birds with a Memory to Envy

Job 38:41
*"Who provideth for the raven his food? when his young
ones cry unto God, they wander for lack of meat."*

The shy bird called Clark's nutcracker collects food during
the growing season and stores it for the cold winter months. In one
year, a bird will store between 22,000 and 33,000 thousand seeds
in as many as 2,500 locations, which can be more than 10 miles
apart. But does the little bird remember where he put all those
seeds?

Biologists tracked the activity of Clark's nutcrackers in the
San Francisco Peaks in northern Arizona. A small army of
researchers tracked the birds' seed gathering and storing activities.
One of the first things they discovered was that the birds quickly
figured out that they were being observed. Some refused to store
food when researchers were watching them. Others faked storing
seeds when they were watched. Back in the lab, researchers
studied the storing activity of Eurasian nutcrackers. After the birds
stored seeds in a large sand floor, the birds were removed. Then
the seeds they stored were dug up. When the birds were allowed to
return, they quickly discovered that their seeds had been stolen, so
they refused to store any more seeds. In the end, researchers
concluded that the nutcrackers recover as many as two-thirds of
their stored seeds within 13 months.

The remarkable memory of these little birds is their gift
from God that enables them to be fed all year around.

**Prayer: Father, I thank You because You are gracious
and generous, not just to the birds, but also to me. Amen.**

Ref: *Science News*, 2/14: 2004, pp. 103-105, Susan Milius, "Where'd I Put That?"

Baby May Be in Charge of His Own Birth

Galatians 4:19
"My little children, of whom I travail in birth again until Christ be formed in you...."

Is it the mother's body or the unborn baby's body that triggers the birth process? Those who advise that the baby will come when it's ready may be correct.

Researchers studying mice have found that a protein called SP-A, which coats the inside of a newborn's lungs, begins to rise in concentration in the amniotic fluid shortly before birth. Normally, the protein is used by the newborn to fend off lung infections. SP-A causes the release of the unborn child's immune cells, called macrophages. These macrophages leave the amniotic fluid and go to the uterus. Once there, they produce inflammation that eventually causes the cervix to open and contractions to begin. It seems that this entire sequence of events that leads to a successful birth is controlled by the unborn infant's own body. If the researchers' findings with mice also apply to humans, many premature births might be prevented by manipulating levels of SP-A in the mother's amniotic fluid.

Every step of this system must be in place and working if there is to be a next generation. This fact in itself argues against this carefully tuned system having evolved through trial and error. Rather, it is the gift of our loving God, Who also gave us the new birth into His kingdom by calling us through the Gospel of the forgiveness of sins in His Son, Jesus Christ.

Prayer: Lord, I thank You for my birth into this world, and I thank You for my new birth into Your kingdom. Amen.

Ref: *Science News,* 3/27: 2004, p. 198, J. Travis, "It's Time!"

Seismic Sayings

Speaking, singing, writing, and body language are all familiar ways of communicating. Science has now learned of another means of communication that has been going on all around us – yet, we are not even aware of it.

A vast range of creatures communicate through vibration. This vibratory communication goes on at frequencies beyond human hearing. Researchers have learned that a number of insects communicate with other members of their species on the same plant by quivering the plant. A tree hopper will call its friends with a specific type of vibration when it finds a good place to feed. The cape mole rat spends nearly its entire life underground. When a solitary male is ready to mate, he thumps against the side of his burrow and then listens for a female's response. The female's burrow may be nine feet away, but she'll sense the vibration. Golden moles are completely blind, but they hunt for live prey. Further, they live in a desert environment where there are only small stands of grass. They hunt by sensing ground vibrations generated when the wind blows through a stand of grass where the next meal is likely to be found.

Communication is God's gift. However, we want to be clear in our communication of our faith. To do that, our communication of our faith needs to center on Jesus Christ.

Prayer: Thank You, Father, for communicating Your love for me in a way I can understand – in Jesus Christ. Amen.

Ref: *Science News*, 3/24: 2001, pp. 190-191, Susan Milius, "Things that Go Thump."

Old MacDonald Has a Shell

Genesis 4:2b
"And Abel was a keeper of sheep, but Cain was a tiller of the ground."

Until recently, it was thought that – excluding mankind – only a few insects, beetles, ants and termites actually farmed crops for their food supply. Then an amazing snail was found.

The snail lives on the leaves of plants growing in East Coast salt marshes. This amazing snail cuts long gashes down the leaves of cord-grass. It doesn't eat the cord-grass. Rather, it waits. Before long, a fungus begins to grow on the gash, aided by the snail's own droppings. Moreover, without the fungus the snails do not thrive, hardly even grow, and almost half of their young die. However, when the fungus is available, they thrive and grow, losing almost none of their young.

Now the question must be asked: How could this arrangement evolve? How did these snails exist before they discovered that they needed this fungus? How did they learn to grow the fungus? If they evolved from snails that didn't need the fungus, how did they discover that they all-of-a-sudden needed the fungus? The most straightforward answer is that the same Creator Who taught us to farm also taught these snails to farm when He made them and the fungus they need to survive. He knows all of our needs before we do and provides what we need, including the forgiveness of sins, eternal life and salvation through His Son, Jesus Christ.

> *Prayer: Father, thank You for the productivity of the earth. I pray that You would continue to provide for our needs. Amen.*

Ref: *Science News*, 12/6: 2003, p. 358, S. Milius, "New Farmers."

The Dead-Horse Arum

Isaiah 40:8
"The grass withereth, the flower fadeth: but the word of our God shall stand for ever."

A flower called the dead-horse arum has a problem. The individual flowers are able to receive pollen for only one day. To make matters worse, its male parts are not mature that day. The next day, the male parts of the flower produce pollen, but the female parts of the flower have shriveled up and cannot receive it.

The dead-horse arum, which grows on islands in the Mediterranean, has a unique solution to this problem. When it's ready to pollinate, the flower begins to generate heat and scent. The scent smells like rotting flesh, which attracts blow-flies. The flies, looking for a place to lay their eggs, crawl into a pocket around the base of the flower stalk. There, the blow-flies are trapped by spines and filaments. If these flies had previously visited another dead-horse arum, they transfer the pollen they picked up there to the female parts of the plant. The next day, when the male parts of the flower are producing pollen, the flies, now coated with this pollen, are released to pollinate another arum.

The complex dependence of the arum on the blow-flies – with its custom-designed features to lure and hold the flies just long enough to ensure pollination – had to come into existence all at the same time and in perfected form. It is a testimony to the genius of our Creator.

Prayer: Father, I thank You that the entire creation glorifies You. Help me to glorify You with my life. Amen.

Ref: *Science News*, 12/13: 2003, pp. 379-381, Susan Milius, "Warm-Blooded Plants?"

Bright Camouflage

Psalm 146:6
"Which made heaven, and earth, the sea, and all that therein is: which keepeth truth for ever...."

Most people have seen the beautiful colors of reef fish. However, all those bright colors would be expected to make them attractive to predators.

Researchers have learned that while we appreciate all the bright colors, when we see fish as other fish see them, most of these fish are perfectly camouflaged. Almost 50 percent of the fish so far studied can see ultraviolet light. Further, fish such as the damselfish have markings that can only be seen in the ultraviolet range. Researchers studying the effect of water depth on light color and the pigments in various fish's eyes have concluded that fish cannot see, for example, the subtleties of all the shades of yellows around them. What appears to us as a bright yellow trumpet fish is seen by fish eyes to be the same color as a coral reef 10 feet away. What appears to us as a bright yellow and blue-striped angel fish appears to fish eyes several feet away like the reef itself. Several species of cleaner fish sport a similar shade of blue even though they may not be related. Perhaps this color is a code to other species that need cleaning.

God has here designed a color scheme that brings delight to the eye, and yet offers his creatures protection so that they can continue from generation to generation.

Prayer: Thank You, Father, for the beauty You have built into the creation even as You protect Your creatures. Amen.

Ref: *Science News*, 11/6: 2004, pp. 296-297, 300, Susan Milius, "Hide and See."

The Most Interesting Sounds You've Never Heard

Psalm 77:17
"The clouds poured out water: the skies sent out a sound: thine arrows also went abroad."

We are surrounded by sounds, some of which can be louder than an airliner taking off. Yet, we never hear these sounds. It's called infrasound. It's real sound that can be recorded, if you have the right equipment.

Infrasound waves are below 20 hertz, the lowest frequency we can hear. Because the sound waves are long, they can travel hundreds or even thousands of miles. Volcanic eruptions regularly generate infrasound and so does the wind. But, perhaps, most interestingly, those beautiful Northern Lights that often color the night sky also generate infrasound. The sound is produced when the incoming solar particles push the air outward. While we are not able to hear infrasound, it does influence us. Researchers in England placed an infrasound generator in a concert hall and, during the performance, infrasound was added at selected points. After the concert, the audience was asked about their emotions during certain passages of music, or if they had experienced any strange feelings during the concert. Researchers concluded that infrasound intensified whatever emotional state the music had produced in people. So if you have ever watched the Northern Lights and thought you were almost hearing something, it was likely the infrasound you were sensing.

The more we learn about the creation God has given us, the more we find to marvel at how excellent is His workmanship.

Prayer: Father, You have been so generous to us, both in the creation You have given us, but also in Your love in Christ.

Ref: *Science News*, 1/10: 2004, pp. 26-28, Kate Ramsayer, "Infrasonic Symphony."

The Social Lives of Bacteria

Genesis 11:6a
"And the LORD said, Behold, the people is one, and they have all one language; and this they begin to do...."

About 300 years after the Genesis Flood, when all people spoke the same language, they decided to work together to build a great city. Working together for a common goal is called "social intelligence." Do animals practice social intelligence? Of course, there are the bees, the ants and the beavers – but the bacteria, one of the lowliest of all creatures, also shows social intelligence!

Several types of common bacteria have shown evidence of social intelligence. Contrary to expectation, sometimes this cooperation takes place between unrelated types at the expense of genetically related individuals. Bacterial colonies where cooperation is taking place always attract freeloaders. Such colonies often find ways to discourage or even kill the freeloaders. One such cooperative community is a common soil bacterium. When they locate prey, they swarm over the prey like a pack of wolves. Many species of bacteria remain relatively singular until they sense that they have enough to form a community. Then they communicate to each other by releasing certain molecules which the others sense, and they form slime mold colonies, or a biofilm.

Cooperation and a result of social intelligence can be used to do good or evil. But it doesn't matter where they are on the imagined evolutionary tree. God has given social abilities to many of His creatures as a means of helping their kind to survive.

Prayer: Lord, I thank You for the ability to cooperate with others to do good. Help me to better cooperate for the good of all. Amen.

Ref: *Science News*, 11/20: 2004, pp. 330-332, Bruce Bower, "One-Celled Socialites."

Genetic Monkey Business

Genesis 1:27

"So God created man in His own image, in the image of God created He him; male and female created He them."

One commonly heralded claim to the evolution of man from the animal kingdom is the statement that humans and chimpanzees are more than 98 percent genetically identical. Many people think this claim has been proven, but it has always been an assumption made by believers in evolution.

Now geneticists have begun to examine this claim. Researchers recently completed the first detailed map of one chimpanzee chromosome. That alone should tell us that the claim of genetic similarity between humans and chimps has never been proven. They then compared this with the corresponding human chromosome. In a detailed examination, they found 68,000 small differences in the DNA between the two genes. An analysis of the 231 genes of this chromosome showed that 83 percent of them would make proteins that differed from one another. They noted that if this pattern held for all the comparisons between human and chimpanzee genes, they would expect thousands of differences. In other words, rather than humans and chimps being more than 98 percent genetically identical, so far they have proven to be 83 percent genetically different!

There are, of course, more differences between humans and chimps than genetics. Humans were created in God's image, and therefore are morally responsible to God. And most importantly, humans have been redeemed by God's Son, Jesus Christ, on the cross of Calvary.

Prayer: Lord, I thank You that You have made me and redeemed me. Amen.

Ref: *Discover*, 1: 2005, p. 30, Chris Jozefowicz, "Proteins Make the Primate."

What Coral and Humans Share

Psalm 95:6
"O come, let us worship and bow down: let us kneel before the LORD our maker."

According to the theory of evolution, all life is related. There is claimed to be a hierarchy of rising complexity from the earliest simple organisms to man. The earliest organisms are said to include corals, sea anemones and jellyfish that thrived 500 million years ago. These early creatures eventually led to the first creatures to move onto land, and worms were among them.

Based on this supposed evolutionary history, one would expect the DNA of humans to be closer to worms than to coral. However, recent mapping of the DNA of these creatures has produced some surprises. While corals have the simplest nervous system of any animal, their genetic sequences are similar to those in human nervous systems. Even more strange is that worms – which are supposed to stand between us and the corals – lack these sequences. These sequences are called ESTs. Researchers have found that, in general, coral ESTs tended to be closer to human ESTs than to worm ESTs. Baffled by this and still convinced that evolution is true, the scientists simply assumed that worms must have lost these DNA sequences. However, they stressed that more creatures need to be studied.

Would it not be simpler to conclude that corals, worms, people and everything else were made by the same Creator Who created specific DNA coding for each creature without concern for evolutionary history?

Prayer: Father, Who has wondrously made us, You are worthy of all honor and worship. Amen.

Ref: *Science News*, 1/24: 2004, p. 55, John Travis, "Reef Relations."

Music and Language Are Linked

Psalm 40:3
"And he hath put a new song in my mouth, even praise unto our God: many shall see it, and fear, and shall trust in the LORD."

Evolutionists often claim that language and music evolved independently of each other. However, new research along several lines is showing that there is a close connection between music and language.

Researchers have been studying the effect of music on verbal comprehension. Electrical activity within the brain was tracked, using electrodes attached to the scalps of volunteers. They found that those volunteers who had just heard the trilling of flutes, for example, identified the word "bird" a split second faster than those who had not heard the music. This effect is called priming. When volunteers heard a church anthem, they more quickly identified the word "devotion" than those who had not. The study showed that these effects were consistent, whether the words had concrete meanings, were cultural references or were abstract concepts. Other research has shown that when a region of the brain – called Broca's area – is damaged, both recognition of harmonic chords as well as language are impaired, also suggesting a connection between language and music.

Both music and language are gifts of God. As the Psalmist noted, the songs he sang were placed into his mouth by God. Genesis tells us that Adam and Eve could talk the day they were created. While music isn't mentioned, we see that within a couple of generations, men were making musical instruments and must therefore have played music.

Prayer: Father, thank You for the gifts of music and language. Help us to use these to praise You. Amen.

Ref: *Science News*, 2/28: 2004, p. 133, B. Bower, "Song Sung Blue."

God's Architecture Wins Again

Psalm 127:1
"Except the LORD build the house, they labor in vain that build it: except the LORD keep the city, the watchman waketh but in vain."

If you live in a temperate climate, you have probably heard your home pop and crack on cold days. Those sounds are caused by the different materials that make up your house contracting at different rates as the temperature falls. At some point, the growing tensions are released and you hear the result. If you live in a warm climate that is subject to hurricanes, you know that a building is likely to fail at the point where different parts of the house, like the roof and wall, meet together.

Buildings are made up of a large number of things, each of which acts differently under the same conditions. That makes for weak points in any structure. British architects have looked at the structure of living things to find an answer to this problem. They noted that skeletons can work well under conditions that would cause many building materials to fail. One researcher noted that a skeleton is more efficient than any man-made structure. One architect's suggestion was to build structures like walls and bridges out of artificial bone that is formed to the needs of the structure.

We should not be surprised that, once again, man is looking to the living world for solutions to his problems. The living world, after all, was designed by our all-wise God Who does all things well.

Prayer: Father, I thank You that I am wonderfully made. Now help me to build my life on Your Word. Amen.

Ref: *New Scientist*, 9/16: 2000, p. 7.

Drink Your Orange Juice

Genesis 1:29
"And God said, Behold, I have given you every ... tree, in the which is the fruit of a tree yielding seed; to you it shall be for meat."

Presumably, before the fall into sin, we didn't have any bad cholesterol, or at least it didn't do any damage in our bloodstream. The so-called "bad cholesterol" is low-density-lipoprotein. It's called "bad" because it tends to cause our arteries to clog unless countered by the so-called "good cholesterol" – or high-density-lipoprotein.

Based on earlier research, scientists wanted to test the idea that substances in orange juice could improve levels of good cholesterol. Volunteers had their cholesterol levels checked on a regular basis during the test period. After six weeks of a low cholesterol diet, they were to drink one glass of orange juice every day for four weeks. The result was a five percent increase in the good cholesterol. Then they drank two glasses of orange juice per day for four weeks. The result was another seven percent increase in good cholesterol. Then they were directed to drink three glasses per day. The result was a 27 percent overall improvement. Surprisingly, researchers found that five weeks after they stopped the three-glass-a-day portion of the experiment, their good cholesterol remained high.

We can be thankful that in His perfect foreknowledge God created some foods that counter the effects of sin on us. We can be even more thankful that His plan to save us from our sins was in place even before there was sin.

Prayer: Thank You, Father, for providing for all my needs, especially my need for a Savior. Amen.

Ref: *Science News*, 11/18: 2000, p. 327, J. Raloff, "Path to heart health is one with a peel."

How Do Your Opals Grow?

Proverbs 20: 15
"There is gold, and a multitude of rubies: but the lips of knowledge are a precious jewel."

Opals are precious multicolored gemstones made primarily of silica. How do they form? Scientists admit that much of the chemistry is not well understood. However, according to the traditional explanation, their formation begins as water filters through silica-rich rock, dissolving some of the silica. When that water passes through a cavity in a suitable rock the silica precipitates as a film on the wall of the cavity. After tens of millions of years, you will have an opal.

Now opals have been found, along with fossilized soil bacteria similar to typical soil bacteria you find today. With this finding, some scientists have suggested that the acids produced by the bacteria may have helped form the opals. They propose that the acids produced by the bacteria dissolved some the minerals in nearby feldspar, forming the opals. Obviously, this process would not take as long as the purely natural process traditionally thought to form opals. Other geologists are reluctant to give bacteria any credit for opal formation. However, opal expert Dr. Len Cram has been growing opals in a process that takes only a few months.

Creationists do not oppose real knowledge. We know that when truth is discovered it will never contradict Scripture. Actually demonstrating that opals can be produced in a matter of months is far better science than speculating about it taking millions of years.

Prayer: Thank You, Lord, for revealing the truth of salvation in Jesus Christ to us in Your inerrant Word, the Bible. Amen.

Ref: *Creation*, 12/00-2: 2001, p. 5, "Opals from Bacteria?"

Don't Lie to These Wasps

Proverbs 19:5
"A false witness shall not be unpunished, and he that speaks lies shall not escape."

Colonies of Paper Wasps consist entirely of female wasps who are ordered according to a strict hierarchy. After mating, the females fight each other for dominance in the colony. Those who prove to be better fighters have more dominance. This means that they can spend more time laying eggs and less time working.

Researchers studying Paper Wasps found, however, that the situation was more complicated than that. They observed that the stronger fighters generally had more black splotches on their face than the weaker fighters. To test if the black markings were related to hierarchy, researchers painted some of the wasps' faces to make them look higher or lower in the hierarchy than they really were. Researchers found that the rest of the colony would not tolerate the social imposters. Those who were caught lying about their status were harassed continually by the others. This was true whether their faces showed them in a higher or lower status than they really were. Researchers also found that a few wasps had mutated so that their faces inaccurately signaled their status. They were also attacked. The scientists concluded that the wasps' face coloring accurately predicted their strength.

While sin entered the world through the temptation of the father of lies, God's standard is the truth. Those who love God's truth will seek to reflect truth in their lives.

> **Prayer: Father, I thank You for Your Gospel truth. Help me to grow in Your truth and faithfully share it with others. Amen.**

Ref: *Discover*, 2/05, p. 10, Jessa Forte Netting, "The Kind of Face Only a Wasp Could Trust."

Who Do You Love?

1 John 2:16

"For all that is in the world, the lust of the flesh, and the lust of the eyes, and the pride of life, is not of the Father, but is of the world."

We have long been told that a child with high self-esteem will do better in school, get into less trouble and is less likely to smoke or get into drugs. However, after examining the results of a large number of scientific studies that made such claims, independent researchers have come to a very different conclusion.

There have been a large number of scientific studies published on the subject of self-esteem. Researchers went through these studies to evaluate the actual results of self-esteem studies. First, they concluded that having a high self-esteem will not improve a student's grades in school or in job performance. This is true whether the subjects naturally had high self-esteem or went through programs designed to improve their self-esteem. The researchers also confirmed what is generally known – that success at work or in school can build self-esteem. They further found that those with so-called "good self-esteem" were not less likely to smoke, drink alcohol, get involved with drugs, or get into school-yard fights. On the contrary, they found that high self-esteem makes it more likely that some will engage in school-yard bullying, while others will stand up to the school-yard bully.

Earthly wisdom does not lead to godliness. In God's perfect wisdom, He has given us our identity as His own children through the redeeming work of His Son, Jesus Christ.

Prayer: I thank You, Father, that You have given me my identity as Your redeemed child through Your Son, Jesus Christ. Amen.

Ref: *Science News*, 6/7/03, p. 365, "Findings puncture self-esteem claims."

New Snail Doesn't Need to Eat

Psalm 104:25
"So is this great and wide sea, wherein are things creeping innumerable, both small and great beasts."

Some of the strangest creatures you can possibly imagine live around undersea hydrothermal vents known as "smokers" that spew out volcanically heated water and minerals. One of the most unusual creatures is an armor-plated snail that never needs to eat!

The as-yet-unnamed snail was discovered in the Indian Ocean. The sides of the snail's foot have overlapping scales. Like the rest of the shell, these scales are coated in iron sulfide. This coating is the result of bacteria that, it is thought, deposit the iron sulfide on all outer shell surfaces. Most mollusks have a gland in their esophagus that contain symbiotic bacteria. These bacteria turn sulfides in the water passing through the snail's gills into nutrition for the snail. However, in all mollusks known until the discovery of this snail, the mollusks must still eat to have enough nutrition to live. This newly discovered snail has a gland that is 100 times larger than any other snail. It provides the snail with all the nutrition it needs, so it never needs to eat.

This newly discovered snail once again shows us that God's wisdom and power are unlimited. This is comforting, for we are reminded that His greatest wisdom and power are seen through His love toward us in the Gospel. His plan of salvation for us reflects His greatest wisdom and power.

Prayer: Father, I rejoice at Your wisdom and power in creating an amazing living world. Amen.

Ref: *Science News*, 11/8/03, p. 291, S. Perkins, "Cast-Iron Foot."

Gecko Tape

Genesis 1:31
"And God saw every thing that he had made, and, behold, it was very good. And the evening and the morning were the sixth day."

In a previous Creation Moments program we talked about the amazing ability of the gecko to walk up walls and across the ceiling. The gecko can do this because it has tiny hairs, called setae, on its feet. These hairs are so tiny that they actually grip the molecules in the surface of the material upon which the gecko is walking.

Human attempts to duplicate the gecko's ability underscore the excellence of the gecko's design. Scientists recently made a one-square-centimeter patch out of water-resistant plastic that had over a million tiny setae on it. As impressive as that sounds, their gecko tape was only one-third as efficient as the gecko's foot. But it is efficient enough that a glove made out of gecko tape could hold a man to the ceiling. However, man-made gecko tape only works about five times before it refuses to stick. That's because the plastic from which gecko tape is made attracts water. Every time it is applied it picks up a little water from even apparently dry surfaces. This causes its setae to clump together and lose their ability to grip a surface. The gecko's setae repel water so well that they work even on an obviously wet surface.

We should not be surprised that even 21st century science cannot duplicate the wonders created by God.

Prayer: Father, thank You for creating wonders in Your creation which show forth Your glory. Amen.

Ref: *Science News*, 6/7/03, p. 356, S. McDonagh, "Caught on Tape."

Scientific Journal Confirms Creationist Findings

John 17:17
"Sanctify them through thy truth: thy word is truth."

Evolutionary scientists have long maintained that it takes several million years for wood to become petrified or turned to stone as in the famous "Petrified forest." In 1995 the creationist magazine *Creation* published research to show that wood can petrify in a relatively short time. Now a scientific journal, *Sedimentary Geology*, has published a new study that agrees.

Japanese scientists immersed specimens of wood in hot spring water. The mineral-filled, hot water stayed at about 122° F. They noted that some pieces of wood already in the hot spring water looked very much like ancient petrified wood. They compared it to petrified wood found in Miocene era volcanic ash. Such petrifaction had always been said to take millions of years. After one year, they removed some of the wood for study. They did the same every year for seven years, finding that little petrifaction had taken place the first year. But after seven years, over 38 percent of the wood was petrified. Detailed study of the wood showed that it was petrified in the same way that the Miocene wood was. In their published paper, they even cited their agreement with the 1995 *Creation* article!

True science will never challenge anything the Bible says, even when it comes to historical details like the age of the Earth. The Bible is indeed God's truth.

Prayer: I thank You, Lord, that I can trust Your Word, even when it comes to historical details. Your Word is truth. Amen.

Ref: *Impact* (ICR), 1/05, Andrew A. Snelling, "Rapid Petrifaction of Wood: An Unexpected Confirmation of Creationist Research."

Dueling Birdsongs

Song of Solomon 2:12
"The flowers appear on the earth; the time of the singing of birds is come, and the voice of the turtle is heard in our land...."

There is a lot more to bird song than meets the ear. Digital recording and computer technology have enabled researchers to study, in detail, various song-birds' reactions to neighboring birds' songs.

In most species, singing is the male's job. There is much more going on when he sings than simply establishing territory or attracting a mate. Researchers refer to one characteristic of bird song as "song matching." While a male bird doesn't like another male in his territory, he is more tolerant of a related male in a neighboring territory than of a complete stranger. A male will challenge a stranger by repeating the stranger's song. Researchers have concluded from bird behavior that such "matching" is a challenge to the stranger and shows a willingness to increase aggressive behavior. Just as when people argue, birds raise the aggression level by beginning their song before their challenger finishes his. However, as long as the neighbor shows no aggressiveness, male birds seldom match a neighbor's song. Decreased aggression is signaled by singing a song that's different from the neighbor's. Researchers also observed that rather than territory, the challenger is sometimes simply trying to lure away a male's mate.

While we appreciate the beauty of bird song, it is a very complex way of communication. Such complex communication points to the Creator Who gave us His Word.

Prayer: Dear Father in heaven, I thank You for the beauty of the birds and their songs. Amen.

Ref: *Science News*, 12/18 & 25, pp. 397-399, Susan Milius, "Song Fights."

Tool Users That Are Something to Crow About

Genesis 4:22
"And Zillah, she also bare Tubal-cain, an instructor of every artificer in brass and iron: and the sister of Tubal-cain was Naamah."

Many creatures have been found that use sticks, leaves and other items as tools. Chimpanzee parents teach their youngsters to poke sticks in termite holes to get termites. However, no animal has shown an instinctive tendency to make and use tools, until now.

Caledonian crows are among the known tool-users. A pair of captive New Caledonian crows were having trouble incubating their four eggs. So researchers decided to incubate and raise the young crows themselves. Upon hatching, the young crows were separated into two pairs. One pair received lessons on how to use twigs to poke food out of slots. The other pair received no lessons, nor were they allowed to see their siblings using tools. When they were given sticks and leaves, they spontaneously began using the twigs to poke food out of a slot. One of them also tore a leaf into a food poker. After evaluating all the behavioral data, researchers concluded that while crows have a natural tendency to make and use tools, they also learn how to make improved tools from their elders.

Tool making is not what separates man from animals, although we can make tools far superior to those made by animals. The Bible tells us that the earliest man was made in the image of God and that the earliest generations of man were already making iron tools.

Prayer: Father, thank You for making me for a relationship with You and making a relationship possible through Christ. Amen.

Ref: *Science News*, 1/15/05, p. 38, S. Milius, "Crow Tools."

Coots Can Count

Psalm 139:18
"If I should count them, they are more in number than the sand: when I awake, I am still with thee."

Researchers spent every day of four breeding seasons in a Canadian marsh watching the behavior of nesting American coots – a bird that looks very much like a duck. They concluded that coots can count.

The researchers found that 41 percent of the nests were victims of "stealth egg layers." Stealth egg laying takes place when a female coot sneaks into an unattended nest and lays an egg for another couple to raise. This is a problem because the extra mouth to feed increases the likelihood that some of that couple's own hatchlings will starve. It was observed that the mother coot protects her young by rolling the "stealth" egg out of the nest or burying it in the nesting material. The "stealth" eggs are usually a slightly different color, and the mother coot can discriminate between these eggs and her own on the basis of this color difference. However, researchers wanted to know if the coots were actually counting their eggs. Reviewing their data on each nest, researchers discovered the coots who accepted foreign eggs usually laid fewer of their own eggs, presumably to prevent starvation of their own young. From this, they concluded that coots can count.

The Psalmist says that God's thoughts are beyond counting. However, His most important thought toward us is one of love because of His Son, Jesus Christ.

Prayer: Father, I thank You for revealing that Your thoughts toward us are loving for Jesus' sake. Amen.

Ref: *Science News*, 4/5/03, p. 212, S. Milius, "Careful Coots."

Bacteria Busy Maintaining Your Good Health

Psalm 22:26
*"The meek shall eat and be satisfied: they shall praise the
LORD that seek him: your heart shall live for ever."*

Scientists are beginning to get a better picture of how
digestion works and have identified 500 to 1,000 different kinds of
bacteria that live in our large intestine. The human body actually
works in a symbiotic relationship with these bacteria – we are their
host and provide them with a warm environment while they work
to benefit us, including digestion of our food.

These bacteria carry out many jobs. Some protect our
digestive system from bad bacteria. Others specialize in helping to
break down food. One of the most common bacterium breaks
indigestible complex carbohydrates down into easily digested
sugars. It also produces vitamins and other nutrients our body can
absorb. Researchers now believe that this busy bacterium also
turns-on some of our genes, so that more blood is able to absorb
food. Laboratory mice bred to be germ-free must eat 30 percent
more food than regular mice because they lack this bacterium.
What's more, when there is little sugar to work with, the bacteria
prompts intestinal cells to make sugar. Yet another bacterium
makes proteins that manage sugar production.

Scientists now believe that most bacteria benefit us. They
are part of God's creation, designed for the good of the creation.
God always has our good in mind, our greatest good being our
salvation that He has prepared for us in Jesus Christ.

*Prayer: I thank You for Your love, Father, and ask that
You would bring me health, both physically and
spiritually. Amen.*

Ref: *Science News*, 5/31/03, pp. 344-345, John Travis, "Gut Check."

"It Still Moves"

Genesis 1:16
"And God made two great lights; the greater light to rule the day, and the lesser light to rule the night: he made the stars also."

One doesn't have to study the history of science very long before one learns of the Roman Catholic Church's persecution of Galileo when he publicly declared that the Earth revolves about the sun. However, the Church of that day was not as ignorant as we have been led to believe. In fact, many churches of Rome in Galileo's day had long had their own astronomical observatories.

On the practical side, the Church of Rome had a great need to keep its liturgical calendar accurate, since many important church festivals, like Easter, depend on the phases of the moon. It is not generally known that the circular pavement in front of St. Peter's Basilica in Rome is actually the largest sundial in the world. The church of St. Mary of the Angels and Martyrs has an intricate brass sundial 144 feet long that tells both the date and the time. The roof of St. Ignatius in Rome houses the observatory where Angelo Secchi, the father of astrophysics, discovered a dark spot on Mars called Syrtis Major. Galileo's final words of protest when placed under house arrest – "and it still moves" – are inscribed on the sundial at Collegio Romano where the Pope asked his astronomers to confirm Galileo's conclusions.

Despite some errors in judgment, which are common to man, Christians have always valued accurate knowledge about God's creation.

Prayer: Father, I thank You for the gifts which You have given us through our growing knowledge of Your creation. Amen.

Ref: *Discover*, 3/05, p. 79, Joseph D'Agnese and Denise Kiernan, "Heavenly Astronomy."

Another Theory on the Origin of Life

Genesis 1:20
"And God said, Let the waters bring forth abundantly the moving creature that hath life, and fowl that may fly above the earth in the open firmament of heaven."

Deep beneath the waves of many of our oceans, superheated water gushes from the ocean floor. The water is so loaded with minerals, especially with black iron sulfide, that it looks like black smoke.

As the hot, mineral-rich water encounters the colder ocean water, some of the minerals precipitate, forming a black chimney around the escaping water. These chimneys are literally honeycombed with hollow compartments. Evolutionary scientists have proposed that these hollow compartments provided a kind of nursery shelter for the first life forms forming from the exotic chemistry of the hot mineral water. They know that living cell walls have an extremely complex structure, and this proposal is thought to solve the problem of the first life forming without its own cell walls. Some research has shown that iron sulfide may be able to support some of the chemistry related to life. However, one must assume that the right mix of ingredients for life had to be present. One must assume that amino acids were somehow available. Nor is there an explanation in the proposal of how biologically meaningful DNA information developed in these circumstances, nor any hint how cell walls would have developed.

Life is made possible by a very complex information system and the complex chemistry it controls. The Bible still offers the best explanation for the origin of life.

Prayer: Father, I thank You for life and especially for eternal life through the forgiveness of sin through Jesus Christ. Amen.

Ref: *Science News*, 4/26/03, pp. 264-266, Kendall Morgan, "Rocky Start."

Fishy Decorators

Psalm 90:17
"And let the beauty of the LORD our God be upon us: and establish thou the work of our hands upon us; yea, the work of our hands establish thou it."

The male bower bird is not the only creature who decorates his nest to attract a female mate. Biologists have discovered that male three-spined sticklebacks decorate their nests to attract females. What's more, the females appear to like a well-decorated nest.

Male sticklebacks build their nests and then wait for a female to stop by and lay eggs. Typically, their nests are built of algae. It has long been thought that fish, including sticklebacks, build their nests in such a way as to be hidden from predators. But researchers in Norway noticed that some sticklebacks placed red algae around the door to their nests. Some used red algae that had died and turned orange. This observation caused the scientists to wonder if the fish were actually decorating their nests and whether this attracted females. So they cut some small foil strips and put them into their research aquarium. They offered the fish five different colors of foil. They also offered the fish some sequins. The fish quickly collected foil strips, especially red ones, for their nests but showed no interest in the sequins. Follow-up research showed that females preferred the most brightly decorated nests.

Beauty and the love of beauty is also evidence of our Creator, for Scripture links beauty with His holiness. That beauty is ours by grace, through faith in Jesus Christ.

Prayer: Father, I thank You for the beauty of Your creation. I look to Jesus Christ for my holiness in Him. Amen.

Ref: *Science News*, 3/15/03, pp. 165-166, S. Milius, "Fish That Decorate."

Tiles and Glue Make Fine Mother-of-Pearl

Psalm 127:1
"Except the LORD build the house, they labour in vain that build it: except the LORD keep the city, the watchman waketh but in vain."

The mother-of-pearl found in abalone shells is both beautiful and exceptionally strong. Scientists wanted to find out how the shell formed in the hope that they could discover the secret of the shell's strength.

Researchers invented a clever way to do this, using only a couple of abalones growing in saltwater tanks. They placed a number of glass slides on the growing abalone shells. The new shell material thus formed on the glass slides as the abalones grew. Researchers removed a slide at intervals to study it using an electron microscope, leaving the remaining slides to collect more shell material. The microscope showed the well-known six-sided calcium carbonate tiles stacked like bricks. These tiles are cemented together with a protein. However, they found that the protein "cement" did not continue right to the edges of the stacks of "tiles." Unlike normal cement, the protein "cement" stretches, and this permits the stacks to slide sideways rather than shattering when, say, a predator tries to break the shell. The shell can thus absorb a great deal of force without breaking, and this is the secret of its strength.

The ordered structure of the abalone shell is difficult to explain as the result of unordered chance. The intricate genius of not gluing the edges of the stacked tiles to add strength to this design points directly to our Creator.

Prayer: Father, I rejoice that You do all things well. Help me to build my life on Your plan, which I read about in Scripture. Amen.

Ref: *Science News*, 2/12/05, p. 110, "Tiles stack for shell strength in abalone."

The Champion of Frozen Frogs

Job 38:29
"Out of whose womb came the ice? and the hoary frost of heaven, who hath gendered it?"

In previous Creation Moments programs we have told you about frogs that produce antifreeze in the winter. But the Wood Frog is the absolute champion at surviving below-freezing temperatures.

Most frogs that survive northern winters cannot withstand more than a few degrees below freezing before they begin to suffer cell damage. Researchers placed Wood Frogs into an industrial freezer where they became stiff and hard on the outside, and partially liquid on the inside. The frogs' metabolism stopped, and they became brain-dead. When they were thawed out, however, they returned to life as if nothing had ever happened. Wood Frogs avoid cell damage caused by the formation of ice crystals by generating glucose – a highly effective antifreeze. Other species of frogs produce glycerol, a less-effective type of antifreeze. However, the levels of glucose generated by the Wood Frog would cause cell damage in most other frogs, but these frogs limit the damage by shutting off their metabolism. What's more, should the Wood Frog suffer any cell damage by ice crystal formation, its blood contains a special fibrinogen that seals any leaks in its cell walls.

It is unlikely that all these different systems would evolve perfectly all at the same time. The Wood Frog is an example of a creature where everything had to work perfectly the first time – a testimony to our Creator.

Prayer: I thank You, Lord, that You care for all Your creatures. Amen.

Ref: *Discover*, 2/05, pp.20-21, Elizabeth Svoboda, "Waking From a Dead Sleep."

Be Careful What You Say About "Stone Age" People

Genesis 4:17
"And Cain knew his wife; and she conceived, and bare Enoch: and he builded a city, and called the name of the city, after the name of his son, Enoch."

When a conversation turns to Stone Age people, we tend to think of technologically clueless cave-dwellers. On the other hand, the Bible describes the first people as creative city-dwellers.

Scientists had always assumed that four Neolithic stone axe blades discovered in China had been polished smooth with quartz. However, one researcher decided to study the axe heads in more detail. As he did so, he marveled at the high degree of polish on the axe surfaces and noted that these surfaces were as smooth as the silicon wafers on which we etch electronic circuits. The axe blades turned out to be made of corundum – a form of aluminum oxide, the second hardest mineral on earth. Quartz was far too soft to have polished these axes! Only diamond could do the job. It turns out that there are two known diamond deposits within 200 miles of where the axes were found. To prove his theory, he cut some material from one of the axes and polished it with three different materials, including diamond. Careful measurements by an atomic force microscope showed that only diamond could duplicate the smooth surface of the axes.

These axes show that so-called Stone Age man had a sophisticated knowledge of materials, even using diamond to polish the second-hardest material on Earth – exactly what might be expected of creative city-dwellers.

Prayer: Father, I thank You for all the gifts and abilities You have given us. Amen.

Ref: *Science News*, 2/19/05, p. 116, A. Goho, "In the Buff."

Trees May Pollute More than Cars

Romans 8:22
"For we know that the whole creation groaneth and travaileth in pain together until now."

We have long been led to believe that the automobile and the power stations are the primary source of hydrocarbons and nitrous oxide pollutants in our atmosphere. On the other hand, the trees clean up the air. Now – surprise, surprise – the oak trees in California's Sierra Nevada have been found to release hydrocarbons into the air!

Scientists have also discovered that Scotch pine trees in southern Finland emit nitrogen oxides. These oxides react with atmospheric hydrocarbons to make nitric acid, a component of acid rain. Nitrogen oxides can also help make ozone, the primary part of smog. This discovery was made accidentally as researchers investigated whether the trees used nitrogen from the air. As part of their research, they sealed living tree branches in plastic bags and measured the changes in the air inside the bags. They expected to see a decrease in the amount of nitrogen. To their amazement, they saw the amount of nitrogen double! Some scientists estimate that the amount of nitrogen oxides produced by such northern forests may be as much, if not more than, the amounts produced by all of man's industry.

Sin is a greater pollution in our world, and because of sin, this world is wearing out. Thankfully, one day Christ will return and give believers a new creation, for He has been victorious over sin for us.

Prayer: Thank You, Father, for rescuing me from sin. Help me to be ready for Christ's return. Amen.

Ref: *Science News*, 3/15/03, p. 166, K. Morgan, "Fallen Trees?"

Fish Communicate on Secure Channel

John 19:38
"And after this Joseph of Arimathea, being a disciple of Jesus, but secretly for fear of the Jews, besought Pilate that he might take away the body of Jesus...."

The Bible most frequently associates the idea of secret communications with something evil. But sometimes, God uses secret communication for His purpose, as He did when Joseph of Arimathea secretly went to Pilate to secure the body of Jesus.

God has also given some animals the ability to communicate secretly. Take, for example, the Swordtail fish – like the one you might have in your aquarium. In the wild, this fish has a problem. They share their habitat with the Mexican tetras that are an aggressive predator and favor a meal of Swordtail. Yet, like many other fish, the male Swordtail must conduct a conspicuous male courting dance to mate. Even so, at mating time while the male is conducting his dance, the aggressive tetras pay no extra attention to his show. Researchers were puzzled until they discovered that the Swordtail conducts his mating communication on a secure channel that the tetras cannot see. They found that Swordtails have a stripe down the length of their body that reflects ultraviolet light essential to their mating communications. Examination of the tetras' eye lenses show that they cannot see ultraviolet light. So the tetras miss the whole show.

Now that the Swordtails' secret is revealed, we have additional reason to appreciate the work of our Creator. Thankfully, He has revealed to those with eyes to see His greatest secret: Salvation.

Prayer: Father, thank You for revealing the secret of the plan of salvation in the Bible. Help me not to keep it a secret. Amen.

Ref: *Science News*, 3/29/03, pp. 196-197, S. Milius, "Secret Signal."

Insect Parasites

Genesis 1:24
"And God said, Let the earth bring forth the living creature after his kind, cattle, and creeping thing, and beast of the earth after his kind: and it was so."

The Fire Ant can be aggressive and deliver dangerous venom, but in the perfect world originally created by God, insects such as this would not be expected to be so troublesome.

Scientists have been studying an insect parasite that may be helpful in controlling troublesome insects. This parasite, itself an insect, is capable of killing even Fire Ants. The parasitic order called Strepsiptera consists of over 500 species. They are known to prey on insects in 34 different families. In its larval stage, it seeks out a victim. When it finds one, it burrows through its hard outer layer to the first layer of cells. Here, it hijacks the insect's immune system, which rather than attacking it, encloses it in a layer of skin. Males of one species of the parasite attack ants while the females attack grasshoppers. Another species, which attacks a species of katydid in New Guinea, has no males at all. Once they mature inside their host, they poke the top of their body out of the skin bag and release some 800,000 larvae. The new generation sets out to find more hosts, and the host dies.

Scientists are studying these insect parasites in the hope of learning how to use them to control troublesome insects. In doing so, they are following God's command given in Genesis for man to subdue the Earth.

Prayer: Father, help us to understand Your creation so it may be productive. Amen.

Ref: *Science News*, 6/7/03, p. 358, S. Milius, "Skin Scam."

Anti-Evolutionary Butterflies

Psalm 59:8-9
"But thou, O LORD, shalt laugh at them; thou shalt have all the heathen in derision. Because of his strength will I wait upon thee: for God is my defense."

Most of the world's 17,000 species of butterflies are delicate, colorful creatures. Geneticists have been studying the various patterns found on their wings, hoping to relate their findings to evolution. But so far, all their findings have failed to support evolution, and some even contradict evolution.

Butterfly wings are covered with small scales. Some butterflies have scales containing molecular structures that look like tiny Christmas trees; these structures bend the light to create those iridescent colors. Other butterflies have scales containing pigment that produce the insects' various colors and patterns. But color has another function. Clouded Sulfur butterflies are found at various altitudes in Colorado's Rocky Mountains. Females of this species are generally darker than the males. In fact, the females tend to become darker in color as the altitude of their habitat rises. This has survival value because darker colors absorb more heat from the sun in the cooler, higher altitudes, enabling the normal rate of metabolism to be retained. However, the male butterflies prefer the lighter-colored females. This means that the advantage of having a darker color at higher altitudes would not be passed on to another generation. This is simply an example of rapid adaptation and is of no value to the theory of evolution.

As Scripture says, the foolishness of God is greater than man's wisdom – in this case, evolution.

Prayer: Father, I thank You for Your wisdom. Grant me understanding. Amen.

Ref: *Science News*, 2/15/03, pp. 104-106, Susan Milius, "How the Butterfly Gets Its Spots."

Big-Hearted Snakes

1 Kings 4:29
"And God gave Solomon wisdom and understanding exceeding much, and largeness of heart, even as the sand that is on the sea shore."

Burmese pythons have been described as "your basic couch-potato hunter." Most of the time they are not very active and don't need to eat for weeks or even months. But when the need to eat arises, they can eat whole wild pigs or any animal that weighs as much as the python does.

Large pythons will eat an entire wild pig at one time. Scientists have long recognized that digesting such a large animal is quite an athletic workout. Its metabolism increases as much as 40 times faster than normal while it is digesting the animal. Amazingly, two days after eating, its heart has increased in volume by 40 percent to handle the extra workload. Research shows that this increase is additional muscle mass. The snake does this by making a specific messenger RNA that makes heart muscle fiber. When the snake is not eating, this RNA returns to normal levels. The python will take about 14 days to digest a large animal, after which its heart and metabolism return to normal.

Obviously, the python knows nothing about RNA, metabolism or even its own heart. Scripture describes Solomon's wisdom as "largeness of heart," which refers to a broad understanding of how things work. Clearly, the python's large heart is the work of our Creator, Who is the source of all wisdom and understanding.

Prayer: Father, I marvel at Your wisdom in all things, and I ask that You would give me clear understanding. Amen.

Ref: *Science News*, 3/5/05, p. 149, S. Milius, "Shortcut to Big Heart."

The Healing Kiss of the Vampire

Leviticus 17:11
"For the life of the flesh is in the blood...."

A stroke – sometimes called a brain attack – happens when a blood clot prevents blood circulation in the brain. Unless the clot is quickly dissolved, the brain cells will die. There is currently only one approved drug to dissolve these clots, but it must be given within three hours of the stroke. Unfortunately, most stroke victims don't get to the hospital that quickly.

A new drug called desmoteplase has now proven safe and effective when given up to nine hours after a stroke. This is a preliminary conclusion after limited human testing. Most amazingly, this drug is made from the saliva of vampire bats! These bats must feed on blood. Typically, they pierce the skin of a cow or some other mammal. The bat saliva contains the working chemical in desmoteplase and keeps the blood from coagulating while the bat is feeding; when it is finished, the blood clots in its host quite naturally. Not only is the critical time in which desmoteplase can be applied much greater than that of the man-made drug, but it appears to carry no risk of causing a hemorrhage.

Again, man has gone to one of God's designs and found something that is better than anything man could devise. That this happens every day should send the message to everyone that we are the result of a wise Creator.

Prayer: Thank You, Father, for all the gifts you have given us in the creation. Help us to learn to use them wisely and for good. Amen.

Ref: *Science News*, 2/19/05, p. 126, "Vampire spit give strokes a licking."

Dinosaur Blood

Job 40:15
"Behold now behemoth, which I made with thee; he eateth grass as an ox."

A short while ago, Creation Moments reported the case of blood cells being discovered in a fossilized T. rex bone. Today, we report on another case. While most fossil bones have lithified, or turned to stone, occasionally identifiable bones are found that are only partially lithified.

Scientists had been studying the fossilized upper leg bone of a T. rex they date at 68 million years. The study consisted of dissolving the minerals from the fossilized bone with slightly alkaline solutions. They were completely surprised, for what remained was a soft, pliable material that proved to be high in carbon. Closer study of the pliable material revealed what appeared to be a network of blood vessels. Researchers were then amazed to find that this network was very similar to the networks found in modern ostrich bones. What's more, they found bone cells as well as red blood cells in this material. Such findings would never be expected in 68-million-year-old biological material, but the researchers could offer no other interpretation for what they saw. They are now hoping that the discovery might shed light on dinosaur physiology and metabolism.

Researchers are still puzzled at how 68-million-year-old biological material could be preserved for so long. Of course, the obvious answer is that the material is not nearly that old and that dinosaurs were even part of human history.

Prayer: Father, I thank You for all the wonders of Your creation, including the great dinosaurs. Amen.

Ref: *Science News*, 3/26/05, p. 195, S. Perkins, "Old Softy."

Dr. Beewolf

Titus 2:1, 4

*"But speak thou the things which become sound doctrine:
... That they may teach the young women to be sober, to
love their husbands, to love their children...."*

It took medicine thousands of years to discover antibiotics
and learn how to use them. Now it appears that a wasp called the
European Beewolf has been using an antibiotic all along.

The Beewolf builds a burrow in sandy ground to lay its
eggs, where the hatchlings will spend four to nine months after
they hatch. She also leaves a spot of white goo in the nursery
chamber. Then the Beewolf catches a bee, paralyzes it with a sting,
and returns it to her burrow. She will stock each nursery chamber
in the burrow with up to five bees. Scientists have long wondered
what the white goo was. Now research has shown that this
substance is laced with a new species of bacteria that live on the
wasp's antennae. It turns out that this species of bacteria makes an
antibiotic that apparently protects the hatchlings. When scientists
separated a clutch of 15 wasp larvae from the goo, only one made
it to adulthood. On the other hand, in a clutch of 18 larvae who had
access to the goo, 15 made it to adulthood.

Obviously, the Beewolf did not discover this use of an
antibiotic and learn how to use it to protect its children. Rather, the
Beewolf's Creator – Who created antibiotics in the first place –
built this behavior into the Beewolf to help it survive.

***Prayer: Father, I thank You for Your love and care of
Your entire creation. Help me to see Your love for me in
Jesus Christ. Amen.***

Ref: *Science News,* 3/12/05, p. 166, S. Milius, "Bacterial Nanny."

Six-Legged Law and Order

Romans 13:4a
"For he is the minister of God to thee for good. But if thou do that which is evil, be afraid; for he beareth not the sword in vain: for he is the minister of God...."

Like human society, many social insects have laws, lawbreakers and law enforcement. Researchers have now established that at least 15 species employ law enforcement.

While these insects rely on a queen as the only egg-layer of the colony, the workers are also capable of laying eggs that can hatch. One of the most common crimes in these nests is "rogue egg-laying" in which one of the workers tries to sneak some of her eggs in among the eggs laid by the queen. This is strictly forbidden. The other workers – or even the queen herself – will enforce nest law that requires the death of the offender. Then, the offender's eggs are searched out and destroyed when found. In one experiment, researchers planted worker-laid eggs in a honeybee nest. Within 24 hours, workers had found and destroyed all but 1 percent of the eggs that had not been laid by their queen. Another researcher offered nursemaid ants a mixture of eggs, some from their queen and others laid by the workers. The nursemaids quickly stacked most of the queen-laid eggs and began to care for them. However, when they discovered a worker's egg, the nursemaids would typically pass the egg around among themselves and then finally crush it.

Law and order is a gift of God to both man and animals for which we owe God thanksgiving.

Prayer: I thank You, Lord, for those who enforce the law among us. Keep them under Your protection. Amen.

Ref: *Science News*, 3/19/05, pp. 184-186, Susan Milius, "Cops With Six Legs."

Lungfish Take a Bite Out of Evolution

Genesis 1:21a
"And God created great whales, and every living creature that moveth, which the waters brought forth abundantly, after their kind...."

According to evolution theory, there were no four-limbed creatures living on land until 360 million years ago. That is supposedly when Lungfish appear in the fossil record. Lungfish can breathe air, have four fins arranged rather like legs and can even climb trees. Long ago, evolutionists declared that all four-limbed creatures that live on land, including man, evolved from the Lungfish.

As we look at the variety of land-living creatures, evolutionists are here claiming a great deal of change from our lowly Lungfish ancestry. It is interesting, however, that the Lungfishes themselves have changed very little in the supposed 360 million years of their existence. Lungfish hatchlings today have small teeth, which, as they grow to adulthood, fuse into a bony dental plate. In this adult plate, the individual teeth are fused to one another. There are thousands of well-preserved fossils of both hatchlings and adult Lungfish that supposedly lived 360 million years ago. A study of these fossils shows that even the dental development of Lungfish has not changed since the first Lungfish appeared among the fossils.

One cannot escape the conclusion that there has been no evolution of Lungfish since they first swam the seas. This agrees with Scripture. It also poses a problem in logic to suggest that such a stable creature could produce the variety of four-limbed creatures we see today.

Prayer: I thank You, Lord, that I have been specially made by Your hand. Amen.

Ref: *Nature*, 31/5/01, Vol. 411, p. 548, Robert R. Reisz, Moya M. Smith, "Lungfish dental pattern conserved for 360 Myr."

Jumbo Fairy Shrimp

Psalm 136:4
"To him who alone doeth great wonders: for his mercy endureth for ever."

There are about 300 species of a delicate creature known as Fairy shrimp. Unlike the shrimp that might end up on your plate for dinner, Fairy shrimp are typically very small.

Fairy shrimp usually live in pools of water that may dry up and remain dry for years. When the pool is dry, they exist as egg-like cysts, sometimes for years, before the rains begin to fill the pool. Early in 2005, biologists announced the discovery of a new species of Fairy shrimp swimming in two lakebeds of the Idaho desert. The new species is much larger than most Fairy shrimp, growing as long as three inches. It has spines on its front legs for capturing prey. While they look frilly and delicate, they prey on smaller Fairy shrimp. When the larger Fairy shrimp finds a smaller shrimp, it bites it to immobilize it. If it's not hungry at the moment, it stores its catch by attaching it to velcro-like patches on it abdomen. A full-grown member of the new species can store up to four smaller shrimp for later use.

The beauty of these Fairy shrimp is a testimony to God's unlimited creativity. At the same time, its cannibalism is a witness to the effects of sin. We thank God that He has sent His Son, Jesus Christ, to save us from the ultimate consequences of our sin.

Prayer: Thank You, Lord, for carrying my sin on the cross and bringing this Gospel to my ears and heart. Amen.

Ref: Associated Press, 3/16/05, "New fairy shrimp species discovered in Idaho."

Self-Correcting Genetics

Genesis 1:12
"And the earth brought forth grass, and herb yielding seed after his kind, and the tree yielding fruit, whose seed was in itself, after his kind: and God saw that it was good."

Charles Darwin's natural selection as the driving force for evolution was abandoned almost a century ago and replaced by random mutations. Every textbook since then has therefore claimed that all the varieties of extinct and living plants and animals have been the result of random mutations. However, the Bible teaches us that plants and animals reproduce "after their kind." Plant biologists at Purdue University recently made a startling discovery that supports the Bible's teaching.

Researchers were working with a species of mustard plant commonly used in genetic experiments. This plant sometimes has a mutation that causes deformed flowers. Since it is a recessive mutation, such plants have no genetic information that would enable them to have normal flowers. To their amazement, the scientists found that 10 percent of these plants were producing offspring with normal flowers, even without the correct genetic information. The plants were put through all sorts of genetic testing to see if the correct genetic information might be found hiding in unexpected places within the plants. None of the correct genetic information was ever found, and they ruled out the possibility that the wrong genetic information changed back into the correct kind.

God created living things to reproduce after their kind. He has made DNA so that it can correct itself. Apparently, He has included other ways for living things to do this, too.

Prayer: Father, I thank You that living things reproduce after their kind, to our good and to Your glory. Amen.

Ref: *Science News*, 4/9/05, p. 235, "Plants fix genes using copies from ancestors."

Calculating Owls

Isaiah 43:20
"The beast of the field shall honor me, the dragons and the owls: because I give waters in the wilderness, and rivers in the desert, to give drink to my people, my chosen."

It's a dark, moonless night. A barn owl perches, silently as a shadow, in a tree. A hundred feet away, a deer mouse scampers over a dry leaf, producing a slight rustling sound. Within seconds, the owl's talons grab the mouse.

We all know that owls have excellent vision in the darkness. Researchers at Cal Tech in Pasadena have learned that there is much more to the barn owl's abilities than vision. To get their data, they wired up 14 barn owls with headphones and then studied their responses to pairs of sounds. Their results convincingly show that barn owls construct a detailed map of their surroundings inside their brains. To locate the source of a sound, owls don't simply add together the incoming sound signals, as would be expected. Rather, the owl's auditory nerve cells calculate the distance of incoming sounds, then apply this information to its mental map in a process researchers could only describe as "multiplication." Up until this time, humans were thought to be the only living beings whose thought processes used such "multiplication." Researchers said that this "multiplication" is a much more powerful way for the brain to process information.

God knew that owls would need this ability to successfully make their living, so God – as the source of all intelligence – gave it to them. Evolution cannot design intelligence.

Prayer: Dear Father, I rejoice that Your creation glorifies You. Help my life to do the same. Amen.

Ref: *Science*, Vol. 292, 13/4/01, Laura Helmuth, "Location Neurons Do Advanced Math."

Grape Weather

Genesis 8:22
"While the earth remaineth, seedtime and harvest, and cold and heat, and summer and winter, and day and night shall not cease."

Some people worry about global warming, but if you think about it, we once had an Ice Age and now we don't ... so warming is not new. Other people argue we are merely seeing the normal cycles of heating and cooling.

Now the Pinot Noir grape may help settle this debate. The harvest date for this grape is so closely tied to weather that average annual temperatures can be determined from the date of the harvest. Harvest dates for the grape have been carefully recorded for centuries in Burgundy, France. These records have harvest dates for every harvest since 1370. Researchers were able to correlate these dates with average annual temperatures. The year 2003 was actually the warmest in over six centuries of data, while the second warmest years were in the 1520s and again in the 1650s. No modern warming cycle has yet lasted as long as those of 350 years ago. The findings also show that there was a long cold period that lasted from the 1750s until the 1970s.

After the Flood, God promised that the seasons, with their seed time and harvest, would not cease while the world is here. However, He did not promise that there wouldn't be cycles. We can be comforted by the fact that He has promised that the weather will always allow crops to be grown.

Prayer: Father, I thank You that You provide the weather we need to grow food. Help me to trust always that You will provide. Amen.

Ref: *Nature*, Vol. 432, 18/11/04, pp. 289-290, "Grape ripening as a past climate indicator."

Sometimes Brain Size Doesn't Count

2 Timothy 2:8
"Remember that Jesus Christ of the seed of David was raised from the dead according to my gospel...."

You look up a telephone number and dial it. You didn't write it down, you simply remembered it. But an hour later, you will probably not be able to remember the number. That kind of memory is known as "working memory."

Honeybees may not have much for a brain, but researchers at the Australian National University in Canberra have found that honeybees have a surprisingly good working memory. Researchers constructed a tunnel, connected to a pipe with openings to different destinations. They marked these openings with simple signs – like wavy lines. They trained the bees to learn that an opening with a specific sign offered a treat, while the other opening – also marked by a sign – offered nothing. After the bees had learned which sign marked the goodies, the scientists made the tunnel longer to learn how long the bees' working memory lasted. They also began offering differing signs to learn how flexible the bees' working memory is. Their conclusion is that honeybees have a working memory that lasts about five seconds, the same as birds. But more amazing is that their memory proved as flexible as a rhesus monkey.

Gathering pollen from a range of flowering plants requires a good working memory. Honeybees' sophisticated working memories have nothing to do with evolutionary ascent. It's a needed ability given them by a loving Creator.

Prayer: Father, I remember Your love and mercy toward me in Jesus Christ, Whose innocent suffering and death saved me. Amen.

Ref: *Science News*, 4/2/05, p. 213, S. Milius, "Little Brains That Could."

The Problem of Genius

Genesis 1:26
"And God said, Let us make man in our image, after our likeness..."

The piano you hear in the background was being played by Matt Savage. He wrote the music and called this piece "Ladybug bounce." Matt is an autistic boy, does piano concerts and was just 12 years old when this piece was recorded.

How does evolution explain such extraordinary talent? Certainly it cannot be ascribed to "survival of the fittest," since musical or mathematical abilities are not related to survival. Textbooks based upon evolution generally remain silent about genius. However, when the question is considered from a biblical perspective, a reasonable explanation does present itself.

God created Adam and Eve and declared them to be "very good." That would mean perfect in every respect – perfect memory, perfect ability to concentrate and so on. Scripture further tell us of Adam's disobedience and Fall. We are the living members of his offspring and note the historical decline in Man's mental abilities. Now, is it just possible that these remarkable qualities exist in everyone's psyche or soul but are normally hidden or covered over? Occasionally, an individual is born – such as Matt Savage – where part of that covering is removed. Science cannot adequately explain these cases, but Creation Moments suggests that God occasionally removes some of the sin-stain on their soul so that a little of the original perfection is revealed to convey to the rest of us what the original creation was like.

Prayer: Dear Lord, teach us to be sensitive to those You may be using to show us the original perfection of Your creation. Amen.

Ref: CD album *Cutting Loose,* track #14. Other CD albums available from: Savage Records, P.O. Box 35, Francestown, NH 03043, www.savagerecords.com. Matt does concert tours with his trio.

Man: The Missing Years

Genesis 2:15
"And the LORD God took the man, and put him into the garden of Eden to dress it and to keep it."

According to the evolutionary timetable, mankind has been on Earth for about 100,000 years. Archeologists and Paleo-archeologists claim that 100,000 years ago the earliest true men began to bury their dead, often with flowers and other trinkets, suggesting that he was capable of abstract thought. Paintings on cave walls and ceilings show that early man was capable of creating exquisite art. Other excavations have yielded scale models, toys and jewelry. It is strange, then, that for these 95,000 years, man left no written record of himself.

We are also told that, according to the evolutionary timetable, it was only about 5,000 years ago that man discovered agriculture. Why would it have taken at least 95,000 years for man to have discovered that when seeds are planted in the ground, they sprout and produce more food? The truth is, even the most lush jungle on earth today cannot produce enough plant material to feed people. Anywhere you find people in the jungle, you will also find gardens to supplement their diet.

The answer to this mystery is simple. Those first 95,000 years never happened. The written record we have of man and our knowledge of his agriculture can be easily accounted for within a literal understanding of the biblical history. And the Bible tells us that Adam was the first to engage in agriculture.

Prayer: Father, I thank You for the blessings of the fruit of the earth and of the written word, especially the Bible. Amen

Ref: *Proceedings of the Second International Conference on Creationism*, vol. 1, pp. 73-78, James O. Dritt, "Man's Earliest Beginnings: Discrepancies in Evolutionary Timetables."

It's a War Out There

Psalm 71:2
"Deliver me in thy righteousness, and cause me to escape: incline thine ear unto me, and save me."

The enemy prowls the night skies, searching. But its would-be victims may have sensitive sonar detectors, allowing it to flee before detection. If the prey is spotted on sonar, the prey has counter measures – even jamming the enemy's sonar.

No, this is not a scene from some modern battlefield. Rather, it is a description of things going on all around us. Many insects – including moths, beetles and katydids – have sensors that can detect a bat's sonar before they are spotted and targeted by the bat. When targeted, moths will either fold their wings and drop to the ground, or they will spiral upward erratically. The bat never knows what to expect. Other moths will send out high-pitched squeaks that some scientists think disrupt the bat's sonar. While most fish cannot hear at the frequency of the dolphin's sonar, the American shad can. Lab tests have shown that the shad will move away from sounds that simulate foraging dolphins. If the sound becomes louder, the shad will form themselves into a tight ball at the opposite end of the tank, making any single fish less likely to be the dolphin's victim.

Our greatest enemies – sin and its results – are not so easily evaded. But thank God that we can flee to the wounds of Christ for forgiveness of our sin so we may know God's love.

Prayer: I thank You, Father, that I can escape Your wrath for my sin through the innocent suffering of Jesus Christ. Amen.

Ref: *Science News*, 5/14/05, p. 315, "Biological Arms Race."

The Monster with 24 Arms

1 Peter 5:8
"Be sober, be vigilant; because your adversary the devil, as a roaring lion, walketh about, seeking whom he may devour..."

A real monster prowls the ocean floor from the Aleutian Islands to Southern California. It is a terror to even relatively large bottom dwellers. It eats many things, including hermit crabs, clams, sea cucumbers, sea urchins, and even abalone. This monster goes by the seemingly innocent name of the Sunflower Star.

The Sunflower Star begins life as a microscopic larva, much like other sea stars. But as it grows, it surpasses anything that other sea stars can achieve. Its five arms become more arms as it grows until it finally has 24 arms. By this time it can be 39 inches across. But its size does not limit its speed. It uses 15,000 tube feet to move over five feet per minute. This is possible because, like other sea stars, the Sunflower Star's skeleton is made up of just a few pieces of skeletal mesh, making it more flexible. It is such a terror to other creatures that when they sense its approach they flee at surprising speed. Even the Northern Abalone, which normally moves sluggishly, flees in the hope that the Sunflower Star will not capture it.

The Bible urges vigilance on our part because our spiritual enemy is a monster who seeks to entrap us in sin. We can be thankful that Jesus Christ has provided both deliverance and protection from this monster.

Prayer: Lord, I thank You that You have rescued me from the devil. Help me stay vigilant so I may resist his traps. Amen.

Ref: Royal British Columbia Museum, Victoria, British Columbia, "The Sunflower Star," http://www.royalbcmuseum.bc.ca.

Oxygen Optional Carp

Psalm 77:14
"Thou art the God that doest wonders: thou hast declared thy strength among the people."

The long cold winters of Scandinavia not only freeze the lakes, but pile so much snow on the lake ice that no light can penetrate to the cold, unfrozen water beneath. This means that the creatures below the ice can use up all the oxygen in the lake water.

As a result of the lack of oxygen, lactic acid builds up in the bodies of these creatures as they metabolize sugar to get energy. However, turtles can stand levels of lactic acid in their systems that would kill you or me, and they lower their heartbeat to 10 percent of normal. The Crucian carp, similar to a goldfish, takes a unique approach to this lack of oxygen. As the oxygen disappears, the carp slows its heartbeat. The fish then changes its entire metabolic chemistry to a process that can get energy from sugar without oxygen. This oxygen-free metabolism turns the lactic acid into ethanol, which the fish releases through its gills. The members of this carp family are the only vertebrates that can continue normal life without oxygen.

That God's wonders seem without number and often seem impossible tells us of God's unlimited creativity and His ability to do anything. His plan of salvation – in which His Son, Jesus Christ, carried our sin on the cross – makes us thankful for His creativity and wisdom.

Prayer: I rejoice, dear Father, for Your great wisdom and power are used in love toward us. Amen.

Ref: *Science News,* 10/2/04, p. 213, S. Milius, "Beat Goes On."

Fresh Dust?

1 Corinthians 15:40
"There are also celestial bodies, and bodies terrestrial: but the glory of the celestial is one, and the glory of the terrestrial is another."

The last few years have seen a good deal of excitement among astronomers over the possibility of discovering planets orbiting distant stars. Astronomers are looking at stars that are surrounded by disks of dust and debris.

The idea is that planets form over millions of years from the dust and rock that orbits a star. This was supposedly how the Earth formed billions of years ago. Hundreds of such stars have so far been identified. Often, these debris fields extend further from the star they orbit than, say, Pluto is from our sun. The question is, are the discovery of planets and debris around other stars proof of evolution's story of the formation of the Earth? Scientists believe that it takes two or three million years for planets to form out of the orbiting debris. However, they also recognize that it only takes a few thousand years before a star's gravity draws the dust into itself, or the pressure of its radiation forces the dust away from itself. This leaves the hundreds of stars with dusty debris fields a mystery. Astronomers believe that all these stars still have their dust after millions or billions of years because they are getting fresh dust from somewhere else ... but scientists don't know where.

Perhaps a better explanation is that these stars are really only about 6,000 years old.

Prayer: Father, I thank You for Your trustworthy Word, which tells me of the forgiveness of sins through Your Son. Amen.

Ref: *Science News,* 7/2/05, pp. 10-12, Ron Cowen, "Panning Distant Dust."

The Master of Light

Psalm 96:9
"O worship the LORD in the beauty of holiness: fear before him, all the earth."

Over hundreds of years, science has learned a lot about manipulating light. And while lasers and liquid crystals might seem pretty sophisticated, some of God's creatures show us how much more there is to learn.

The Morpho butterfly is one of the brightest butterflies in nature, but looked at closely in artificial light, it appears dull gray-brown. However, in the sunlight its color changes to a bright blue. It can do this because the scales on its wings form a type of diffraction grating called a photonic band gap. This diffraction grating is formed by a precise spacing of the scales so that they are similar to the wavelength of sunlight. When white light hits the grating, it breaks down into its various colors. The red light waves cancel each other out and all the other colors are scattered, except the blue. As a result, the blue color never fades, and it is so intense that it can be seen up to half a mile away. Scientists comment that we do not yet know how to make an optical structure this complex.

The Morpho butterfly, with all its precise engineering, is a testimony to our Creator's skill and love of beauty. He considers holiness the greatest of beauties – a beauty given us through the suffering and death of His Son, Jesus Christ.

Prayer: Thank You, Father, for the light of Your truth and giving us the beauty of Christ's holiness. Amen.

Ref: *Discover*, 8/05, pp. 42-47, George M. Whitesides, "Illuminated Life."

Chickadee-Dee-Dee Danger

Matthew 8:20
"And Jesus said unto him, Foxes have holes, and birds of the air have nests; but the Son of man hath not where to lay his head."

Millions of North Americans are familiar with the call of the Black-Capped chickadee. However, most bird-watchers know that the little chickadee communicates danger with its "chickadee-dee-dee" call. Bird-watchers also know that chickens use different warnings for dangers from the air or from the ground.

Scientists decided to see if chickadees used specialized calls for different dangers. In their first experiments they used a stuffed hawk to see what the chickadees in an outdoor aviary would do. However, they were only fooled once, and after that researchers had to use live hawks. After studying over 5,000 responses, a pattern emerged. Small, agile raptors like hawks are more dangerous to chickadees than, say, a large, horned owl – which the chickadees can easily evade. When confronted by a smaller raptor, the birds' "chicka" call added up to four "dee"s in rapid succession, instead of two more leisurely "dee"s. Even more "dee"s might be added if the chickadees evaluated the danger as greater. Most frightening to the little birds was a pygmy owl that rated 23 "dee"s.

God cares for all His creatures and knowing that predation would enter the creation with man's sin, provided them with ways to warn each other. He also gave man His Word to warn us how to avoid sin and how to escape from it through Jesus Christ should we become entrapped.

Prayer: I thank You, Lord, for Your protection from all the dangers we face, especially the danger of our sin. Amen.

Ref: *Science News*, 6/25/05, pp. 403-404, S. Milius, "Dee for Danger."

The Importance of Being Father

Ephesians 6:4
"And, ye fathers, provoke not your children to wrath: but bring them up in the nurture and admonition of the Lord."

How important is father to a child's religious growth? Due to the way in which census information is gathered in Switzerland, researchers were able to find out. And while their conclusions might shock modern sensitivities, they are really not too surprising.

If both mother and father attend church regularly with their children, 33 percent of those children will grow up to attend church regularly. Another 41 percent will grow up to attend church irregularly, and the remaining 25 percent of the children will end up not going to church at all. Amazingly, if only the father is regular in his church attendance and the mother is irregular or doesn't go at all, the number of children who grow up to attend church regularly or irregularly actually increases. On the other hand, if only the mother attends church regularly and the father doesn't go at all, only two percent of the children will grow up to attend church regularly. Researchers concluded that a father's practice of his faith has 12 times more influence upon his children than the mother's. Similar studies in England showed the same trend.

While no one would dispute that mothers are a great blessing and provide things that fathers cannot provide, it's clear that fathers are essential to healthy spiritual development. This is why, in Scripture, God charges fathers with spiritual leadership.

Prayer: Lord, I thank You for faithful fathers everywhere. Help Christian fathers to take their responsibilities seriously. Amen.

Ref: *Touchstone Magazine*, 2003, Robbie Low, "The Truth About Men and Church."

Busy Mushrooms

Joel 1:17
"The seed is rotten under their clods, the garners are laid desolate, the barns are broken down; for the corn is withered."

If it weren't for mushrooms, there would be so many un-decayed dead trees that there would be no room on Earth for anything else to grow. But mushrooms don't just recycle dead trees. They help make the trees grow in the first place.

The mushrooms that we see are merely the part of the fungus that produces the fruit. Most of the mushroom is unseen. If you were to peel back the bark of a decaying tree you'll see white tissue called mycelia. That is the main part of the mushroom plant. Many species of mushrooms combine efforts to help trees grow. Their mycelium forms a sheath around tree roots that help to deliver water and nutrients. In return, they get excess sugar produced by the tree. This relationship is so close that both the fungi and the tree depend upon each other. For example, researchers estimate that the Douglas Fir has about 1,000 species of fungus working together for its support. The fungi will even form underground mycelial networks to move nutrients between different kinds of tree.

Clearly, God has designed a finely balanced partnership between trees and fungi for their mutual survival. In the Old Testament, God punished His people through the loss of their planted crops. Is it just possible He tipped the fine balance of other such partnerships to do His bidding?

Prayer: Father, thank You for the beauty of trees and especially for the tree on which our Lord died to take away our sins. Amen.

Ref: *Discover*, 2005, pp. 48-53, Greg Mueller, "Dr. Mushroom."

Dancing Infrared Ground Squirrels

Numbers 21:9
"And Moses made a serpent of brass, and put it upon a pole, and it came to pass, that if a serpent had bitten any man, when he beheld the serpent of brass, he lived."

The last creature a rattlesnake wants to see is the California ground squirrel.

When an adult ground squirrel finds a rattlesnake, it begins to taunt the snake. The squirrel dashes into striking range, whips its tail about, bites the snake's tail and kicks sand on it. While a rattlesnake can strike with lightning speed, the little ground squirrel is even faster and well able to dart out of the way. Even if it was bitten, the venom wouldn't kill it, since these squirrels have proteins in their blood that detoxify the poison. Frustrated snakes have been known to simply retreat when faced with this treatment. Researchers have learned that the squirrels' bag of tricks is even deeper. Rattlesnakes can see heat as infrared light. When the ground squirrel is taunting the rattlesnake, it sends additional blood to its tail, causing it to heat up and producing a very obvious infrared image for the snake, further confusing it. Interestingly enough, when the ground squirrel taunts a gopher snake – which cannot detect the infrared – it does not heat its tail.

How does the squirrel know that the rattlesnake can be confused with an infrared show while the gopher snake cannot? The only explanation is that the Creator Who made them both – and calls us to saving faith in His Son, Jesus Christ – designed the ground squirrels' unique display.

Prayer: Father, I thank You for the wonders You have made and for the innocent death of Your Son to take my sins away. Amen.

Ref: *Science News*, 6/26/04, p. 403, S. Milius, "Hot Bother."

Ancient Hummingbirds Were Quite Modern

Genesis 1:20
"And God said, Let the waters bring forth abundantly the moving creature that hath life, and fowl that may fly above the earth in the open firmament of heaven."

Today, hummingbirds are found only in North, Central and South America. Of course, since Noah's Ark landed in the mountains of Ararat, they had to cross Europe and the Atlantic or Asia to get there. However, until now, there was no evidence for this migration.

Scientists have now discovered two hummingbird fossils in a clay pit in southwestern Germany. These tiny fossils are remarkable in many ways. Until now, evolutionists claimed the earliest hummingbird fossils to be one million years old. The new fossils are said to be 30 to 34 million years old. While we would not agree with the evolutionary dating, we would expect the hummingbird fossils in Europe or Asia to predate those in the New World. Even more interesting is that the fossils suggest that these older birds are fully functional hummingbirds. Their wing bones are like those of modern hummingbirds, which suggest that they could hover and fly backward just like the hummingbirds we know today. Their beaks were twice as long as their skulls, suggesting that they drank nectar just like modern hummingbirds. In other words, there is no sign of any evolutionary development, another fact we would expect.

While the evidence for the history of hummingbirds is what we would expect, we do not need scientific evidence to uphold Scriptural truth. We have God's Word on it.

Prayer: I thank You, Lord, for the beauty of Your creation, which remains beautiful, despite our sin. Amen.

Ref: *Science News*, 5/8/04, p. 292, S. Perkins, "Ancient Buzzing."

Can Monkeys Count?

Ecclesiastes 3:21
*"Who knoweth the spirit of man that goeth upward, and
the spirit of the beast that goeth downward to the earth?"*

Listeners will know from our Creation Moments programs that the scientific establishment is firmly convinced that man evolved from the higher apes millions of years ago. For this reason, rhesus monkeys have long been used not only for pharmaceutical trials but in psychological tests to determine how man's intelligence evolved.

Researchers at Duke University, North Carolina, wanted to know if rhesus monkeys could count, and they set up an experiment to find out. Using two television screens, one showed two monkeys vocalizing and the other showed three. However, the audio of each television could be controlled so that in some trials two monkeys could be seen but three voices heard and vice versa. Each one of the 20 test monkeys spent more time watching the matching number of monkeys and voices. The researchers concluded that the rhesus monkeys could tell the difference between the numbers two and three.

They also pointed out that the monkeys can count small numbers because this ability relates to their social worlds. Yes, and by the same token Creation Moments would add that some insects can count to hundreds, but none of this means that man is related to insects or monkeys! Scripture carefully distinguishes between man and animals. God placed man over the animals and gave him an eternal soul that is saved by His Son, Jesus Christ.

Prayer: Father, I thank and praise You that You have made me because You wanted to love me through Your Son, Jesus. Amen.

Ref: *Science News*, 7/2/05, p. 14, "Monkeys keep track of small numbers."

Getting Rid of the Trash

Psalm 139:15

"My substance was not hid from thee, when I was made in secret, and curiously wrought in the lowest parts of the earth."

Years ago, evolutionary scientists labeled 180 human organs, such as the appendix, as vestiges left over from evolution. The fact is, they did not know the function these organs actually served. Since that time, it has been learned that every one of these organs has useful functions and has nothing to do with evolution.

Now, a similar situation is shaping up with DNA. As scientists learned what the different segments of DNA do, they also found segments that appeared to have no function. These segments have often been referred to as "junk DNA." Predictably, evolutionists have suggested that these apparently useless segments of DNA are left over from our evolutionary history. Now, researchers at Jackson Laboratory in Bar Harbor, Maine, have discovered that they may have a function after all. They were studying early mammalian development in fertilized mouse eggs and early embryos. As they traced the genes at work in these early stages of development, they discovered that about 10 percent of the so-called "junk DNA" was actively making protein during the first cell divisions of the egg. Further research is planned.

Like the so-called vestigial organs, at least some so-called "junk DNA" has a purpose and has nothing to do with evolution. Once again, as ignorance is replaced with knowledge, we gain a greater appreciation of what our Creator has made.

Prayer: Father, I thank You that I am fearfully and wonderfully made by Your loving design. Amen.

Ref: *Science News,* 10/16/04, p. 243, C. Brownlee, "Trash to Treasure."

Being Right About Right and Wrong

Romans 2:15
"Which show the work of the law written in their hearts,
their conscience also bearing witness, and their thoughts
the mean while accusing or else excusing one another..."

Ethicists who believe in evolution are trying to figure out an evolutionary explanation for why people universally have a sense of right and wrong. This line of study is so new that it doesn't yet have a name, although some have suggested "neuroethics" or "moral neuroscience."

Much of this study began by looking at the theories of philosophers John Stewart Mill and Immanuel Kant. Mill taught that moral good is defined by those actions that do the most good for the most people, even if some individuals must suffer in the process. Kant said that moral good could be defined by pure reason. Then they add in philosopher David Hume who taught that people consider an action to be good if it makes them feel good. However, researchers in this field noted that even monkeys, who don't read philosophy, have a sense of fair play. In one experiment, monkeys who had been accepting cucumbers as a reward began rejecting the cucumbers after they saw other monkeys getting much tastier grapes. At this point in this new "science," some researchers have concluded that right and wrong are nothing more than the instinctive firing of brain neurons.

Scripture, on the other hand, says that God has written His law on our hearts. This is a much more logical explanation of man's universal sense of right and wrong.

Prayer: I thank You, Father, for Your law, but I find
comfort in the Gospel of forgiveness. Amen.

Ref: *Discover*, 4/04, pp. 60-65, Carl Zimmer, "Whose Life Would You Save?"

Global Positioning Lobsters

Isaiah 40:22
"It is he that sitteth upon the circle of the earth, and the inhabitants thereof are as grasshoppers; that stretcheth out the heavens as a curtain, and spreadeth them out as a tent to dwell in..."

Homing pigeons are valued because of their highly developed sense of direction, and this includes the ability to read the Earth's magnetic field. Some other birds, turtles and even a few salamanders have also shown this same ability. However, bees, ants or people are not born with this ability.

Until now, those animals classified as "lower animals" on the evolutionary scale were not expected to have such navigation abilities. However, this ability has now been confirmed in – of all things – the Caribbean spiny lobster. Researchers collected more than 100 lobsters from various locations; each lobster was tagged with a number indicating the exact location of their discovery. They were then placed in closed containers and boated about in circuitous routes for an hour so that they would not remember the direction of home. To further confuse the lobsters, some of the containers contained magnets. Each lobster was then fitted with a removable hood so that they were effectively blindfolded. They were then placed in a large tank to see which direction they would naturally seek. Typically, the lobsters would begin trying to walk home, aiming to within three compass degrees of where they were captured.

Scientists were surprised that a so-called "lower invertebrate" has a navigation system as sophisticated as a homing pigeon. But they shouldn't be surprised. The same wise Creator made both creatures.

Prayer: Lord, I thank You for Your goodness toward us and all Your creatures in giving them their survival abilities.

Ref: *Science News,* 1/4/03, p. 4, S. Milius, "Homing Lobsters."

From Mozart to Einstein

1 Chronicles 15:16
"And David spake to the chief of the Levites to appoint their brethren to be the singers with instruments of music..."

Scientists have shown that the so-called "Mozart effect" of music in young children is just a myth. This popular idea said that exposing young children to classical music improves their ability in non-verbal tasks. Nevertheless, researchers did find a more interesting effect of classical music on students.

At the beginning of the school year, researchers from the University of Toronto randomly assigned 132 first graders into one of four groups. Some received piano or drama lessons while others took chess lessons or joined science programs. At the end of the school year, the students' IQ was evaluated. Those who had taken piano lessons showed a 7 point increase in IQ. Those involved in the other programs showed only a 4¼ point increase in IQ. Researchers believe that the focused attention that learning music requires for extended periods is a major factor in the greater increase of IQ among the music students. They also suggest that the memorization required in a musical education also helps IQ. Further research into these and other factors will be the subject of long-term study.

Music is a gift from God, and the study of music has traditionally been considered an essential element of a good education. Modern research is showing us that this traditional approach to music has more wisdom than is offered by a purely materialistic approach to education.

Prayer: Father, I thank You for the gift of music. O, Lord, open my lips that I might sing forth Your praises. Amen.

Ref: *Science News*, 6/19/04, p. 389, B. Bower, "Tuning Up Young Minds."

A Cage of Light

Psalm 27:1
"The LORD is my light and my salvation; whom shall I fear? the LORD is the strength of my life; of whom shall I be afraid?"

Ask any evolutionist and he will tell you that the Venus Flower-basket is one of the least-evolved animals. This animal is actually a sponge that is made up of a colony of creatures, and it does some amazing things.

The Venus Flower-basket builds a basket-like skeleton made up of glass-like silica covered only by a thin layer of cells. The intricate internal structure of this skeleton is reinforced to provide the greatest strength, using the least amount of material. The resulting skeleton turns out to be a fiber-optic network whose sophistication has been compared to modern fiber optics used for telecommunications networks. Symbiotic luminescent microorganisms make a home inside the base of the sponge, sending their light throughout the Flower-basket's fiber-optic skeleton. The Flower-basket traps shrimp inside this skeleton, where they spend their entire lives. The food they drop feeds those luminescent microorganisms at the bottom of the basket. The purpose of the light pulses is to attract prey to feed the shrimp who, in turn, feed the source of the light pulses! All of this is even more impressive given the fact that the Flower-basket has no nervous system whatsoever.

That this beautiful creature with no nervous system is designed and works in such an intricate manner is a powerful testimony to our Creator, the only One Who could design this.

Prayer: Father, in the beginning You created light which brings beauty, but nothing like the beauty of Your salvation. Amen.

Ref: *Discover*, 8/05, pp. 42-47, George M. Whitesides, "Illuminated Life."

One Generation After the Flood

Genesis 8:11
"And the dove came in to him in the evening; and, lo, in her mouth was an olive leaf pluckt off: so Noah knew that the waters were abated from off the earth."

Many listeners will recall the volcanic eruption that rocked Washington State as Mount St. Helens exploded in May of 1980. Fortunately, there was plenty of warning, and the event was recorded in detail. Since that time, many studies have been made by the Park service and by creationists – including Creation Moments – on the rate of recovery. We are now about a generation – over 25 years – later and this should give us a good idea of how the Earth had recovered a generation after Noah's Flood.

The volcano destroyed 230 square miles of forest. Much of that area was literally sterilized by hot pyroclastic flows. Twenty-five years later, 150 species of plants have established themselves in this area. This includes five species of conifers, such as the Western hemlock and Pacific silver fir. This is contrary to current ecological theory, since these trees are supposed to sprout only after generations of other plants have improved the soil. Many trees are already 15 feet tall. In addition, birds, frogs, toads, mammals and even elk have returned. Again, many of these species were not expected to have returned to the area for a long while yet.

The Bible mentions the appearance of green plants within two months of the rain stopping at the end of the Flood. Mount St. Helens illustrates such a speedy recovery after the Flood.

Prayer: Thank You, Father, for making the living world that is so resilient and for preserving it for our good.

Ref: *Smithsonian*, 5/05, David B. Williams, "Phenomena and Curiosities: Rising from the Ashes."

The Fastest Flower in the West

Psalm 105:5

"Remember his marvelous works that he hath done; his wonders, and the judgments of his mouth..."

Can you imagine a plant that moves so fast that science didn't know what it was doing until recently? The plant is a forest wildflower found in North America and called the Bunchberry dogwood.

A few botanists had noted a strange "poof" associated with a plant, but no one knew what was going on. Researchers at Williams College in Williamstown, Massachusetts, were studying the plant when they experienced the "poof." Wanting to track down what the plant was doing, they got a high-speed video camera that can shoot 1,000 frames per second. Amazingly, that camera was too slow to clearly catch what the plant was doing. So they got a higher-speed camera that could shoot 10,000 frames per second. When they reviewed the video, they discovered that the flower was releasing pollen at an amazing speed. They calculated that the gravitational force on the pollen as it is released is 800 times the force astronauts endure when they blast into space. This wonder is accomplished by the flowers' very elastic petals which are part of a design that looks like a trebuchet – a medieval catapult.

The amazing wonders of God's creation should lead us to unceasingly praise Him, something which belief in evolution does not allow. Even if you try to add God to evolution, chance and natural forces still get the credit.

Prayer: I praise You, Father, for all the wonders of Your creation. Help my life praise you before others as well. Amen.

Ref: *Science News*, 6/11/05, p. 381, "World's Fastest Plant Explodes with Pollen."

Love Your Anemones

Psalm 46:9
"He maketh wars to cease unto the end of the earth; he breaketh the bow, and cutteth the spear in sunder; he burneth the chariot in the fire."

The world that God created for us and intended us to live in had no wars and no death because there was no sin whatsoever. Once the first man, Adam, brought sin into the world, murder, wars and disease descended upon the entire creation, including the animal world.

While sea anemones might seem to be relatively peacefully creatures, researchers have discovered that they have a sophisticated army with warriors as well as scouts. The California anemones that were studied live in colonies of genetically identical individuals. Often, another colony of such clones – but genetically different from the first colony – lives quite close. The colonies are separated by a narrow patch of non-clone anemones. While genetically identical individuals get along with each other within each colony, they engage in warfare with the neighboring colony. Some of the individuals, the warriors, have tentacles that are not used for catching food but rather for lashing invading anemones with stinging cells. Sometimes, scouts will enter the non-clone no-man's land between the colonies. The non-clones appear to be guards that sting any scout that enters their territory from either colony. Researchers were flabbergasted to find such a complex social system and penchant for war among anemones.

While warfare is something we added to the creation when we sinned, only Jesus Christ can bring us true peace with God.

Prayer: Prince of Peace, give me Your peace in the midst of a world filled with wars and rumors of war. Amen.

Ref: *Science News*, 6/4/05, p. 355-356, S. Milius, "Anemone Wars."

Whales' Wails Spook Seals

Genesis 11:7
"Go to, let us go down, and there confound their language, that they may not understand one another's speech."

You hear a bird sing. Can you tell by its dialect where it spends the winter? Birds – like some other creatures – do have different dialects, depending on where they live. However, for most of us, animal dialects are not easy to detect.

Killer whales also have dialects that are reflected in their 17 different calls. Some killer whales are homebodies, staying in the same area for all of their lives. These whales create few problems for local harbor seals on the North American west coast since they stick to a diet of local fish. Other killer whales form groups that cruise up and down North America's west coast, hunting cooperatively. These gangs are not satisfied with fish, and they particularly like harbor seals. Researchers have recorded the calls of both groups and have noted that the calls of each group have differing qualities – which amount to differing dialects. They also found that harbor seals know about this. Though the calls are at a frequency that fish cannot hear, the seals can hear them very well. They ignore the calls of local, fish-eating whales. But when a killer gang appears in their neighborhood, harbor seals tend to vacate the area rather quickly.

The ability to communicate and interpret communication are gifts from God, not just to us humans but clearly also to His other creatures.

Prayer: Thank You, Lord, for the gift of language. Let my words always bear witness of Your love to us in Christ. Amen.

Ref: *Science News,* 11/16/02, p. 308, S. Milius, "Ear for Killers."

Some Moms Are Green

Luke 13:34

*"O Jerusalem, Jerusalem ... how often would I have
gathered thy children together, as a hen doth gather her
brood under her wings, and ye would not!"*

Chickens aren't the brightest creatures in the animal
world, but the mother hen knows to protect her eggs and keep
them warm. Many species of snakes also care for their young.
Amazingly, scientists have learnt that even some plants have been
designed with "motherly" instincts.

The plantain is a common North American weed. When it
blooms, the warmer it keeps its developing seeds, the more seeds
its offspring will produce. Researchers have found that cooler air
temperatures cause the mother plant to produce a darker bloom
cluster. The darker color adsorbs more radiant energy from the
sun, and this gives its offspring a boost in life even before they
sprout. The shooter plant, as it is commonly called in America's
southeast, does something similar. It blooms for several months
over the southern summer. The leaf-like bracts that sheathe each
flower cluster have a brown pigment. Researchers observed the
plants over several months and found that the bracts that formed in
cooler April were darker than the bracts that formed in warmer
June. The increased levels of brown pigment in April enabled the
bracts to absorb more infrared light that helps to warm the flowers.

Just where did those plants learn the necessary physics –
not to mention the genetics – to produce these motherly
provisions? Of course, the answer is God's intelligent design from
the very start.

**Prayer: Father, I thank You that You are a loving God
Who teaches us love ultimately through Jesus Christ.
Amen.**

Ref: *Science News*, 7/23/05, pp. 59-60, Susan Milius, "Mommy Greenest."

A Tuck and a Nip

1 Thessalonians 4:6
"That no man go beyond and defraud his brother in any matter: because that the Lord is the avenger of all such, as we also have forewarned you and testified."

Most listeners have heard of the little "cleaner fish" or wrasse that clean the teeth of larger fishes. New research on the behavior of these fishes show that they are not always honest-business fish. Other fish, including those who might ordinarily consider a meal of "cleaner fish," actually stand in line for their services. That's because they need to have parasites and diseased tissue removed. They also know that the little "cleaner fish" offer massages.

It's amazing enough that even potential predators will become clients for a good cleaning and massage. Researchers from the University of Cambridge in England observed 28 cleaning stations and discovered some unexpected behavior. Now and again, as a "cleaner fish" nibbles parasites off a customer, it might also bite out a chunk of healthy flesh. Wisely, they avoid this behavior when cleaning predators that could bite them back. Researchers also observed that potential customers were aware of this risk and closely watched how the current customer was being treated. They were more likely to seek services from a wrasse that didn't nip any of the customers ahead of them. Of course, the wrasses were also aware of this and were observed to offer those customers they were likely to nip four-star treatment, including a massage.

Scripture teaches that man's sin infected the whole creation. Thankfully, Christ came to bring us forgiveness.

Prayer: Father, I thank You for Your laws, but as a sinner, I thank You even more for forgiveness in Jesus Christ. Amen.

Ref: *Science News,* 11/2/02, p. 277, S. Milius, "Fish Fraud."

Big Bang Boom?

1 Corinthians 15:41
"There is one glory of the sun, and another glory of the moon, and another glory of the stars: for one star differeth from another star in glory."

The Big Bang theory holds that in the very early stages of our universe, there were few galaxies, and they were small by today's standards. In this theory, no star can be older than its home galaxy.

But this tidy model of our universe appears to be in trouble. For this discussion we are going to use the inflated ages used by astronomers. When astronomers look through their telescopes at a star that is, say, 10 million light years away, they say they are looking at what was there 10 million years ago. Now, the universe is said to be 14 billion years old. Galaxies formed nearly that long ago are a very long way off, expected to be small, and their stars young – just as it was supposed to be after the Big Bang. Work with the Hubble telescope during the past 18 months has revealed many such young galaxies, including one only 800 million years old, but it is six times more massive than our own galaxy, the Milky Way. Most significantly, these young galaxies contain some old red stars. It's said to be like looking in a nursery of cooing babies and finding a few grown men!

These findings not only call the Big Bang theory into question but support the view that God created a mature universe, just as Scripture teaches.

> **Prayer: Thank You, Father, for the glory, beauty and variety You have created in the heavens which praise You. Amen.**

Ref: *Science News*, 10/8/05, pp. 235-236, Ron Cowen, "Crisis in the Cosmos?"

Plants with Perches for Pollinator Birds

Psalm 148:7, 10
"Praise the LORD from the earth, ye dragons, and all deeps ... Beasts, and all cattle; creeping things, and flying fowl..."

Could a plant devise a special growth for itself so that it becomes inviting to its only pollinator? If evolution were true, how could such a plant survive until it could learn enough about its pollinator – and about genetics – to evolve a special growth just for that pollinator?

Those sound like silly questions, but if evolution is true, they must be answered, and answered scientifically. A South African plant called the "Rat's Tail" grows a seemingly purposeless spear that extends near its flowers. Theorizing that the spear might be a bird-perch for a pollinator, scientists closely watched some of the plants in the wild. They learned that the only bird that seems interested in pollinating the plant is a bird called the "Malachite Sunbird." The scientists then removed the spikes from some of the plants. The result was that male sunbirds were far less likely to visit and pollinate those plants. As a result, perchless plants only produced half as many seeds as plants with perches. Researchers pointed out that this arrangement makes sense because male sunbirds have long tails that can be damaged by ground landings.

However, if we conclude that the Rat's Tails were created for the sunbirds, and the sunbirds for the Rat's Tails, we don't have to find natural explanations for such silly questions. This is simply another of God's clever designs.

Prayer: Lord, Your caring hand is all around us. I thank You especially for caring for me by forgiving my sins. Amen.

Ref: *Science News,* 6/4/05, p. 365, "Built-in bird perch spreads the pollen."

Plants Add More Greenhouse Gas

Genesis 8:22
"While the earth remaineth, seedtime and harvest, and cold and heat, and summer and winter, and day and night shall not cease."

Those who fear global warming blame any climate changes upon man's activity, including the raising of cattle for food. The digestive system of all ruminants, including cows, produce methane gas as part of the digestive process. Methane is considered one of the greenhouse gases that change the earth's climate. Some have even suggested ways of limiting the methane produced by cows.

Methane is produced in a chemical reaction that scientists have always believed must take place in the absence of oxygen. That's why they were surprised to find living plants making methane. It should be added that the researchers took great pains to ensure that the methane they were measuring was produced by the plants and trees and not by microbes in the soil. While they are unsure of the chemistry involved, they did find that more methane was produced with higher atmospheric temperatures. This finding explains large methane plumes that were recently identified over tropical forests. Based on their finding, they estimate that 20 percent of all atmospheric methane comes from plants and trees. That's about 150 metric tons a year!

Since God has created the Earth for life, He has built balances into it that can deal with the byproducts of life, including methane. We can trust God's promises that man will be here on Earth, planting and reaping, until its history ends.

Prayer: Father, I praise You for giving us a creation that balances itself so that we might live within it without fear. Amen.

Ref: *Science News*, 1/14/06, p. 19, S. Perkins, "Greenhouse Plants."

This Shrimp Packs a Punch

Psalm 104:25
"So is this great and wide sea, wherein are things creeping innumerable, both small and great beasts."

If you enjoy keeping tropical fish, the Mantis shrimp is one creature you may not want to keep in your aquarium. While this creature is related to common shrimp, it has a very unusual and specialized feature.

In the wild, if the Mantis shrimp finds a tasty snail, it cocks its spring-loaded forearm and shatters the snail's shell. The forearm has moved through the water at 50 miles per hour, so fast that it causes cavitation as well as heat and a flash of light as the bubbles collapse. And, yes, the Mantis shrimp can break the glass walls of an aquarium! To do this, the shrimp must generate over 200,000 watts of power per pound of muscle, something no other muscle can do. The shrimp accomplishes this seemingly impossible task by storing the energy generated by the muscles. The shrimp first locks the arm and then contracts its muscles. The energy stored in this way would damage the arm if it weren't for a very clever spring design. This saddle-shaped spring can accumulate enormous quantities of energy without breaking as it compresses. When the shrimp is ready to strike, it simply releases the spring.

The Mantis shrimp's forearm is only an effective working unit when all of its specialized parts are working together. It is difficult to imagine how it could have evolved.

Prayer: Father, I thank You for all the wise designs You have put into Your creation – especially Your plan of salvation. Amen.

Ref: http//www.USA Today.com. 1/9/06, April Holladay, "Shrimp spring into shattering action."

Could a Bee Pick You Out in a Police Line-Up?

Psalm 81:16
"He should have fed them also with the finest of the wheat: and with honey out of the rock should I have satisfied thee."

Given the size of its brain, could a honeybee recognize a specific human face? And if a bee could recognize specific human faces, how would the evolutionist explain this kind of ability?

Researchers who study honeybee and human vision point out that there would have been no evolutionary pressure for bees to learn to recognize specific people. The scientific prediction would therefore be that bees would not recognize human faces. To test this prediction, researchers placed pictures of human faces above bee-feeders. The same human face was always above the feeder that dispensed a sugar solution. A variety of other faces were placed above feeders that dispensed, say, quinine, a bitter-tasting solution. The bees quickly learned to associate one particular human face with the sweet solution. Even when researchers shuffled the feeders around, the bees quickly homed in on the sugar feeder with the familiar face. Then they removed the feeders and left only the pictures for the bees to find. Eighty percent of the time, the bees still focused on the face that had been on the sugar feeder. Evolution would predict random results, that is, the pictures of faces would have no effect.

However, our powerful Creator could be expected to give bees any abilities He wished. In this case, He apparently saw a good purpose to give bees this unexpected ability.

Prayer: Father, I thank You for all the good gifts You give us through Your creation. I especially thank You for salvation. Amen.

Ref: *Science News*, 12/3/05, p. 360, S. Milius, "Face Time."

Abortion and the Mother's Mental Health

Psalm 127:3
"Lo, children are an heritage of the LORD: and the fruit of the womb is his reward."

Over the past several years, scientific studies of women have shown that those who have had abortions increase their risks of infertility, breast cancer and other problems. Now, a new study – released by the Population Research Institute – reveals a whole new category of risks associated with abortion.

The researchers learned that among girls from 15 to 18, pregnant or not, for those who have had an abortion the chance of major depression rises from 31 percent to 78 percent. The same pattern appeared for anxiety, where for young girls who had had an abortion the likelihood of anxiety neuroses were doubled. The pattern also showed a doubled rate of thoughts of suicide for girls who had an abortion as compared with those who became pregnant but did not have an abortion. A similar study of women in New Zealand had the same results. Two studies by the Elliot Institute showed that women who had an abortion were three times as likely as those who had not to be plagued with anxiety and to abuse drugs.

These studies show scientifically that it is time to stop accepting the mental health of the mother as justification for abortion. Researchers find that abortion *causes* mental health problems, it does not prevent them. More than this, of course, abortion is contrary to God's will because it takes a life.

Prayer: Lord, I thank You for the gift of life, and I ask that You would turn the hearts of our countrymen to treasure life. Amen.

Ref: Population Research Institute, 20 January 2006, Vol. 8, No. 3, Joseph A. D'Agostino, "Why Think Abortion Good for Anyone?"

Geckos Don't Need Flashlights

Psalm 146:8

"The LORD openeth the eyes of the blind: the LORD raiseth them that are bowed down: the LORD loveth the righteous...."

You get up early. The illumination isn't very good, so you put on your socks anyway, only to find out, in the light of day, that you have one blue and one gray sock on. That's because our eyes have cone cells to detect color as well as rod cells that are sensitive to light but cannot see color. So as the light level becomes lower, we have a decreasing ability to detect colors.

Not so with the hooded gecko. Based on their study of gecko eyes, some scientists wondered whether they could see in the dark. To test this, they made cards with a checkerboard pattern of blues and grays. Geckos were then trained to take crickets labeled with one of the cards. Then, when they offered the geckos crickets labeled with a blue card, they rewarded the geckos with the expected cricket. Crickets labeled with gray cards, however, were made bad-tasting by being placed in salt water. During these tests, the light level was so low that researchers could not tell the difference between colors. However, the geckos took the crickets labeled with blue cards more than twice as often, proving that they could see the color differences.

While we marvel at God's unlimited creativity in providing for His creatures' needs, we see this truth by faith. Faith also shows us that God redeemed us through His Son.

Prayer: I thank You, Lord, for the gift of sight. Help me to see more clearly through the eyes of the faith You have given me. Amen

Ref: *Science News,* 11/27/04, p. 342, S. Milius, "Color at Night."

The Squid Without a Shadow

Psalm 18:28
"For thou wilt light my candle: the LORD my God will enlighten my darkness."

Many marine creatures reflect surrounding light. They can do so because of tiny light-reflecting platelets. Typically, these crystalline platelets are made of purine, one of the building blocks of DNA, but these particular crystals cannot change how much light they reflect.

The Hawaiian bobtail squid, however, needs to be able to reflect different levels of light because of its unique lifestyle. This squid glides through moonlit waters, but without its special reflective tissue, its shadow would be seen as it passes over the bottom. The bobtail squid has light-generating tissue on its underside facing the bottom, and this produces just sufficient light to make its shadow disappear. In other words, it can generate variable levels of light. What's more, the squid can move its light-generating platelets around so that they might be scattered among its cells or concentrated where needed. Rather than being composed of just one amino acid, this squid's platelets are made up of six amino acids.

God is the source of all light, including spiritual light. According to evolution, the squid is closely related to some of the first animals that evolved in the sea. Yet, its technically sophisticated camouflage, which perfectly fits its environment and lifestyle, is a testimony to God's wise design – not the early stages of mindless evolution. The spiritual light of God's truth makes that clear.

Prayer: Father, we are surrounded by the darkness of the world. Let the light of Your truth shine in our hearts and minds. Amen.

Ref: *Science News*, 1/10/04, p. 20, A. Goho, "Moonlighting."

Relax

Genesis 6:3
"And the LORD said, My spirit shall not always strive with man, for that he also is flesh: yet his days shall be an hundred and twenty years."

Before the Flood, people were living hundreds of years. As man grew more evil, God declared that man's lifespan would be reduced to 120 years. Modern biology has learned that we do indeed have built-in timers in each of our cells that limit the number of times they can divide. When enough cells can no longer divide, we die. We can even do things to speed up the timers.

The timers are called telomeres. However, every time a cell divides, a small part of each telomere is lost. When these telomeres are worn down to nothing, the cell no longer divides and soon dies. Researchers studied 58 healthy women between the ages of 20 and 50. All the women had children, but 39 of them had a child that was seriously chronically ill. Stress levels were measured through questionnaires, while blood samples provided information about their cell health. Among other things, scientists checked for levels of an enzyme that maintains the health of telomeres. The mothers who saw their stress levels as high proved to have much shorter telomeres than those who reported little stress. They reported that cells from stressed women had telomeres that were as short as unstressed women 10 years older.

Scripture tells us to cast all our cares on the Lord. Among the many blessings of doing so are healthy telomeres.

Prayer: Father, I cast all my cares on You. You have loved me through Your Son, Jesus Christ. I trust Your love. Amen.

Ref: *Science News*, 12/4/04, p. 355, C. Brownlee, "Stressed to Death."

Which Came First, the Defense or Countermeasures?

Luke 11:21
"When a strong man armed keepeth his palace, his goods are in peace...."

Our Lord recognized that in a sinful world we must be prepared to protect ourselves. The same is true in the animal and plant world. When it comes to trying to explain this truth using evolutionary thinking, there are some serious difficulties.

There are many plants that have effective defenses against the insects that attack them. For example, a plant called Bursera defends itself with poisons that squirt from its leaves when a certain beetle larva attempts to feed on it. However, the larvae have learnt to chew on a particular part of the leaf first. When they do this, they disable the plant's defense system and can munch away on the leaf without fear of harm. According to evolution, the plant's defense mechanism and the beetle's countermeasures had to evolve simultaneously: countermeasure perfectly matching defense. Otherwise, the countermeasure would be quite useless. The probability of this happening, even if evolution were true, is extremely remote. Even evolutionists have realized this problem and have published their attempts to explain how this could happen. But such explanations are based on a complex foundation of evolutionary assumptions and little evidence.

According to evolution, such unlikely interrelationships had to evolve by chance many times when one looks at all the defenses that plants use and predators can outsmart. Creationists see these systems as created fully formed by our Creator.

Prayer: Lord, I thank You that although You created a perfect world, You provided for our needs in a sinful world.

Ref: *Science News*, 11/15/03, p. 318, "Chronicling a war of beetle vs. leaf."

Some Birds Do Mental Time Travel

Matthew 13:4
"And when he sowed, some seeds fell by the way side, and the fowls came and devoured them up...."

Episodic memory – the ability to remember something that happened in the past – is called mental time travel. It has long been thought that only humans are capable of episodic memory. New research suggests that some birds are also capable of mental time travel.

Researchers gave captive Western scrub jays one of their favorite foods – wax worms. As they usually do, the jays made their selections and hid the worms in the trays of sand provided. Five days later, the birds were allowed to recover their treats. The jays discovered that after the five days, the worms had begun to decay. The researchers fooled a second batch of jays by replacing their decayed worms with fresh worms just before the birds were allowed to find their treats. Then both batches of birds were again allowed to take and hide a choice of worms. Those birds that had had experience with the decayed worms would no longer take new worms to hide. But the birds that had been fooled took the worms and buried them, still expecting them to be good later. In other words, the birds remembered what happened in the past and adjusted their behavior. Other tests offered similar results.

God has given all His creatures the abilities they need to make a living without regard to where those creatures are on the manmade evolutionary ladder.

Prayer: Father, I thank You that You have given me and all creatures what we need for life here. Amen.

Ref: *Science News*, 2/14/04, pp. 103-105, Susan Milius, "Where'd I Put That?"

What Value Is Music?

Genesis 4:21
"And his brother's name was Jubal: he was the father of all such as handle the harp and organ."

The Bible tells us that the earliest generations of human beings were making music. By the time the eighth generation of man came along, Jubal – a member of that generation – was able to make his living providing musical instruments. On the evolutionary side of things, however, musical ability would seem to provide no survival advantage. Yet, the human brain devotes considerable resources to the processing of music.

Our love of music is wired into our brain. Each of our sense organs is important to our enjoyment of music. And each of these organs is linked to its own part of the brain, which is responsible for how we experience the music. Parts of the brain are reserved for memory which stores the music. Other parts of the brain are dedicated to trying to understand the entire piece of music, referencing back to parts of the music stored in the memory. Even more interesting is that one need not hear music to activate the various parts of the brain devoted to music. Positron-emission tomography reveals that a person only needs to imagine music for these portions of the brain to become active.

The ability to make or appreciate music offers us no apparent survival value, and therefore, according to evolutionary theory, should not have developed. Yet, our brains, and indeed, all our senses are designed to make and appreciate music. The obvious message here is that evolution had nothing to do with the formation of human beings. Rather, we were created by God, Who loves music and wants us to praise Him with music.

Prayer: Father, I thank You for the gift of music and the ability to appreciate it. Amen.

Ref: *Science Frontiers*, No. 141, 5-6/02, "Why Music?"

Friendship Is No Friend of Evolution

John 15:13
"Greater love hath no man than this, that a man lay down his life for his friends."

It has long been argued that animals do not make friendships. According to evolutionary thinking, animals only make friends among relatives because it benefits another creature that shares the same gene pool. Survival of their gene pool is said to be the driving force for every living creature, although animal knowledge of gene pools is still a mystery!

A detailed study of select animal populations calls this thinking into question. The Atlanta Zoo had two female and one male giraffes. After nine years together without mating, the male was sent to another zoo. This produced much agitated behavior among the females and raised the question: had these animals developed a friendship? A study was made at the San Diego Zoo where there were 12 giraffes. Among other things, it was found that mother giraffes with young ones often hung around with each other. Certain animals would spend 15 percent of their time with the same giraffe. It was further noted that, among another population of giraffes, certain females were seen with the same female one-third to one-half of the time. Similar signs of friendship have been noted among rhinos, dolphins and even vampire bats.

It would appear that friends are a gift that God has not only given to man, but to many of His creatures, and it has nothing to do with evolution or gene pools.

Prayer: Lord, I thank You for the good friends that I have, but most of all I thank You for Your love for me. Amen.

Ref: *Science News*, 11/1/03, pp. 282-284, Susan Milius, "Beast Buddies."

Genetic Variation Can Fly

Genesis 8:17

"Every beast, every creeping thing, and every fowl, and whatsoever creepeth upon the earth, after their kinds, went forth out of the ark."

Noah saved a pair of each kind of unclean creature and seven pairs of every kind of clean creature on the Ark. Generally speaking, the classification of "kind" is broader than today's species. Creationists believe that today's species developed from those creatures, staying within the kind. For example, while there are many species of fruit flies, they are all of the same kind.

But how could all the species we know today have developed so quickly? In 1978, a few European fruit flies were accidentally introduced to Chile. They have now spread their population over much of North America's west coast. In that short time, they differentiated within their kind. For example, those found in more northern latitudes have the longer wingspans, while those in the more southerly latitudes have shorter wingspans. Tests have shown that these differences are due to differences in genetic makeup. Amazingly, the same pattern of longer wingspans in more northerly fruit flies is very much like the pattern observed in European fruit flies. Even more astonishing is the fact that the American fruit flies achieve the longer and shorter wing spans through the lengthening of a different part of the wing than their European cousins.

That these differences, down to the genetic level, have developed in a mere quarter of a century illustrates how, in the few thousand years since the Flood, the various species we know today could have easily developed from their basic kinds.

Prayer: Lord, thank You for the variety You have placed in Your creation. Amen.

Ref: *Creation*, 9-11/00, p. 5, "Fruit flies spread wings."

Nanobugs Amaze Scientists

Psalm 139:8
"If I ascend up into heaven, thou art there: if I make my bed in hell, behold, thou art there."

A series of unlikely discoveries have scientists shaking their heads. They have discovered the smallest creatures ever seen three miles below the Earth's surface, happily living where the temperatures go as high as 338° Fahrenheit.

The creatures were discovered as part of the Deep Subsurface Microbiology Program. This scientific effort is searching for subsurface microbes which might feed on and break down underground pollutants. At 20 to 150 nanometers in length, they seem too small to be alive. A nanometer is one billionth of a meter. The average human hair is 10,000 nanometers across. Atoms average 3-5 nanometers in size. So a creature only four or five times the size of an atom doesn't seem as though it should be alive. After all, a cell wall is five to seven nanometers thick. DNA alone is five to six nanometers thick. So with just two cell walls and a little DNA, the smallest of these creatures – called "nanobes" – seem too small to be living creatures. For this reason, scientists decided they can't be alive. But after study, scientists have found that these creatures do indeed have DNA and are made of the elements of life: carbon, nitrogen and oxygen. And they do grow like other living things.

Nanobes are another demonstration that nothing is too hard for God, nor is there anywhere He is not. This is a comfort for us, since God has spared nothing – including the life of His own Son – to bring about our salvation.

Prayer: Lord, You can do all things. Let me be comforted by this truth and the truth that You have loved me in Jesus Christ. Amen.

Ref: *Discover*, 1/01, p. 58, "It's a Small World After All."

Amoeba Midwives

Genesis 35:17
"And it came to pass, when she was in hard labour, that the midwife said unto her, Fear not; thou shalt have this son also."

Ever since Old Testament times, midwives have been helping mothers during the birthing process. They are especially valuable should there be difficulties, since they not only offer an extra set of hands, but experience in dealing with common problems. Some of the scientists who were studying amoeba behavior observed some very strange behavior which suggests that some amoebas, too, employ midwives.

The scientists were studying an amoeba that lives in the digestive tract of reptiles. As all amoebas, they reproduce by splitting in half. Scientists noted, however, that this particular species is not very good at it. Up to a third of the time, the amoebas fail to split. They begin the process but never manage to complete it. When that happens, the amoeba is doomed to exist as long as it can with two sets of genetic information. But as scientists watched, when an amoeba had difficulty dividing, other amoebas would move in on it and help the division process, thereby serving as a midwife. Further study revealed that the amoeba having difficulty dividing releases a chemical which apparently summons help to finish the process. The midwife amoeba have been seen traveling up to 40 times their own length to help in the birthing of a new generation.

The Bible teaches us that God cares for all of His creatures. Here we see that He provides even for the needs of the lowly amoeba. How much more does He love us and will provide for our needs!

Prayer: Thank You, Lord, for the helping professions. Help me to see where I can help someone else. Amen.

Ref: *Science News*, V. 159, 3/31/01, p. 200, "Distressed amoebas can call for help."

A Scaled Mammal

Psalm 105:5
"Remember his marvellous works that he hath done; his wonders, and the judgments of his mouth . . . ."

Its long, slender, scale-covered body glides along the ground on four short legs, each of which has sharp claws. Its slender head has no teeth. It will not seek to hurt you, but if it feels threatened, it will lash out with that scale-armored tail.

While this creature sounds very much like a reptile, it is, in fact, a mammal called the pangolin. There are seven species of pangolins scattered throughout Africa and Asia. Typically, the female pangolin will give birth to a single young one after a 140-day gestation period. When fully grown, the young one will, like its parents, be almost two feet long and weigh about 20 pounds. In addition to using its tail for defense, it can spray a bad-smelling liquid like a skunk. If all else fails, it can roll into a tight, armored ball. Its feeding behavior is similar to a nocturnal anteater. The pangolin's highly developed sense of smell can actually sniff out ant and termite mounds. When it finds a nest, it uses its long, sticky tongue to collect a meal. Unfortunately, the endangered pangolin is prized as a delicacy as well as medicine among the hill tribes where it lives. Lions and tigers also feed on pangolins.

Pangolins are another example of God's unlimited creativity and His power and wisdom which allows Him to bring about whatever He desires. His greatest desire is for our salvation through the innocent suffering of Jesus Christ.

Prayer: Dear Father, I stand in wonder at Your creation and the variety You have made. Amen.

Ref: "Pangolin," World Book Multimedia Encyclopedia (2001).

Ironclad Evidence

Exodus 20:11
"For in six days the Lord made the heaven and earth, the sea, and all that in them is, and rested the seventh day; wherefore the Lord blessed the sabbath day, and hallowed it."

While evolutionists can't explain how life originated, they have proposed theories of how inorganic matter became biological molecules. Each of these theories require the assumption that the Earth had no oxygen in its atmosphere when life first began. Oxygen would destroy the chemistry they propose.

However, Neil Phillips, an Australian geologist, has discovered iron oxide in South Africa. The iron oxide was discovered in rock layers that are dated to a time long before the first appearance of life, according to evolutionary theory. The form of iron oxide he found, pisoliths, are only known to form in the presence of oxygen. Based on his study, Phillips has concluded that the Earth has had enough oxygen in its atmosphere to react with geological features since the beginning of geological history. That's enough oxygen to destroy any of the products of the chemistry evolutionists have proposed for the origin of life.

Part of the scientific power of any model of origins is its ability to predict what kind of evidence to look for. The creation model says that there was air-breathing life within the first week that Earth's geology existed. The discovery of iron oxide in the most ancient rocks is no surprise to those who accept creation.

Prayer: Father, help me to worship You in spirit and in truth by also making a faithful witness to Your work of creation. Amen.

Ref: *Discover*, 4/02, p. 11, Lauren Gravitz. "Early Breath of Fresh Air."

Teaching Ants

Psalm 25:5
"Lead me in Thy truth, and teach me: for Thou art the God of my salvation; on Thee do I wait all the day."

Researchers in England have, for the first time, identified an example of true human-like teaching in the animal world.

Their definition of teaching goes beyond simple "monkey-see, monkey-do." First, the teacher must show the student how to do something, doing it less efficiently than they normally would. Next, the student must learn the task faster than it would without the teacher. Finally, to be true teaching, there must be student-teacher feedback.

They found that a small ant on England's southern coast meets these criteria. In their experiments, they placed a sugar solution about six inches from the ants' nest. They videotaped what happened next. After an ant discovered the sugary treat, it returned to the nest to get a friend. The teacher ant would then lead its student to the sugar, going four times more slowly than it normally would. During the lesson, the student would periodically stop and turn around, as if to get its bearings. Feedback between student and teacher took place when the student would tap the teacher with her antennae to keep her moving.

God is, of course, the ultimate Teacher Who gives both the ability to teach and to learn wherever it is needed. The greatest truth He teaches is the truth of salvation by grace through faith in Jesus Christ, His Son.

Prayer: Father, thank You for teaching me the truth that Jesus Christ died for my sins so that You could truly be my Father. Amen.

Ref: *Science News*, 1/14/06, pp. 20-21, S. Milius, "Little Professor."

New Light on Radiometric Dating

2 Peter 3:5
"For this they are willingly ignorant of, that by the Word of God the heavens were of old, and the earth standing out of the water and in the water:"

Most people find the subject of radiometric dating too technical to understand. Until recent years, scientists who believe in creation haven't had the necessary resources to explore radiometric dating in detail.

Now that has changed, and some important discoveries are being made. When granite rock hardens, it freezes radioactive elements in place. The most common radioactive element in granite is Uranium-238. This element is locked in tiny zircons within the granite. As part of the decay process, helium is produced. While it stays within the zircon for a period of time, being a very small atom, helium escapes the zircon within a few thousand years.

When creation scientists studied granite samples, they made interesting discoveries. The samples were from a mile below the earth, which, according to inflated evolutionary years, were 1.5 billion years old. The helium still locked in the samples was studied as well as the rate at which the helium diffused from the rock. They concluded that the helium in the rock was 100,000 times more plentiful than it should have been if the rocks were actually 1.5 billion real years old. They concluded that their findings are consistent with an Earth that is about 6,000 years old.

As our knowledge continues to grow, what we know continues to be in agreement with Scripture.

Prayer: I thank You, Father, for those things in the creation that bear witness to You. Help me to be a faithful witness, too. Amen.

Ref: *Answers*, 7-9/06, pp. 22-24, Don DeYoung, "Raising the Bar on Creation Research."

Which Came First . . . or Did They?

Genesis 1:21
"So God created man in His own image, in the image of God He created him; male and female created He them."

We have all seen those illustrations supposedly showing the stages of human evolution from some ape-like creature. Progressing from the earliest ape-like creature to modern man, you see *Homo habilis* and, closer to modern man, *Homo erectus*.

Although this illustration continues to adorn textbooks, paleontologists have known for some time that it is an inaccurate depiction of even their own theory. While digging in Africa in 2000, a paleontological team headed by the Leakeys found bones of both *erectus* and *habilis*. Not only were they within walking distance of each other, they were in the same level and, thus. have the same dates. The evolutionary dating of the jaw from the *habilis* as well as the *erectus* skull were dated at 1.44 million evolutionary years. This was long after *habilis* was supposed to have evolved into *erectus*.

Evolutionists also once thought that modern humans evolved from Neandertals. But then they found clear evidence that modern humans existed at the same time as Neandertals. Commenting on the finding, one evolutionary scientist cautioned that this finding should not be considered a weakness in evolutionary theory. However, real science is all about evidence. And there is no evidence that modern humans evolved from some early ape-like creature.

While evolution views man as just another animal, God made us in His image to be His children.

Prayer: Father, I thank You that You have made me and redeemed me through the suffering and death of Your Son. Amen.

Ref: http://www.foxnews.com/printer_friendly_story/0,3566,292572,00.html

The Light-Emitting Swallowtail

Genesis 1:3
"And God said, 'Let there be light;' and there was light."

Though tiny, the scales of the swallowtail butterfly's wing are similar in design to light-emitting diodes. We say similar because the design is closer to a specialized light-emitting diode that puts out six times as much light as a standard LED.

The blue-green wing of the swallowtail is covered with millions of tiny scales. Each microscopic scale has three layers. The top layer is made up of thousands of hollow cylinders shaped in a honeycomb pattern. There is fluorescent pigment within the sides of those cells. The second layer adds the blue-green color to entering light and the bottom layer reflects it back out. As the light enters, the top layer focuses and reflects all the blue-green light that enters it. The second layer turns any other color entering light – including ultraviolet light – blue-green, and the bottom layer reflects it back out.

The efficiency of the delicate structure has been compared to LEDs that have two-dimensional photonic crystals that put out six times as much light as a regular LED. As one scientist put it, they had no idea that the design would be so "precise" and "refined."

Of course it's precise and refined, showing an understanding of light! It was designed by the same Creator Who created light in the first place.

Prayer: Thank You, Father, for creating light with its beauty and especially for the beauty of the light of the Gospel. Amen.

Ref: *Science News*, 11/19/05. p. 324, A. Cunningham, "Way to Glow."

Did Solomon Really Marry a Pharaoh's Daughter?

1 Kings 3:1a
"And Solomon made affinity with pharaoh king of Egypt, and took pharaoh's daughter, and brought her to the city of David...."

Scripture notes, several times, that King Solomon married a pharaoh's daughter in the tenth century B.C. His dowry for this marriage was the city of Gezer which he received from the pharaoh.

Many Egyptologists and biblical critics have claimed that this was simply impossible. They base their argument on a 14th century B.C. Egyptian inscription. The inscription shows a pharaoh speaking with his daughter with the caption, "From of old no [Egyptian] king's daughter has been given to anyone." However, in 1 Kings 11:19-20 we read of a pharaoh giving his sister-in-law in marriage to an Edomite prince. This took place just a few years before Solomon's reign. Extra-biblical sources tell of another pharaoh who gave his daughter to a Libyan noble later in Solomon's reign. We would have to conclude that the Egyptian royal traditions in the 14th century B.C. had changed by the tenth century B.C. After all, that is 400 years later.

While many scholars doubt that the Bible presents history accurately, believers know that the Bible presents us with the story of our salvation. That salvation is based on real people and real events in history. So we thank God that He has given us an accurate account of how our salvation came about, beginning in Genesis.

> **Prayer: Father, I thank You that Your Word is true and that it reveals Your forgiving love for me in Your Son, Jesus Christ. Amen.**

Ref: *Biblical Archaeology Review*, 9-10/01. pp. 32-37, Kenneth A. Kitchen, "How We Know When Solomon Ruled."

Remember Your Turmeric

1 Chronicles 9:30
"And some of the sons of the priests made the ointment of the spices."

Many ancient peoples made various ointments from spices, including ancient Israel. In India, they have been using a spice called turmeric for medicinal purposes for 3,000 years.

Turmeric is made from the roots of a broad-leafed plant that grows well in the warm, moist climate of southern Asia. Ancient healers in India used turmeric to treat skin wounds, jaundice, indigestion and several other ailments. Turmeric is found in most curry dishes. Modern medical science has now begun to study the spice. Preliminary research shows that turmeric lowers total blood cholesterol by 11 percent and increases good cholesterol by 29 percent. But the most hopeful and dramatic medical use of the spice may be in treating, even reversing, Alzheimer's disease. The active ingredient in the spice is curcumin. In lab tests, curcumin has been shown to aid the body in ridding itself of the amyloid-beta plaques that result in Alzheimer's. These results are supported by a population study done in India. A study of people over 65 in that country who ate turmeric showed an incidence of Alzheimer's that was a quarter what it is in the West.

In His foreknowledge, God knew that man would sin and bring death and disease on himself. In His mercy, He stocked the creation with natural medicines to help us.

Prayer: Thank You, Father, for providing for our needs in this life. Prosper all useful science. Amen.

Ref: *Science News*, 9/15/07, pp. 167-168, Patrick Barry, "Curry Power."

Hornet Stranglers

Psalm 118:12a
"They compassed me about like bees...."

We all know that when bees swarm they are in defensive mode. However, not all species of bees have stinging in mind when they swarm.

We did a program about an Asian honeybee species that engulfs an invading wasp and cooks it to death. That's what scientists thought Cyprian honeybees were doing when they engulf an invading hornet. However, further study showed that the bees could not kill the attacking hornet with heat. They simply didn't generate enough heat to kill it in the hour they were observed killing a hornet.

Further observation showed that the bees favored encasing the hornet's abdomen. It appeared that they knew that the hornets have an unusual breathing arrangement for insects. The hornet in question actually breathes through holes in its abdomen by contracting the abdomen. The bees appeared to be suffocating the hornet. So researchers placed tiny plastic blocks under a hornet's abdominal plates. This propped the hornet's breathing pores open when the bees tried to smother it. Sure enough, the next time the bees attacked, the hornet survived twice as long.

In His love for His creation, God knew that when sin entered His creation, His creatures would need to know how to defend themselves. So He gave the Cyprian honeybee the knowledge to protect itself against its worst foe.

Prayer: I thank You, Father, that You love your creation and have especially loved me through your Son, Jesus Christ. Amen.

Ref: *Science News*, 9/29/07, p. 205, "Honeybee Mobs Smother Big Hornets."

The David Inscription

2 Samuel 2:4a
"And the men of Judah came, and there they anointed David king over the house of Judah."

There are two major schools of thought among biblical archaeologists. Many archaeologists go about their work with the goal of providing background to biblical accounts with their finds. But another school, called "minimalists," refuse to accept anything the Bible says unless they find solid evidence for it.

For example, minimalists argued for years that David never existed except as a mythical figure. They even went so far as to argue that Jerusalem wasn't even a city at the time David was supposed to have lived. However, in 1993 archaeologists made a huge contribution to this debate. While cleaning up an excavation at the biblical Dan, one of the team members noticed an inscription on a stone that was sticking out of the ground. It turned out to be part of a victory monument erected by an Aramean ruler celebrating a victory over Israel and possibly Judah. It is written in the type of Hebrew letters used before the destruction of the first temple in 586 BC. It boasts of the victory over a king, whose name is missing, but mentions the "House of David/King of Israel."

Believers don't need such evidence to know that the Bible is trustworthy, even when it talks about historical events. However, now there can be no question that David was a real person.

Prayer: I thank You, Lord, that the history reported in Your Word is accurate, for it also records the history that saves me. Amen.

Ref: *Biblical Archaeology Review*, March-April 1994, pp. 26-39, Herschel Shanks, "'David' Found at Dan."

Intimidating Duets

Ecclesiastes 12:4b
"... and he shall rise up at the voice of the bird, and all the daughters of musick shall be brought low..."

Precision in communication is highly important. This is especially true of the type of communication called music, whether you are talking about Mozart or magpie-larks.

Only about three percent of bird species are known to sing duets. In a duet, one mate begins singing, and the other mate begins a half second later. Among Australian magpie-larks, pairs that are newly mated usually lack that precision. However, in pairs that have been together for two years, the lag time of the duet usually varies by only a few hundredths of a second.

Researchers also discovered that this precision serves a purpose. Male magpie larks respond to perceived threats by increasing their singing. When they played the less-precise duets to 12 pairs of other magpie-larks, the males only responded in this way seven times in five minutes. However, the more-precise duets resulted in nine responses in five minutes. In short, other magpie larks are more intimidated by pairs that sing with precision than by those who do not. This is important in preserving an established couple's territory from invasion by new couples.

Communication with precision is yet another fingerprint of God on the creation. In Scripture, the ultimate in precise communication, God even points us to the birds as He urges us to recognize His involvement in the creation.

Prayer: Thank You, Father, for taking care of all Your creation and especially for sending Your Son to save me. Amen.

Ref: *Science News*, 6/9/07, p. 357, S. Milius, "Scary Singing."

Accounting for King Solomon's Gold

1 Kings 6:22
"And the whole house he overlaid with gold, until he had finished all the house."

Scripture tells us that Solomon's temple was overlaid with gold inside – the walls, the ceiling and even the floor! Solomon even decorated the Temple with gold, including over two U.S. tons of golden shields. Given the dimensions of the rooms, this would take a huge amount of gold.

For this reason, many modern scholars have expressed doubt about what the Bible reports. Scripture does report that Solomon's annual income was 25 tons of gold. We know that other world rulers in the ancient world held huge amounts of gold. We have all seen the golden treasures that were found in King Tut's tomb. Reliable Greek sources report that Alexander the Great discovered a hoard of 1,180 tons of gold in Susa. So there was obviously a great deal of gold in the ancient world. But what happened to all of Solomon's gold? The Bible records that after Solomon's death Shishak, king of Egypt, invaded Jerusalem and hauled away the Temple treasure. After his death, a year later, his son Osorkon I became king. Three years later, Osorkon made an offering to the gods of Egypt of 383 tons of gold. Was some of that from Solomon's Temple?

There is no reason to doubt the Bible's lavish descriptions of Solomon's Temple. There was more than enough gold in the ancient world to do the job.

> *Prayer: Lord, You are the generous giver of all good gifts. Help me always to hold Your Word as the greatest treasure. Amen.*

Ref: *Biblical Archaeology Review*, 5-6/89, pp. 20-34, Alan R. Mallard, "Does the Bible Exaggerate King Solomon's Golden Wealth?"

Randomness and Life

Genesis 1:12
"And the earth brought forth grass, and herb yielding seed after his kind, and the tree yielding fruit, whose seed was in itself after his kind."

Charles Darwin knew nothing about genetics. In his day the cell was thought to be filled with nothing more than a watery jell. Darwin also thought that characteristics picked up during life could be passed on to the next generation.

After over a century of genetic studies, including the discovery and growing understanding of DNA, evolution looks more impossible than ever. For example, cystic fibrosis is caused by a random mutation at three small points in one protein. This means that one random change in one ten-millionth of the entire human genome is fatal. There are 4,000 known mutations in the human genome, and none of them are beneficial. One so-called good mutation that has been cited is sickle cell anemia since it gives some protection against malaria. However, without medical intervention, even this mutation is fatal.

After studying mutation rates among humans, scientists have concluded that if an unlikely good mutation were to happen, there would be 10,000 fatal mutations before another good mutation would happen. By this math, if life began over 3 billion evolutionary years ago, it would have all died off by now from bad mutations. Random mutations are not the way to turn paramecia into people!

That there is nothing about life or its preservation that is random shows God's love in preserving life.

Prayer: I thank You, Father, for creating life with order so that it is protected and provided for. Amen.

Ref: *Acts and Facts*, 9/07, pp. 10-13, Barney Maddox, "Mutations: The Raw Material for Evolution?"

A Young and Active Moon

Genesis 1:16
"And God made two great lights; the greater light to rule the day, and the lesser light to rule the night; He made the stars also."

According to the inflated evolutionary time-scale, the Earth's moon is 4.5 billion years old. A rocky body the size of the moon would be expected to be geologically active for about 1.5 billion years. This means that for the last 3 billion years the moon has been geologically settled or dead. If it is indeed that old.

In the first half of the 20th century there were reports of color changes, bright spots, hazes and other unexplained things being seen on the moon. These sightings were dismissed since it was accepted that the moon was far too old to be geologically active. But the sightings increased to such a level that in 1968 NASA published a report on the sightings titled the *Chronological Catalog of Reported Lunar Events.*

But this shouldn't be so surprising. Back in 1787 the famous astronomer William Herschel recorded a volcanic eruption on the moon. He reported that he had identified three volcanoes on the darkened limb of the moon. One, he observed, erupted, ejecting luminous material for at least two days. Interestingly they were in the Aristarchus region of the moon where more than 300 sightings of apparent volcanic activity have been reported.

These reports offer good evidence that the moon is more likely thousands of years old, rather than billions, thus fitting in nicely with the biblical chronology.

Prayer: I thank You, Father, for the beauty of the night sky which shows forth your glory. Amen.

Ref: *Answers Magazine*, 1-3/08, pp. 32-33, Ron Samec, "The Moon Is Still Alive..."

Jay Caching

Matthew 6:26a
"Behold the fowls of the air: for they sow not, neither do they reap, nor gather into barns; yet your heavenly Father feedeth them."

A cat crouching at a mouse hole is already hunting. Until now, no animal has ever been observed actually planning for the future.

Recent studies of western scrub jays have now shown undeniable planning behavior by the jays. To see if the jays engaged in true planning, individual jays were moved into a special cage in the lab. It had a main room with two side rooms. A jay would be moved into one or the other of the side rooms every morning. One side room never offered food for the first two hours the bird was in it, while the other consistently offered food. After each bird learned this pattern, they were allowed into the main room in the evening to eat their fill. All of the eight test subjects also provided the no-breakfast side cage with generous caches of extra food, clearly in anticipation of the morning. In a second test, different food supplies were available in each side cage. When they were allowed to freely cache, they cached supplies of the missing food in each side room, again clearly anticipating the next morning.

God has provided for His creatures' needs by giving them the abilities they need to make their living. That includes giving seemingly advanced abilities to creatures that are supposedly far less evolved than we are.

Prayer: I thank You, Father, that Your provision for all Your creatures is evident in Your creation, just as Your Word says. Amen.

Ref: *Science News*, 2/24/07, p. 117, S. Milius, "Bird Plans."

Wood Contradicts Rock

Psalm 118:8
"It is better to trust in the Lord than to put confidence in man."

Radioactive carbon, carbon-14, accumulates in all living things when alive. Once they die, half of any given amount of carbon-14 in a once-living thing decays to non-radioactive carbon in 5,730 years. Thus, by measuring the amount of carbon-14 left in a once-living thing, scientists can get a rough idea of when it died. It can be used to date things that are only thousands of years old, not millions.

In Colorado there is a formation caused by volcanic activity in the distant past out of which much gold has been mined. Evolutionists date the last volcanic activity at this formation at 27 million inflated years ago. When the eruption took place, it apparently engulfed a forest. As a result, many pieces of carbonized wood are found sealed in the hard rock. Working from deep within a mine, researchers drilled down even further, looking for an uncontaminated piece of carbonized wood. They hit their target over 3,000 feet from the actual surface. They found several fragments which were decontaminated as a precaution. After four separate carbon datings and corrections were worked out, they turned out to be about 4,300 years old.

After four separate carbon datings were obtained – similar to inflated dates for coal beds that must have formed during or shortly after the Flood – we can be confident that they are likely only about 4,300 years old. Besides, the wood cannot be millions of years younger than the lava around it. Evolutionary claims of great age for the creation have scientific problems as well as contradicting the Bible.

Prayer: Lord, I believe Your Word. Help me to overcome my unbelief, and help me to better know Your truth. Amen.

Ref: *Acts & Facts*, 1/08, pp. 10-13, Andrew A. Snelling, "Radiocarbon in 'Ancient' Fossil Wood."

Caterpillars Remember

Matthew 6:19
"Lay not up for yourselves treasures upon earth, where moth and rust doth corrupt, and where thieves break through and steal."

The metamorphosis of a caterpillar into a moth or butterfly completely restructures the creature internally and externally. Scientists at Georgetown University in Washington D.C. wondered whether that included the caterpillar's brain as well.

To find out, they placed tobacco hornworm caterpillars inside a hollow tube shaped like a Y. Scientists then put a bad-smelling gas in one of the arms of the Y. When a caterpillar went down that arm of the tube it received a mild shock. Since the caterpillars go through several molts, researchers performed the experiment on caterpillars at various stages of their moltings.

They found that caterpillars that underwent the experience before their fifth and final molt did not remember their experience with the gas after metamorphosis. However, 77 percent of those caterpillars that encountered the gas and experienced a shock after their final molt remembered their dislike of the gas after metamorphosis. Scientists point out that caterpillars, moths and butterflies are not social creatures. This means they have more need for memory because there is no division of labor among them.

Just because the Bible associates moths with decay doesn't mean that God didn't provide them with all they need to live successful lives. To God, no creature is unimportant.

Prayer: Father, I thank You that You are generous with Your gifts. Let me never forget Your goodness. Amen.

Ref: *Science News*, 3/22/08, p. 189, Rachel Ehrenberg, "Moths' Memories."

What Languages Did Jesus Speak?

John 7:35b
"...will He go unto the dispersed among the Gentiles, and teach the Gentiles?"

What languages did Jesus speak during His ministry on Earth? Of course He spoke Aramaic, since that was the common language of the people He taught. When He read from Isaiah in the synagogue in Nazareth, He would have read it in Hebrew. But did Jesus also speak Greek?

Greek was in common use in Israel in the First Century. Greek inscriptions are frequently found in Jewish graves from the period. This is evidence that many Jews knew the Greek language. Some scholars point to some of the terms in Jesus' recorded sayings that have Greek origins; however, their arguments are not universally accepted.

But Jesus did grow up in Nazareth, which is in "Galilee of the Gentiles," where Greek as well as Aramaic would have been spoken. Nazareth was only an hour's walk from Sepphoris, where one would have to speak Greek to do business. As scholars point out, Jesus was educated and as a carpenter, He was a skilled artisan. He would have to speak Greek to deal with customers. At one point His disciples wondered whether He would go to teach the Gentiles, a task that would require Greek.

Language is a gift of God. It is through this gift that God gives us the greater gift of His saving Gospel which assures us of the forgiveness of sins through Jesus Christ.

> **Prayer: Thank You, Father, for the gift of language, for this is how You give us Your Word of salvation in Jesus Christ. Amen.**

Ref: *Biblical Archaeology Review*, 9-10/92, pp. 58-63, Joseph A. Fitzmyer, "Did Jesus Speak Greek?"

Glass Insects in Space!

Psalm 9:1
"I will praise Thee, O Lord, with my whole heart; I will shew forth all Thy marvelous works."

Brine shrimp and water bears are tiny animals that are able to basically freeze dry into a state of suspended animation and then return to active life. Scientists have learned that they do this by replacing the water in their cells with a sugar called trehalos.

The larvae of a fly native to Africa makes its living eating organic material that settles at the bottom of puddles. During periods of drought, the larvae replace the water in their cells with trehalos. The sugar acts just like other sugars, solidifying into a glasslike state. In this state, the sugar acts to stabilize the larvae's tissues. The larvae can remain in this state for up to 17 years and still come back to life when water is again available.

Scientists would like to learn more about this ability. Their hope is to apply such knowledge to preserving blood for transfusion in a dry form. They may also learn how to preserve organs for transplant. As part of their research, they have sent dry larvae to the International Space Station. They want to see if the larvae can be revived after they have been exposed to space outside the space station.

Not only are the wonders God has created marvelous, but we can learn from them for our own betterment.

Prayer: Father, I praise You for the wonders that You have made and that we can learn from how You made things. Amen.

Ref: *Science News*, 3/29/08, p. 197, Davide Castelvecchi, "Live Another Day."

How Old Is Human DNA?

Genesis 11:8
"So the Lord scattered them abroad from thence upon the face of all the earth: and they left off to build the city."

Mitochondria generate energy inside each of your cells. They have their own DNA, which is passed directly from mother to child. This fact and the known rate at which mitochondrial DNA mutates has led to some conclusions which would be expected by those who accept the biblical history of mankind.

Both creationists and evolutionists who study mitochondrial DNA are agreed on several conclusions. They agree that at some time in the past there was a single dispersal of humankind. They also agree that there are three mitochondrial DNA lines represented in all of mankind. (Evolutionists, however, would not connect these three lines to Noah's three sons' wives.)

Both are also agreed that the dispersal of the human population happened fairly recently in the Middle East. The pattern indicates that this dispersal from a common place led to small, related groups or clans moving into new territory. Creationist researchers, seeing a parallel between the agreed-upon scientific conclusions and biblical history, have explored the evidence further.

Human mitochondrial DNA mutates at a known rate. Based on this known rate, the human genome is very young – much younger than evolutionary theory says it should be. It is only thousands of years old.

Prayer: Father, I thank You that You have loved us so much that You have saved us and given us the Gospel in Your Word. Amen.

Ref: *Acts/Facts*, 5/08, p. 6, Larry Vardiman, "Mitochondrial DNA and a Recent Human Origin."

Abimelech the Watermelon

Judges 9:53
"And a certain woman cast a piece of a millstone upon Abimelech's head, and all to brake his skull."

In the book of Judges we read of how "a certain woman" gave the Philistine leader Abimelech a skull fracture when she threw a millstone on him from a tower. Some biblical scholars concluded that no woman could lift a millstone to throw it. Besides, what would a millstone be doing at the top of a tower?

However, archaeologists easily answered these questions. First, the large round stones, often powered by a donkey, weren't invented until a thousand years later. The type of millstone in use at the time of this incident was a round, loaf-shaped stone that weighed between four and seven pounds. Archaeologists have found many of them in the Holy Land. It was used to grind flour in a stone base at a time when every household ground their own flour every day. This job was often done on a roof, in the cool breeze, under an awning.

To test the story, archaeologists in Israel assembled the type of stones that would have been used and a watermelon. They used a magic marker to give the melon a face and named it Abimelech. Then, with the help of several women volunteers, they tossed their stones from an ancient two-story tower. Abimelech did not survive.

Whether the Bible is talking about salvation or history, we know we can trust it as God's Word.

Prayer: Lord, I thank You for Your love to me in Jesus Christ and Your love in giving us Your Word, faithfully preserved. Amen.

Ref: *Biblical Archaeology Review*, 1-2/02, pp. 34-37, 62, Denise Dick Herr and Mary Petrina Boyd, "A Watermelon Named Abimelech."

Midnight Migrating Moths

Genesis 12:1

"Now the Lord had said unto Abraham, 'Get thee out of thy country ... unto a land that I will shew thee.'"

It was a moonless night over England. A specially designed radar picks up something that has never been seen before.

The radar is picking up silver Y moths as they migrate south for the winter. What has never been seen before is evidence that the moths actually navigate very precisely. It doesn't seem to matter whether the stars or moon are out or whether it is a cloudy, moonless night. This, scientists say, is the first evidence of a compass in night-migrating insects.

The special radar, which can track individual moths at altitudes of 500 to 4,000 feet, revealed how precise their navigating skills are. The moths only fly on nights when they can proceed south-southwest. If the wind is blowing in that direction, the moths need to make no course corrections. If the wind is blowing within 20 degrees of south-southwest the moths will very precisely modify their flight direction so that their overall progress is south-southwest. If the wind is more than 20 degrees off the desired direction, the moths don't fly.

Scientists believe that the moths winter somewhere in North Africa. Nocturnal moths that must migrate great distances under only select conditions require very special abilities. But just as God could lead Abram to a land he did not know, He can lead moths thousands of miles through the darkness.

Prayer: I thank You, Lord, that You have the power to keep Your promises, no matter how great they are. Amen.

Ref: *Science News*, 4/5/08, p. 212, Susan Milius, "Night Flights."

Meerkat School

Exodus 4:15b
"... and I will be with thy mouth, and with his mouth, and will teach you what ye shall do."

Behavioral researchers define teaching very specifically. First, of course, a teacher must have pupils. Then the teacher must be less efficient in doing whatever he is doing than he normally would be if he were alone, as a means of showing the pupils how to do the task. And finally, the pupils must learn the task more quickly than they would on their own.

By that definition, humans, of course, are teachers. Among animals, only a species of ant meets this definition of teaching. But now researchers from the University of Cambridge in England say that meerkats also qualify as teachers. They found that experienced hunters will take young, inexperienced pups with them when they hunt. They will let the youngsters watch them as they catch prey. Of course, when they catch some small prey, the youngsters will vocally beg for a handout. However, only 35 percent of those handouts are served to the youngsters dead. The rest of the time they have to learn how to subdue the caught prey themselves. On the other hand, older, more experienced pups received already-killed handouts only 10 percent of the time. Further tests involving live and dead prey show that those given live prey could learn to subdue it in only three days.

Despite the researchers' presupposition that teaching evolved, God is still the One that teaches the teachers.

Prayer: Father, I pray that you would provide Your church with faithful teachers of the forgiveness we have in Jesus Christ. Amen.

Ref: *Science News*, 7/15/06, p. 36, S. Milius, "Live Prey for Dummies."

God Helps Design a Better Submarine

Psalm 69:34
"Let the heaven and earth praise Him, the seas, and everything that moveth therein."

Engineers who design vehicles to move through fluids face a quandary. A torpedo-shaped vehicle can move quickly and efficiently through a fluid like water, but is difficult to maneuver precisely or get to hover. A boxier vehicle can be designed to hover and move with more precision but lacks speed and efficiency.

Engineers at the University of Colorado at Boulder have now solved that problem. For their solution they went to the design found in jellyfish and squid. These creatures move through the water very efficiently by expelling water in a vortex ring. So the engineers experimented with various designs until they had small but efficient vortex ring generators. Then they tested them on small vehicles. One of their designs was used to successfully parallel park an unmanned underwater vehicle. This design is expected to be used in much more than underwater vehicles. Engineers also envision tiny capsules equipped with tiny vortex jets cruising through the digestive tract to find or treat diseases.

As ingenious as this design is, this design really gives glory to its original Designer – God. This glory is not just in God's original design of jellyfish and squid but His design of the human brain, which can understand and copy His designs.

Prayer: Father, I join Your creation in glorifying you for Your designs, including our brains, which can learn from them. Amen.

Ref: http://www.colorado.edu/news/cgi-bin/print.cgi?year=2006&id=428

This Carbon-14 Discovery Is a Gem

Job 28:16
*"It [wisdom] cannot be valued with the gold of Ophir,
with the precious onyx, or the sapphire."*

Because half of the radioactive carbon-14 in anything decays to nonradioactive material in 5,730 years, things that are supposedly millions of years old cannot possibly have any. At least that's what evolutionary scientists always thought.

On the other hand, scientists who believe in a young creation, realized that nothing that has carbon in it should be too old to date. So they decided to see what results they would get dating coal and oil, which are supposed to be tens to hundreds of millions of years old.

Ten coal samples that were supposedly 34 to 311 million years old were tested. All 10 samples contained traces of carbon-14. Then they tested diamonds, which are supposed to be at least a billion years old. Again, they found carbon-14 in every sample tested. Keep in mind that they found carbon-14 in *every* coal, oil and diamond sample they tested. Evolutionary theory says that not one of these samples could possibly have carbon-14! Clearly, evolutionary claims about the ancient ages of these substances have scientifically and conclusively been proven wrong.

Scripture says that wisdom is more precious than even the most precious gems. Scripture also tells us that the fear of the Lord is the beginning of wisdom. True fear of the Lord is engendered by His love to us in Christ Jesus.

Prayer: Father, I thank You for bringing Your wisdom, the knowledge of Your mercy and forgiveness, into my life. Amen.

Ref: *Answers*, 7-9/06, pp. 22-24, Don DeYoung, "Raising the Bar on Creation Research."

God's Gifts and God's Gift

John 15:1
"I AM the true vine, and My Father is the husbandman."

The evolutionary story of man's history tells us that it took man tens of thousands of years to figure out he could farm crops for himself. Yet, today we know that some termites, ants and ambrosia beetles actually cultivate food crops.

In the world's oceans there are simpler approaches, called protofarming, among a few creatures. Protofarming is nothing more than where limpets and some damselfish graze on established algae. Now scientists have found an example of true farming among one species of damselfish. This fish feeds on a species of red alga that grows in a brown carpet. It protects it from other creatures looking for a salad. It also weeds its patch of any other algae, actually moving the interloping algae out of its patch. When a damselfish was removed from its patch, it was quickly devoured by other creatures and could not replace itself. A survey showed that the brown carpet alga only grows where there is a damselfish to tend it. It actually depends on the damselfish to survive.

Farming is not an invention of man, but a gift of God. It is clear that God gave the gift of farming to those creatures He wished to have this gift. God often compares Himself with a farmer in Scripture. Ultimately, He calls Himself a farmer, and Jesus Christ the vine, and believers in Christ the branches.

Prayer: Thank You, Father, for grafting me into Your Son, Jesus Christ, so that I may know Your forgiveness. Amen.

Ref: *Science News*, 8/12/06, p. 102, S. Milius, "Fish as Farmers."

When a Bug Is Not an Engineering Problem

Isaiah 54:11
"O thou afflicted, tossed with tempest, and not comforted, behold, I will lay thy stone with fair colours, and lay thy foundations with sapphires."

Squid and chameleons change colors. So does the golden tortoise beetle. But it does so in a way never before seen.

Squid and chameleons change colors by signaling pigment cells in their skin to shrink or expand. The golden tortoise beetle uses an entirely different method. The beetle is normally a very shiny golden color. But when disturbed, it turns blood red. The secret of its color change lies in the unique structure of its shell. It is made up of transparent chitin. The chitin is arranged in three levels, each with their own layers. In between the layers are microscopic channels, connecting them together. Normally, the beetles' body fluid fills the layers, smoothing them into perfect mirrors. But when disturbed, the body fluid flows out, making the shell transparent and revealing a bright red fourth layer.

Scientists quickly recognized that this design could lead to some important new technology. "Nature never stops surprising us with elegant solutions to everyday problems," said a chemist at GE Global Research Center in Niskayuna, New York.

This design is such an "elegant solution" to some engineering problems that "nature" must be given credit as if it were a being. Why not just recognize that the Designer of this "elegant solution" is the Triune God Who created it and uses color to show His glory to His creation?

Prayer: Thank you, Lord, for using color so generously to beautify Your creation and show forth Your glory. Amen.

Ref: *Science News*, 8/18/07, p. 99, C. Barry, "Mood Bugs."

Real Roots

Genesis 13:8

"And Abram said unto Lot, Let there be no strife, I pray thee, between me and thee, and between my herdmen and thy herdmen; for we be brethren."

People and animals recognize their siblings and generally treat them differently than unrelated acquaintances. Scientists wanted to know, do plants do the same thing?

Researchers from McMaster University in Hamilton, Ontario, studied the Great Lakes sea rocket with the hope of finding out. This member of the mustard family grows on the sandy beaches of lakes and the Atlantic coast. First, they collected seeds along a beach. They kept a record of which seeds were collected from the same mother plant. Then they planted the seeds in groups. Some of the groups had unrelated plants, while other groupings were all siblings.

After the plants had grown long enough to develop good, aggressive root systems, researchers carefully removed the root systems from the sand in which they were growing. After rinsing and drying the roots, they weighed each plant's root system. They learned that unrelated plants growing in a group had 15 percent more root system than siblings growing together. In other words, unrelated plants grew a more aggressive root system for gathering water and nutrients. Siblings were less aggressive toward each other. In short, sibling plants seemed to have recognized each other.

Just as godly Abram did not wish to aggressively compete with his nephew, apparently some plants do the same.

Prayer: Thank You, Lord, for my family. I also thank you for the heavenly family of believers who are united in Christ. Amen.

Ref: *Science News*, 6/16/07, p. 372, S. Milius, "Easy There, Bro."

How the Dinosaurs Died

Genesis 7:21
"And all flesh died that moved upon the earth, both of fowl, and of cattle, and of beast, and of every creeping thing that creepeth upon the earth, and every man."

The Bible says that when the flood waters came upon the Earth, all living things that have the breath of life were killed. While many of them drowned, some were encased in mud while still alive, as some fossils show. What they all had in common is that they died from lack of oxygen.

Paleontologists have long noted that many animal fossils are found with their heads thrown back. This is called the "dead bird" position. Some paleontologists assumed that the fossilized creature had fallen into the water when it died where the current pushed its head back. Others suggested that when rigor mortis set in, the head was pulled back. A third suggestion was that as the body decayed, drying tendons in the back of the neck pulled it back.

A little research ruled out rigor mortis as the cause of the "dead bird" position. Experiments using tendons from several different animals ruled out the "drying tendons" explanation. Finally, a credible explanation was found. Nerve damage. Specifically, the kind of nerve damage caused by lack of oxygen. While there are several causes for hypoxia, the most common cause is drowning.

That the "dead bird" position is so common among fossils paints a picture of the death that was a result of God's judgment in the Flood. His mercy to Noah shows us His love.

Prayer: Father, I thank You for Your Word, which tells me of Your love for me in Your Son, Jesus Christ. Amen.

Ref: *Science News*, 6/23/07, p. 390, C. Barry, "Jurassic CSI."

Darwin Was No Geologist

Psalm 46:2

"Therefore will not we fear, though the earth be removed, and though the mountains be carried into the midst of the sea."

Charles Darwin's ignorance of geology, a science he never studied, probably resulted in the biological errors he made in formulating his theory of biological evolution.

As he sailed on the *Beagle* to the Pacific, Charles Darwin read Charles Lyell's book, *Principles of Geology*. That book, of course, theorized that the Earth's geology was the result of the slow processes we see today working over millions of years. On the way to the Galapagos he had a 16-day stopover in Argentina. He spent some of the time exploring the valley of the lower Santa Cruz River. He later wondered in his journal how the small and lazy Santa Cruz River could have carved the 300-foot-deep valley. But he allowed that Lyell's idea of long ages could solve that problem.

Later, at the Galapagos, he tried to explain plant and animal diversity based on those same long ages. Today, geologists believe that melting glaciers at the headwaters of the river formed a huge lake behind a natural dam. When that dam broke, the rushing lake water quickly cut a spillway that became the valley through which the Santa Cruz River gently flows today.

It appears as though Darwin's assumption that Lyell knew what he was talking about when he wrote of long geological ages influenced his biological interpretations.

Prayer: Lord, when I am intimidated by evolutionary challenges to the truth of Your Word, comfort me with Your promises. Amen.

Ref: *Acts & Facts*, 7/08, pp. 10-12, Steven A. Austin, "Red Rock Pass: Spillway of the Bonneville Flood."

The Heavens Declare the Glory of God

Genesis 1:16
"And God made two great lights; the greater light to rule the day, and the lesser light to rule the night: he made the stars also."

Astronomers who believe in evolution tell us that the stars formed when gas in a nebula began to gather due to gravity. Eventually, that gravity became strong enough to collapse the gas into a star.

Astronomers who believe in creation point out that this is unlikely, if not impossible. As we all know, compressed gas wants to expand by moving to areas of lower pressure. A cloud of gas that was large enough to begin compressing under gravity would begin to rotate faster. Magnetic forces would also increase. The increase in pressure, magnetic forces and centrifugal forces would overcome the forces of gravity, preventing the formation of a star.

At the same time, blue stars are common in the arms of the galaxies we can see. These stars are considered young because they burn their fuel so fast that they could only last a few million evolutionary years. On the evolutionary scale, they must have formed long after the Big Bang. The number of blue stars would then indicate to an evolutionist that star formation is common. Yet, as we have seen, the forces at work to form a star in this way make these stars either unlikely or younger than millions of years.

Perhaps God created the blue stars to serve as a clear indicator to scientists that He created the stars fairly recently.

Prayer: I thank You, Father, for the beauty of the created heavens. The very existence of the stars praises Your Name. Amen.

Ref: *Answers Magazine*, 10-12/07, pp. 78-80, Jason Lisle, "The Stars of Heaven Confirm Biblical Creation."

Fish Birth Amazes Evolutionists

Job 12:8
"Or speak to the earth, and it shall teach thee: and the fishes of the sea shall declare unto thee."

It was nice day on a tropical reef in what is now Western Australia when an armored fish began to give birth. Before she could finish, the violence of the Genesis Flood encased her in mud.

Of course, that's not how evolutionists interpret the evidence. Our mom-to-be is a member of a newly discovered species of placoderm, a family of now-extinct armored fish. Not only were these fish armored, their jaws could apparently crush bones. Evolutionists say that these fish lived between 354 and 417 million inflated evolutionary years ago. This discovery pushes back the first-known example of a fish giving live birth 200 million evolutionary years ago. After the discovery, scientists went back and studied the fossils of another placoderm and discovered that it, too, had a uterus with three apparent unborn pups in it. Scientists say that the partially born youngster was already a quarter of its mother's ten-inch length. This helped its survival in a fish-eat-fish world. Scientists admit that the fish had an unexpectedly sophisticated reproductive system. Such systems, they say, are found only in supposedly much more evolved fish.

Of course, like all other living things, the placoderms did not evolve but were created. Their so-called advanced reproductive system does not show evidence for evolutionary progression, but it *does* show evidence of a caring Creator.

Prayer: Lord, the entire creation declares the excellence of Your handiwork. Help me to do so, too. Amen.

Ref: http:www.livescience.com/animals/080528-fossil-embryo.html

Security Mites

Psalm 20:1
"The LORD hear thee in the day of trouble; the name of the God of Jacob defend thee...."

The potter wasp is a solitary wasp that makes a mud nest with several rooms in it. At egg-laying time, the wasp lays one egg in each cavity and leaves some food in each cavity. She also leaves behind a security force!

You see, there is another species of parasitic wasp that seeks out a potter wasp nest to lay its eggs. When it is successful, the baby potter wasps would have no chance of survival if it wasn't for the security force. The mother potter wasp has very specialized pockets on its back. Tiny mites live within those pockets, causing no harm to the wasp. Then, while the potter wasp lays her eggs, some of the mites exit and remain in each room with the egg. These mites will remain in the nest after it is sealed, feeding on the food left for the hatchlings. They also mate at this time, which conveniently provides a population of mites as food for the young potter wasps. While these mites are peaceful creatures, they are the security force, and should a parasitic wasp get into the nest, they eagerly attack it.

This arrangement that benefits both the potter wasp and the mites is too intricate to have come about by accident. It was designed by the same Creator Who protects His children.

Prayer: Thank You, Father, for Your care and protection, especially Your protection from the devil through Christ's victory. Amen.

Ref: http://www.sciencenews.org/view/generic/id/33774/title/Mighty_mites

Homer May Have Been Smarter than We Thought

Psalm 147:4
"He telleth the number of the stars; he calleth them all by their names."

Homer, the blind Greek poet, spoke of Odysseus's return to Ithaca and describes some astronomical events that seldom happen in the order he describes. Yet, the setting of the events he writes about took place 400 years before it is thought Homer lived.

As Odysseus sails home five days before a banquet, he notes that both the constellations Boötes and Pleiades are visible. Because of their placement in the sky, they are very rarely visible in the same sky in Greece. Homer also mentions Odysseus's sighting of Venus just before dawn. Then, on the day of the banquet there is a solar eclipse. Some have dismissed these details as just colorful descriptions in a fictional poem. However, a solar eclipse did take place in that part of the world on April 16, 1178 B.C., just the time period Homer is writing about. Researchers then figured out the positions of the other astronomical features Odysseus is reported to have seen, and they were indeed happening on and within days of that date as described. The problem is, Greek astronomy at Homer's time was not believed to be sophisticated enough to figure out where these astronomical bodies were 400 years earlier.

Perhaps man, who has made astronomical observatories since before most historic cultures were established, was originally given such knowledge by his Creator.

Prayer: Father, I thank You for the beauty of the night sky that so gloriously sets forth Your glory and power. Amen.

Ref: http://www.sciencenews.org/view/generic/id/33683/title/Too_much_information_in_the_Odyssey

A Serpent Can Point to Christ

John 3:14
"And as Moses lifted up the serpent in the wilderness,
even so must the Son of man be lifted up...."

The Tiger Keelback snake has a bite that delivers slow-acting venom and prevents the victim's blood from clotting. An adult human could bleed to death from a bite, but it takes a while for the snake to deliver a lethal dose.

When threatened, the average Keelback will raise its head and display its colorful swollen neck. Should the attacker bite the snake near its head, it will get a mouth full of a much stronger poison from glands in its neck. Where does that poison come from? For years scientists have debated whether the Keelback produces its own poison, or does it get the poison from some other creature that it ate? Now research has revealed that the Keelback actually does store the poison of a poisonous toad that it eats. Moreover, it seems to know that it has this poison stored. For example, on an island where there are some Keelbacks but no toads, these Keelbacks when threatened do not display their neck to an attacker. Rather, they flee from their attacker.

God has used many ingenious designs in His creation, knowing that some would recognize this and, by doing so, acknowledge His existence, power and glory. His desire is always that we might be driven to His Word to learn of the salvation He has prepared for us in Jesus Christ.

Prayer: Father, I thank You that You desire our salvation and that You have called me to faith in Jesus Christ. Amen.

Ref: *Science News*, 2/3/07, p. 69, S. Milius, "Bite This."

Delicate Beauty

Revelation 21:4
"And God shall wipe away all tears from their eyes; and there shall be no more death, neither sorrow, nor crying, neither shall there be any more pain: for the former things are passed away."

Bacteria and fungi form biofilms on just about every wet surface, like that bowl of water you left out last night! In this biofilm state, bacteria cause 70 percent of all human bacterial infections. On underwater pipelines, biofilms cause corrosion. Such biofilms even form on seaweed. That is, except for the seaweed called Delicate Beauty.

Delicate Beauty, grows off the coast of Australia, and researchers long wondered why biofilms never form on this seaweed. Researchers have now discovered that Delicate Beauty secretes chemicals called furanones. Furanones don't kill the bacteria, but prevent it from colonizing by repelling them. This observation is important because it is believed that since the furanones don't kill the bacteria, the bacteria will not develop a resistance to the furanones. Commercial production of these chemicals are now beginning to be used in water-cooling towers to prevent biofilm buildup and in clinical trials on contact lenses to prevent bacterial growth. So far these trials have been successful, and further applications are under study.

It was not God's desire that disease and death should come into His creation because of our sin. But He knew that it would. So He stocked the creation with things for us to discover to alleviate and avoid some of our suffering in this world. Christians know that there is no disease or death in heaven.

Prayer: Father, while we will experience no disease when we get to heaven, I thank You for giving us tools to prevent it here. Amen.

Ref: *Science Illustrated*, 7-8/08, pp. 62-69, "Inspired by Nature."

No Eyes, But It Can See Light

Psalm 94:9
"He that planted the ear, shall he not hear? He that formed the eye, shall he not see?"

It turns out that not all creatures need eyes to see light. It all depends on what the creatures were designed to do. The roundworm, *C. elegans*, lives below the soil surface where it needs no eyes. At the same time, this roundworm needs to sense light because too much exposure will kill it. Researchers noted that the roundworm has only 302 nerve cells. Study of these cells showed that some of them sense light in the same way that similar cells in vertebrates sense light. Evolutionists suggested that this is an example of an early step in the evolution of eyes. However, there is no evolutionary pressure for this roundworm to evolve eyes, because light will kill it. Besides, animals that supposedly evolved long before *C. elegans* already had eyes. A better explanation is that, like the cave fishes, this roundworm lives in the dark and needs no eyes and would, in any case, be constantly filling with dirt. No, this is not an example of evolution, but of good design by God.

God has designed all things to fit well into their respective environments. The fish that lives in the dark depths of the ocean and has lighted lures, the fishes that live in the darkest caves have no eyes and neither does the roundworm, *C. elegans.* All these show God's fingerprints.

Prayer: Father, You have made all things well, showing Your wisdom and power for all to see. Thank You. Amen.

Ref: http://www.sciencenews.org/view/generic/id/33889/title/Seeing_without_eyes

Smart Slime

Ecclesiastes 4:9
"Two are better than one; because they have a good reward for their labour."

We all know that there is strength in numbers. Many animals have even discovered this and, for example, migrate in large herds. However, one would never expect bacteria to have discovered this or know enough to organize themselves collectively.

Bacteria consist of a single cell that doesn't even have a nucleus. They have no nervous system, and they reproduce by simply dividing in half. Of course, there is no brain; yet, they seem to display a sense of consciousness that totally baffles the neurosciences. Some marine species of bacteria are able to sense when there are other bacteria around them. Then, when a sufficient number have gathered together, their metabolism changes, and they begin to produce a slime that then holds them together. While all this is now known, new research shows that the slime, called biofilm, includes chemicals that are poisonous to the very predators that would ordinarily feed on the bacteria. In fact, the biofilm seems to protect the bacteria. The more bacteria there are, the more biofilm they make and the more protection they have from predators.

There are no simple forms of life. Even bacteria, which are an important part of the ecosystem, have been designed with the ability to protect themselves – something they could never have invented for themselves.

Prayer: Father, while You teach us to help one another, help me to always look to Your strength for my aid. Amen.

Ref: *Minneapolis Star Tribune*, 7/29/08, p. A5, David Brown, "Cellmates: Research shows that bacteria, when under attack, stick together to survive."

Are "Cavemen" Primitive?

1 Kings 19:9
"And he came thither unto a cave, and lodged there; and, behold, the word of the LORD came to him...."

Cavemen. The very word conjures images of bear skin clothing, wooden clubs and perhaps some simple stone tools. We think of the cavemen themselves as part ape and certainly less than modern humans. All of these images help make human evolution look more plausible.

However, in China there are some 20 million people living in caves. The caves there are easily carved in the silty soil of the Western regions of the Yellow River. The caves are generally 10 to 13 feet wide and can extend as far as 25 feet back into the hillside. Sometimes the caves are connected to one another, creating a larger place to live. Many of the people who live in these caves would not think of moving out of them. Caves are warm in the winter, cool in the summer, and they are fireproof. These caves include flues for venting the exhaust from cooking fires. But these caves are not primitive dwellings by any stretch of the imagination. They feature plumbing, electrical wiring and even cable television! Except for windows, some of these cave homes are as modern as anything you'll see in the rest of the developing world.

Throughout the ages, people have taken shelter in caves and even set up housekeeping in them. The fact that they lived in caves does not make them primitive at all.

Prayer: Lord, do not let Your people be misled into unbelief, and enlighten them with Your truth. Amen.

Ref: *Minneapolis Star Tribune*, 12/21/08, p. AA5, Tim Johnson, "Cave, sweet cave: Many Chinese find home is in a hillside."

Australia's Smart Dolphins

Psalm 104:27
"These wait all upon thee; that thou mayest give them their meat in due season."

It was once thought that only man used tools. However, scientists have learned that some monkeys and even some birds use "tools." Now we can add dolphins to the growing list of tool-users.

Researchers studying dolphins in Australia's Shark Bay noticed that some dolphins were swimming around with sponges on their beaks. After some observation, both on the surface and beneath the water, scientists discovered what the dolphins were doing. Holding the sponges in their mouths, they would sweep the sea bottom sand, flushing out fish. Then they dropped the sponge and ate what they had flushed out. When they were finished eating, they retrieved their sponge and repeated the process. Researchers found that about 10 percent of the females obtained their food using sponges as tools. For some unknown reason, very few of the males used this method. Furthermore, most of the females using this method were related to two maternal tool-using dolphins. Researchers debate whether these two taught their descendants this method of obtaining fish or whether the behavior is based in genetics.

Since this is not a widespread behavior among dolphins, it seems likely that it is a learned behavior probably taught to younger relatives by the maternal dolphins. After all, dolphins are known to be very intelligent, and intelligence is a gift from their Creator.

Prayer: I thank You, Lord, that You have given Your creatures an Earth and the ability to make a living on it. Amen.

Ref: Science News Online, 12/10/08, www.sciencenews.org/view/generic/id/39219, Bruce Bower, "Dolphins Wield Tools of the Sea."

Three-Dimensional Thinking

Matthew 22:37
"Jesus said unto him, Thou shalt love the Lord thy God with all thy heart, and with all thy soul, and with all thy mind."

Without a doubt the brain is a marvelous organ, although there is still a great deal to learn about how it works. We do know that brain cells communicate through connections which reach out in three dimensions to other cells. When thought and motion take place, they communicate with each other very quickly. They are even in communication while you sleep.

In contrast to the human brain, the "thinking" parts of a computer are connected in two dimensions to "communicate" with each other. Researchers thought that it might boost performance if a three-dimensional computer chip could be designed. Cell phones already use a three-dimensional chip arrangement, but these are just individual flat chips stacked one on top of another. Researchers wanted to see what true three-dimensional chips (called TSVs), could do. Now several chip manufacturers have developed working TSVs. They have found that three-dimensional chips transmit information faster and use less power than flat chips. In other words, they are more efficient than flat chips and pack more "thinking" power into a smaller space. Chip manufacturers are now working on ways to successfully mass produce the TSVs.

The three-dimensional computer chip does improve chip performance by mimicking the wiring of the brain. However, except in the area of calculation, we are nowhere close to mimicking the power of the human brain.

Prayer: Thank You, Father, for implanting in my mind faith in Jesus Christ as my Lord and Savior. Amen.

Ref: *The Nikkei Weekly*, 12/29/08 & 1/5/09, p. 3, "Semiconductor makers head for third dimension."

Great Travelers Have Great Stories to Tell

Acts 11:19a

"Now they which were scattered abroad upon the persecution that arose about Stephen traveled as far as Phoenicia, and Cyprus, and Antioch...."

Those who widely travel usually have interesting experiences to talk about. That is no less true of animals that migrate. A commonly known example is the monarch butterfly. In the fall, monarchs from all over North America head south to the same small patch of jungle trees in Mexico. Even more astonishing is that each generation finds this exact traditional wintering spot but has never been there before.

Scientists have recently discovered that another migrating creature has an even more interesting story to tell. Bar-tailed godwits, shorebirds with a wingspan of about 12 to 16 inches, summer in Alaska. But they winter in New Zealand, over 7,000 miles away. As you mentally picture their route, you would be right to notice that there are very few places to stop and rest between Alaska and New Zealand. Researchers outfitted seven female godwits with tracking devices to learn more about their migration. They found that the godwits traveled the distance nonstop, without rest or even food or water. That's the equivalent of a nonstop flight from London to Los Angeles, plus 1,000 miles more!

Godwits glorify God as Creator with their amazing migratory paths. As the first Christians scattered across the Roman Empire in fear of persecution and martyrdom, they spread the wonder of God's love for us in the Gospel of salvation.

Prayer: Father, I thank You for the glory of Your creation, but I rejoice in the wonder of Your love and salvation. Amen.

Ref: *Science News*, 11/22/08, p. 14, Laura Sanders, "Nonstop godwit flights."

Stressed Plants Tell Us About It

Ezekiel 47:12b
"...and the fruit thereof shall be for meat, and the leaf thereof for medicine."

When they have a headache or perhaps a toothache many people take an aspirin. It turns out that many plants do almost the same thing when they are under stress.

The plants that do so, however, make their own form of aspirin called methyl salicylate. This phenomenon has been observed in the laboratory, but never in nature until now. Researchers studying air pollution set up their instruments near a California walnut grove. They wanted to see what gases the plants might be emitting. Methyl salicylate was among the gases they detected. Researchers believe that the gas might have some immune function for the plants. It might also warn surrounding plants of a threat. This finding may help farmers and others detect when plants are being stressed by lack of water, insects or disease. Until this finding, those caring for plants could only tell when a plant was stressed once the plant began to show visible signs of stress. With this information, those who tend plants will be able to apply pesticides, for example, in a more timely manner.

God gave us a perfect world where there was no need for medicines. But He knew we would sin and bring death and sickness upon the creation. So, being a loving God, He also gave us medicines to discover and ease our suffering.

Prayer: Thank You, Father, for the gift of medicine. Prosper all good knowledge that brings healing in our midst. Amen.

Ref: *Yahoo! News*, 9/18/08, Randolf E. Schmid, AP Science Writer, "Stressed plants produce aspirin-like chemical."

Dolphins at Play

Job 40:20

"Surely the mountains bring him forth food, where all the beasts of the field play."

Bottlenose dolphins have a reputation as intelligent, playful creatures. A newly released video shows just how intelligent their play is.

The video shows various dolphins creating rotating bubble rings which seem to hover in the water for a few seconds. The dolphins do this by first creating a water vortex with their dorsal fin. The ends of the vortex then come together into an invisible ring. Then the dolphin injects air from its blowhole into the spinning vortex. The vortex has enough energy to hold the ring from rising too quickly for play. Such a vortex bubble is about two feet across. However, dolphins might play with the vortex to create a smaller ring. Sometimes a dolphin will insert a smaller bubble ring inside a larger ring. They also create rings that flip vertically or even flip completely over. Sometimes a dolphin will create two bubble rings that collide and produce a third ring. The video shows one dolphin creating a large ring and watching it rise through the water. Just before the ring breaks the surface, the dolphin swims through the ring and leaps from the water.

Intelligence and such play as this are linked. Our Creator has not just shared intelligence and creativity with man. He clearly has shared some of His intelligence and creativity with His other creatures as well.

Prayer: Father, thank You for the beauty of Your creation and sharing Your creativity with so much of Your creation. Amen.

Ref: http://www.snopes.com/photos/animals/dolphinrings.asp, "Video shows dolphins creating and playing with bubble rings."

Antibiotic Resistant No More

Genesis 22:8
"And Abraham said, My son, God will provide himself a lamb for a burnt offering: so they went both of them together."

One of medicine's greatest challenges are those populations of bacteria that have become resistant to antibiotics.

The ocean is literally a soup of bio-germs, including bacteria, many of which can infect, sicken and kill a wide variety of creatures. These germs often form biofilms which protect them from antibiotics. Marine researchers were investigating the ocean bottom where something had killed all the marine creatures. In the midst of all this death they found a thriving marine sponge. Why wasn't it dead like everything else? Studying the sponge's defenses, researchers discovered a chemical called ageliferin. Further study showed that this compound prevented biofilms from forming. What's more, the chemical makes resistant germs once again susceptible to antibiotics. It has already been proven to re-sensitize bacteria that cause ear infections, food poisoning, whooping cough and a particularly nasty resistant bacteria that causes infections in hospitals.

While God gave us a perfect world, He knew that mankind would sin and bring disease and death into the world. So God provided antibiotics. But He also knew that some germs would become resistant to antibiotics. So He provided His creation with substances to solve that problem, too. Nevertheless, mankind's primary problem is sin, and He provided us with the Lamb of God Who takes away the sin of the world – one repentant sinner at a time.

Prayer: I thank You, Lord, for good medicine, but most of all I thank You for sending Your Son to be my Savior. Amen.

Ref: *Science News*, 3/14/09, p. 16, Laura Sanders, "Sponge's secret weapon revealed."

Evolutionary Model of Early Earth's Atmosphere Fails Test

Genesis 1:31
"And God saw every thing that he had made, and, behold, it was very good. And the evening and the morning were the sixth day."

According to the theory of evolution, the atmosphere of the very early Earth contained no oxygen, but it did contain carbon dioxide. When the plants and trees evolved, they lived on the carbon-dioxide as they still do today and, by metabolizing carbon dioxide, they released oxygen as a waste product.

When sufficient oxygen had been produced, air-breathing animals evolved, but this was supposedly a slow process. Calculations showed that by the time the dinosaurs were beginning to die out, 65 million evolutionary years ago, the Earth's atmosphere only contained 10 to 12 percent oxygen. Today, the atmosphere is 21 percent oxygen. But to complicate the issue, there is much fossil evidence of wildfires during this era. The researchers wondered whether the small amount of oxygen that was supposedly in the atmosphere then could support such fires under realistic conditions. Tests were carried out in an atmosphere containing 12 percent oxygen using paper, matches, wooden sticks and a candle. The results showed that none of these items will burn readily until the atmosphere contains a minimum of 17 percent oxygen. The evolutionary model of the early Earth's atmosphere was proven wrong!

When God finished creating, He declared that everything was "very good." That includes the design of the atmosphere with enough oxygen to support life, but not too much to cause fire to burn explosively.

Prayer: Father, thank You for so wisely designing the Earth's atmosphere so that it supports life and fire serves us. Amen.

Ref: *Science*, 29 August 2008, pp. 1197-1200, C.M. Belcher, J.C. McElwain, "Limits for Combustion in Low CO_2 Redefine Paleoatmospheric Predictions for the Mesozoic."

Designed as a Companion

Genesis 9:2a
"And the fear of you and the dread of you shall be upon every beast of the earth, and upon every fowl of the air...."

When God told Noah that man could now eat meat after the Flood, He kindly filled the animals with a natural fear of man. However, He evidently left a few animals without that fear in order for them to be helpmates and companions for man.

The dog has been man's best friend probably since before the Genesis Flood. Researchers recently tested whether Border Collies were intelligent enough to fetch an unseen item in another room simply by being shown a picture or model of it. Chimps and dolphins had also been tested for this ability and were unable to do it. Collies, both trained and untrained to "fetch", were tested in their own homes. Eight toys they were to fetch were in a second room. Then the dogs were shown either an exact copy of what they were to fetch, a model of it, or a photograph and were told, "bring it here." All retrieved their toy easily after being shown a model of it. Trained dogs did well when shown an exact copy, but the untrained dogs needed a little practice with this task. Some dogs were even able to fetch a toy when shown a full-sized photograph.

Not only does the domestic dog have no natural fear of man, but many of them can relate to us in very helpful ways.

Prayer: Father, thank You for those animals which can be companions and even help us. Amen.

Ref: *Science News* Online, 3/21/09, http://www.sciencenews.org/view/generic/id/419732, Bruce Bower, "Dogs Show a Fetching Communication Savvy."

Salad Spiders

Genesis 1:30
"And to every beast of the earth, and to every fowl of the air... I have given every green herb for meat: and it was so."

In the perfect world that God created there were no meat eaters. In today's sinful world it is hard to imagine meat eaters, like spiders, being vegetarians.

Some spiders have occasionally been observed tasting plants. The male crab spider has been seen tasting plant nectar. Some baby spiders eat spores that they find in their webs. But now a small jumping spider that lives on acacia trees has been discovered that is vegetarian. Acacia trees are often home to vicious ants that protect the tree from other gnawing insects. In return, the tree offers the ants protection and tasty nectar. So the little jumping spider must constantly avoid the guard ants when it heads out for a meal of nectar. One of their strategies for avoiding ants is to build their nests on mature leaves. These leaves are the least guarded on the plant. Researchers noted that they did observe four instances of a spider eating ant larva, but this was out of 140 feeding observations.

Our experiences in a fallen world do not begin to prepare us for what God is able to create, despite all the wonders around us. If it pleases God, He can make vegetarian lions, tigers and even spiders. Who of us would ever have thought of His plan to rescue us from sin through His Son, Jesus Christ?

Prayer: Thank You, dear Father, for providing for all of Your creatures, even in a fallen world. Amen.

Ref: *Science News* online, http://www.sciencenews.org/view/generic/id/35121, 8/12/08, Susan Milius, "Vegetarian Spider."

The Lotus Effect

1 John 1:9
"If we confess our sins, he is faithful and just to forgive us our sins, and to cleanse us from all unrighteousness."

Perhaps you have a self-cleaning oven in your kitchen, and if you have small children in your house, you've probably wished for self-cleaning walls. Self-cleaning clothes would be nice, too!

Lotuses often grow in muddy water where mud can accumulate on leaves. Yet, for efficiency in collecting sunlight, their leaves need to be clean. And, yes, they stay clean despite the environment in which they grow. Close examination under a powerful electron microscope reveals why. The top of the leaves are covered with tiny spikes that feel waxy. They are so tiny that they can even hold up a particle of dust that settles on a leaf. As a result, any water that lands on the leaves rolls right off. As it rolls off, it collects any dirt that may be on a leaf. These leaves are self-cleaning! Researchers realized that this microscopic spike structure could be used to make self-cleaning products. For example, self-cleaning paint for homes is already in use under the product name Lotusan. Self-cleaning food containers are being developed as well. And one day we may even have self-cleaning clothes, including swimming suits that never get wet.

However, when it comes to our standing before God, we are not self-cleaning. We must rely on the cleansing from our sin won for us by our Lord Jesus on the cross.

Prayer: Father, thank You for the forgiveness of sins I have through my Lord Jesus Christ and the life He gives me. Amen.

Ref: *Science Illustrated*, 7/8/08, pp. 62-69, "Inspired by Nature," ("Mr. Clean," pp. 68-69).

"God Bless You" Indeed

Matthew 6:26
"Behold the fowls of the air: for they sow not, neither do they reap, nor gather into barns; yet your heavenly Father feedeth them."

Most people know that if they are stranded at sea without fresh water they should not drink sea water. While we need salt, the amount of salt in sea water would kill a person more quickly than thirst. Have a little too much salt on your popcorn and your kidneys will filter out the extra. But to do so, they need extra fresh water.

The marine iguanas of the Galapagos islands drink too much salt water every day. They feed on the algae that grow in sea water, but they lack a good freshwater supply to flush the salt out using their kidneys. Since God knew what kind of environment this iguana would one day be living in, He gave the marine iguana a special gland. Located in its head, it removes excess salt from the iguanas' blood and holds it. Periodically, the iguana will sneeze, expelling the salt-saturated fluid. As it dries it leaves a salty crown on the top of its head that dissolves back into the sea during the next swim. Several other reptiles also have salt glands, but each of these work very differently. This means that evolutionists must explain how these salt glands evolved at least ten times.

God gave the marine iguana these unique glands because He knew what they would need for the life He gave them.

Prayer: Thank You, Lord, for providing so wondrously for all Your creatures, even as you have provided for my salvation. Amen.

Ref: *Answers*, 3-4/09, pp. 20-22, Mary Mitchell, "Salt-Sneezing Lizards."

Star Smellers

Genesis 27:27a
*"And he came near, and kissed him: and he smelled the
smell of his raiment, and blessed him...."*

Can mammals that spend time in the water smell odors
under water? Of course they can, but no researcher is going to take
a big sniff under water to find out!

Being able to smell helps us to learn important information
about our surroundings – smells can attract or warn of danger. But
it has always been thought that semi-aquatic animals could never
smell odors under water. Animal researchers at Vanderbilt
University were aware that water shrews and star-nosed moles
release bubbles constantly when they are under water, but they
didn't know why. The star-nosed mole is amazing by itself. Its
nose has 16 pink tentacles, giving this strange-looking creature its
name. So they watched the animals under water on high speed
video. They saw the creatures exhaling and then re-inhaling the
bubbles at the rate of ten times a second. That led them to wonder
whether the animals could be detecting odors under water. As a
test, they placed food in the tank but separated it from the test
subjects with a screen so there was no physical contact. As the
animals were tested they excitedly targeted in on the food source,
demonstrating that they were indeed detecting the odor of wanted
food.

Since these creatures make their living under water, God
has given them the amazing and surprising ability to smell under
water.

**Prayer: Heavenly Father, the gifts You give are
wonderful and often unexpected, for which I praise and
thank You. Amen.**

Ref: www.rscc.org/Chemistry World/News/2006/December/20120601.asp, "A breath of
fresh water."

Hot Fungicide

Exodus 37:29
"And he made the holy anointing oil, and the pure incense of sweet spices, according to the work of the apothecary."

Plant seeds are distributed by a number of ingenious methods, including wind, water, mammals and birds. Plants that rely upon these creatures to distribute their seeds often attract them with tasty fruit surrounding the seed. However, tasty fruit contains sugar and other substances that many other creatures also find inviting. Yes, the problem is, everybody likes sugar and that includes insects, molds and fungi, all of which are useless as seed distributors. Some plants make up for this problem by producing large amounts of fruit, just to ensure that some are reproduced.

It has long been said that "hot" chili peppers use spice to deter non-seed distributors from contaminating their fruit. Researchers have now confirmed this and report that the "hot" taste in these chili peppers comes from the amount and types of chemicals in them called capsaicinoids. They studied the Capsicum chili plants in Bolivia that have a range of capsaicinoids. A common fruit pest in this part of the world is a sap-sucking bug whose mouth parts commonly infest plants with a black fungus. Researchers surveyed infestations in different plant populations and analyzed the quantity of capsaicinoids they contain. Sure enough, the hotter peppers had measurably fewer black mold infestations than the more mild peppers.

In providing these plants with protection from pests, God has also provided us with useful and pleasant spices.

Prayer: Father, thank You for not only providing protection for productive plants but for giving us useful spices as well. Amen.

Ref: www.sciencenews.org/view/generic/id/35114/title/Bittersweet_fruits, 8/12/08, Rachel Ehrenberg, "Bittersweet Fruits."

Capuchins Don't Monkey Around

Genesis 3:15
"And I will put enmity between thee and the woman, and between thy seed and her seed; it shall bruise thy head, and thou shalt bruise his heel."

We were once told that tool use is what separates man from the animals. Then it was discovered that some animals use tools. Now, scientists have learned that these animals do more than just grab something from their surroundings; they look for something that would be needed to do the job.

Primatologists studied tool use and selection among wild capuchin monkeys in Brazil. First, they observed natural tool use among the monkeys. They noticed that when monkeys wanted to crack open a nut they examined several types of stones. When they had a choice between a hard rock or a softer sandstone, which would be likely to break, they preferred the harder stone after examining both rocks. One monkey was observed examining two stones of the same hardness and then selecting the larger one. Then he placed a palm nut on a fallen log and cracked the nut open with a rock. Stone selection also varied depending on what type of nut was being cracked open.

Man isn't separated from animals by tool use or making. Rather, he is separated from animals because he was made to have a personal relationship with God. He is also responsible to God for his actions. This is why, when man first sinned, God promised us a Savior Who would show us the way to salvation.

Prayer: I thank You, Father, that through Your Son Jesus Christ I have the forgiveness of sins and salvation. Amen.

Ref: www.science news.org/view/generic/id/39930, 1/15/09, Bruce Bower, "Capuchin Monkeys Choose The Right Tool For The Nut."

Moths Fool Bats

2 Corinthians 11:14
"And no marvel; for Satan himself is transformed into an angel of light."

When one thinks of clever creatures, moths are probably not the first creature that come to mind – in fact, they probably don't come to mind at all!

Researchers at Wake Forest University raised some bats from infanthood in large cages. Their purpose was to carefully control the growing bats' diets and study their responses to various prey. Among the prey offered were Tiger moths. In the caterpillar stage they eat plants which make them unpalatable even as moths. As moths, when a bat is near, they emit a series of clicks. A bat will try to eat the moths only once, spitting out the foul-tasting insect almost immediately after biting it. When the bats were offered a different but equally foul-tasting species of Tiger moth, a few of the bats tried the new species despite their "don't eat me" clicking sounds. They quickly learned to avoid the new species as well. Researchers also offered the bats tasty Milkweed Tussock moths. While tasty, these moths click like the tiger moths when approached by a bat. Three of ten bats tried these moths, but the other seven wouldn't touch them. These tasty moths managed to fool most of the bats into thinking that they were the unpalatable Tiger moths.

Good doesn't usually mimic evil, but Scripture warns us that evil will mimic good.

Prayer: Father, thank You for Your Word which teaches me the truth of salvation and warns me against evil mimicking good. Amen.

Ref: *Science News*, 6/23/07, p. 397. S.M., "Moths mimic 'Don't eat me' sounds."

Man Is Not First to Do Genetic Engineering

Genesis 9:3
"Every moving thing that liveth shall be meat for you; even as the green herb have I given you all things."

"You are what you eat." We've all heard the saying. It doesn't mean that if you eat a lot of chicken, you'll literally become a chicken. But now science has discovered a creature for which the saying is literally true, in part, right down to the genetic level.

The green sea slug called *Elysia chlorotica* is more than just leaf-shaped. It eats algae and after a couple of weeks doesn't need to eat for the rest of its year-long life. It actually photosynthesizes its own food by stealing the genes for photosynthesis from the algae it ate. However, geneticists knew that the genetic information it steals from the algae only gives it one-tenth of the DNA it needs to code for the proteins needed to continue to be able to photosynthesize. In search of the answer to this mystery, scientists closely studied the slug's DNA. They discovered that the missing genetic information was indeed to be found in the slug. What's more, this information was identical to the algae's genetic information. In other words, the slug steals all of the genetic information necessary for photosynthesis. Scientists are mystified as to how the slug accomplishes this wonder!

Of course, it's no mystery when you know that the same Creator Who designed DNA also designed the sea slug who can selectively steal it.

Prayer: Father, I thank You for all the wonders You have created, but the greatest wonder is Your love toward me. Amen.

Ref: www.newscientist.com/article/dn16124-solarpowered-sea-slug-harnesses-stolen-plant-genes.html, 11/24/08, Catherine Brahic, "Solar-powered sea slug harnesses stolen plant genes."

Nasty Nannies

Romans 8:21
"Because the creature itself also shall be delivered from the bondage of corruption into the glorious liberty of the children of God."

There is a species of ant that, although quite small, makes slaves of yet smaller ants. This slave-making ant makes its nest inside acorns, and unlike the species they enslave, they have chemical weapons and powerful jaws.

While they enslave the smaller species, they don't seem to do much else, including caring for their own young. They get their captives by raiding the nests of the smaller species, stealing larvae and pupae. Once these ant babies mature in the acorn, they are expected to do all the work, including taking care of the slave-makers' eggs. Evolutionary scientists have said that such ants could not evolve resistance against their enslavement. However, now they have learned that the slave ants do indeed resist. Once the slave-maker's eggs mature to the pupa stage, the slave-ants will neglect them or even eat them. This is behavior they do not do in their home colony. Researchers say the slave-maker ant queens lay enough eggs. However, between 60 and 80 percent never make it to maturity when cared for by captive slaves. Such population reductions help reduce future raids on their home colonies – home colonies they have never seen! Clearly, an altruistic objective.

But not all slavery is physical. God sent His Son, Jesus Christ, to be our Lord and Savior when we were enslaved by sin, death and the devil.

Prayer: Thank You, Father, for sending Your Son, Jesus Christ, to free me from bondage to sin, death and the devil. Amen.

Ref: www.sciencenews.org/view/generic/id/35309/title/Slave_ants-rebel, Susan Milius, "Slave Ants Rebel."

Birds' Unique Leg Structure Says No Evolution

Genesis 1:21
"And God created ... every winged fowl after his kind: and God saw that it was good."

Countless television programs, museums, textbooks, and popular articles tell us that the birds evolved from dinosaurs. It now appears that this claim is even *less* credible!

Researchers at Oregon State University have made a fundamental discovery about how birds breathe. Unlike other land animals, birds have immovable thigh bones, and they walk and run by bending their knees. All other land creatures can move both their thigh bone as well as bend their knees to walk and run. This included the dinosaurs and other theropods from which birds supposedly evolved. Birds need twenty times as much oxygen as cold-blooded animals. To supply this need, birds are designed with unique lungs and supporting musculature. Researchers found that if birds had the usual muscle structures and could move their thighs, their high-performance lungs would collapse. Even the evolutionists at Oregon State University said that this makes it unlikely that birds evolved from dinosaurs, and they added that birds appear earlier in the fossil record than the theropods from which they supposedly evolved!

There are other transition problems associated with bird evolution that are seldom mentioned. For example, reptiles are cold-blooded and birds are warm blooded; yet, this major transition has seemingly been overlooked.

Of course, the Bible has always taught that birds were specially made by God and did not evolve from any other creature.

Prayer: Lord, You have designed all things well. Do not let Your people be fooled by those who deny Your works. Amen.

Ref: Oregon State University (2009, June 9), "Discovery Raises New Doubts About Dinosaur -Bird Links. *Science Daily*. Retrieved June 16, 2009, from http://www.sciencedaily.com/ releases/2009/06/090609092055.htm.

Monkeying with Genetics

Psalm 7:17
"What is man, that thou shouldest magnify him? and that thou shouldest set thine heart upon him?"

We have all heard the claims – and school textbooks love to include it – that humans and chimpanzees are about 99 percent genetically identical. However, that claim evaporates when the details of what is being compared are examined.

First of all, the DNA sequences that were compared were cherry-picked. Similar sequences in both humans and chimps were compared, while non-similar sequences were ignored. In addition, comparisons were made using only the DNA that codes for making protein. This ignores most of the human and chimp genome. When the DNA that regulates cell operation are included in the comparison, the degree of similarity drops considerably. Important parts of certain chromosomes, like the Y chromosome, are very different. Research has also found that there are major differences between how certain genes express themselves within cells. In addition, the chimpanzee genome is 10 to 12 percent larger than man's, which is quite a difference in itself.

The truth is the entire human and chimp genome has never been properly compared, while if it has, it has never been reported. However, when the spiritual differences are considered, there is an unbridgeable gulf between humans and chimps. Man was made in the image of God, to be responsible before Him and to have a relationship with Him. Jesus Christ died for the salvation of mankind, not for chimps.

Prayer: Thank You, Father, for sending Your Son for our redemption and seeking us out with Your gracious Word. Amen.

Ref: *Acts & Facts*, 6/09, pp. 12-13, Jeffery Tomkins, Human-Chimp Similarities, "Common Ancestry or Flawed Research?"

New Avian Speed Champion Discovered

Job 9:10
"Which doeth great things past finding out; yea, and wonders without number."

A peregrine falcon diving toward its prey reaches a relative speed of 200 body-lengths per second. This is close to the 207 body-lengths that the space shuttle travels as it enters our atmosphere. Thus, the peregrine falcon was thought to easily be the fastest dare-devil bird on Earth.

Scientists have now discovered that a little pink male hummingbird called Anna's Hummingbird is the real Top Gun among the birds. As part of its mating ritual, a male hummingbird will try to impress a female with his speed and acrobatics. First, the male will fly up to about 90 feet above the ground. Then, he begins a power dive. As he nears the female, he pulls up, ascending again. During that near-miss pull-up he experiences more than nine times the force of gravity. His relative speed during descent is 385 body-lengths per second. That's almost twice the peregrine falcon's relative speed, it's faster than the space shuttle entering the Earth's atmosphere and is more than twice the relative speed of a jet fighter running with afterburners!

The wonders of God's creation are still being discovered, and Creation Moments still loves to make them known to our listeners. But God's greatest wonder is His love for us though His Son, Jesus Christ. We are thankful that this wonder is revealed to us in the Bible.

Prayer: Father, I give You thanks for the wonders You create, but I especially give You thanks for the wonder of salvation. Amen.

Ref: *Science News*, 7/4/09, p. 7, Susan Millius, "Hummingbird pulls Top Gun stunts."

Worm's Glue May Fix You

Job 12:7
"But ask now the beasts, and they shall teach thee; and the fowls of the air, and they shall tell thee...."

While materials scientists are always interested in super-strong glues, they are especially interested in super-strong glues that harden under water. It turns out that a small marine worm called the Sandcastle Worm has a few things to teach them.

The Sandcastle Worm builds itself a tube-like shell by gluing together sand particles and bits of shell. It is the glue it uses that is of interest to scientists. This amazing glue not only hardens under water, it hardens in 30 seconds. The glue comes from a special gland in the Sandcastle Worm. While it hardens quickly, after several hours it becomes like leather. After analyzing it, scientists identified several of the proteins that are responsible for its properties. They also found that half those proteins are either very negatively or very positively charged. Attempting to mimic the glue, scientists mixed together some of the same charged proteins to see if they would bond broken bone together in a wet environment. Their glue not only bonded the bone together, but remained neither acid nor alkaline which is crucial for materials used in living bodies. Scientists also report that the glue is not poisonous.

As we study how God created things, we are learning better ways to do things. This is surely evidence that an intelligent Creator is responsible for the creation.

Prayer: Father, prosper all good learning and knowledge, and keep us from falling into false knowledge. Amen.

Ref: Science News Online, http://www.sciencenews.org/index/activity/view/id/46544/title/worm-inspired_superglue, Rachel Ehrenbergm, "Worm-Inspired Superglue."

Magpies Reflect on Themselves

2 Chronicles 9:23
"And all the kings of the earth sought the presence of Solomon, to hear his wisdom, that God had put in his heart."

When you look in a mirror you are conscious of seeing yourself. Bottlenose dolphins, elephants and primates in general have also shown this ability, but that's about it.

Since social birds, like magpies, have larger brains than other birds, researchers wanted to find out if they would recognize themselves in a mirror. To do this, researchers placed a mark on the animal that can only be seen or touched when they look into the mirror. Most animals would have no idea that the creature in the mirror was themselves. Many animals would simply look behind the mirror and be puzzled. Even if they didn't, their lack of recognition of themselves would become evident when they did *not* seek to remove the unnatural spot from the image in the mirror. Researchers found that most magpies recognized the image in a mirror as themselves and sought to remove the unnatural mark from their own body while looking in the mirror. When given a choice, most of the magpies also preferred the compartment with a mirror in a two-compartment cage. The minority of magpies that didn't recognize themselves in the mirror preferred the compartment without a mirror.

It should be clear that attributes such as consciousness, wisdom and knowledge cannot be created by accident and chance. Only God could grant these things as His creatures need them.

Prayer: Father, I thank You for the gifts of wisdom and knowledge. Help me to use these gifts to Your glory. Amen.

Ref: http://www.sciencenews.org/view/generic/id/35462/title/1%2_magpie, Bruce Bower, "I Magpie."

Self-Cleaning Feet

Psalm 148:7, 10
"Praise the LORD from the earth, ye dragons, and all deeps ... Beasts, and all cattle; creeping things, and flying fowl...."

Here on Creation Moments we have often mentioned the gecko's amazing ability to walk up or even upside down on surfaces as smooth as glass. We have pointed out that the gecko can grip even a glass surface as it walks with microscopic hairs on its feet. These minute hairs actually grip the surface at the molecular level.

Noting that geckos never seem to clean their feet, scientists wondered what would happen if the microscopic hairs became fouled with microscopic dust particles. They computed that particles would have to foul between 26 and 59 hairs on each foot to be effective. They then fouled geckos' feet with micro-spheres and observed them as they walked on a glass surface. To their surprise, with each step the geckos' grip on the glass surface became stronger. This result suggested that with each step, the geckos' feet were shedding some of the micro-spheres. To determine if this was what was happening, scientists removed some of the fibers from gecko feet and studied their interaction with the micro-spheres. Their conclusion was that gecko feet are indeed self-cleaning.

Not only is the design of the gecko's feet amazing, but God evidently realized that His design would not work unless it was self-cleaning and able to shed dust. This design certainly cannot be attributed to a hit or miss process like evolution.

Prayer: Father, with all You have made, I praise You, not only for my being, but also for my redemption in Christ. Amen.

Ref: *Science News*, 1/8/05, pp. 21-22, P. Weiss, "Twinkle Toes."

Some Dinosaurs Ate Grass!

Job 40:15
"Behold now behemoth, which I made with thee; he eateth grass as an ox."

The Genesis creation account tells us that in the perfect world that God created there was no death. This means that there were no predators. In fact, Genesis 1:30 specifically states that God gave all the beasts and birds every green herb for food. And, yes, this would include all the dinosaurs. Some discoveries made in 2005 now add strong scientific evidence to support the Genesis account that in the beginning all the beasts ate the green herbs for food.

Of course, evolutionists found great amusement in these Bible claims since even plant-eating dinosaurs didn't have the right kind of teeth to eat, say, grass. And besides, they said, grass did not evolve until long after the dinosaurs were extinct. Scientists from India's Birbal Sahni Institute of Palaeobotony examined fossilized sauropod droppings to see what they were eating. Common in such droppings are bits of silica called phytoliths. These bits of silica were the remains of the plants eaten by those dinosaurs and are unique to each species of plant. To the surprise of the entire scientific community, the phytoliths were made by grasses, including relatives of rice, bamboo and forage grasses.

It is now unquestionably clear that grasses did exist when the dinosaurs lived and that the sauropods ate grass. On this fact, the Bible was right all along, and evolutionary science was wrong.

Prayer: Father, I thank You that Your Word is true in all that it teaches, including my salvation in Jesus Christ.

Ref: *Minneapolis Star Tribune*, 11/18/05, p. A4, Lauren Neergaard, "Rewriting prehistory: Dinosaurs had their grass and ate it, too."

Ants Go Homeless for Cheating

2 Corinthians 8:21
"Providing for honest things, not only in the sight of the Lord, but also in the sight of men."

Many plants give ants special protection and, in return, the ants protect these plants from other insects. In itself, this widespread arrangement offers evidence of design. However, sometimes these arrangements are even more complex than they at first appear.

A small tree that grows in the central Amazon of Brazil, called the *Hirtella*, offers small ants shelter in tiny pouches that form in pairs at the base of young leaves. Scientists prevented the ants from reaching some of the branches of a tree and noted that those branches lost about half of their new foliage to other insects. It appeared that the ants were keeping other pests off the new growth in return for shelter. However, scientists also found that the branches that had no ants also had eight times as many flowers as those branches the ants could reach. Apparently, the ants do a good job at protecting new growth, but once flowers begin to form the ants become the pests. The *Hirtella* doesn't ignore this. Once the new foliage is established and it is time to flower, the leaves drop the ant shelters so that the ants have to find somewhere else to call home.

This elegant defense arrangement is clear testimony not only to God's design, but also His provision for a complex creation with a vast array of creatures.

Prayer: Father, surround me with honest people, and help me to be honest so that my life reflects what I have in Christ. Amen.

Ref: *Science News*, 11/2/02, p. 285, "Ant cheats plant; plant cheats back."

"The Most Perfect Design I've Ever Seen"

Psalm 107:24
"These see the works of the LORD, and his wonders in the deep."

"The most perfect design I've ever seen." Those words were uttered by a materials engineer after studying a deep sea sponge from the Pacific Ocean. And, indeed, the *Euplectella aspergillun*, claimed to be an early and primitive sponge, can teach modern materials engineers a number of useful things.

The sponge's body is made up of a thin layer of cells over an intricate glass skeleton. The sponge grows into a cylindrical shape about 8 inches long and about an inch across. The wonder lies in the glass skeleton that is made up of vertical and horizontal beams of glass. Diagonal beams strengthen this grid. One-third of these beams are thicker than the others, adding the extra strength of ridges to the cylinder. What's more, each of these glass beams is made up of small cylinders of glass glued together with more glass-like tree rings. The result is a structure that spreads the pressures that might crush an ordinary glass structure this size. It is a delicate looking, but nearly unbreakable, glass structure. In a less than scientific test, one researcher noted that one has to jump full weight on one of these cylinders to even produce any cracking, and such jumping will still not break it.

"The most perfect design I've ever seen." There's little we at Creation Moments can add to that.

Prayer: Father, I thank You for all Your wonders, the greatest of which is Your love in forgiving me for Jesus' sake. Amen.

Ref: *Science News*, 3/25/06, pp. 184-185, Aimee Cunningham, "Making the Most of It."

The Worm Turns on Plants

Psalm 59:17

"Unto thee, O my strength, will I sing: for God is my defense, and the God of my mercy."

Regular listeners to Creation Moments are familiar with the many examples we have described of plants protecting themselves from insects.

A wide variety of plants make self-defense insect poisons by first producing the chemical jasmonate. Consideration was being given by the insecticide industry to stimulate plant defenses by spraying crops with this naturally occurring chemical. However, research now shows that this might not be a good idea. A worm – known variously as the corn earworm, the cotton bollworm or the tomato fruit worm – infests more than 100 plant species. This worm has two amazing abilities that probably explain why it's such a pest. First, it can sense when a plant begins to produce jasmonate, the first step in production of its self-defense poisons. When the worm senses jasmonate, it produces enzymes that will detoxify those plant's poisons. Studies have shown that spraying crops with jasmonate will only tip off the worm's detoxification abilities and make it more resistant to the plant's self-defense poisons. It appears that the plants rely on surprise to discourage the worms.

Of course, neither the plants nor the worms know anything about chemistry. It is the Creator of heaven and earth Who has given both the worm and the plants their defense mechanisms and, through His Son, Jesus Christ, has offered mankind protection from sin, death and the devil.

Prayer: Father, I thank You for the protection from sin, death and the devil that I have in Your Son, Jesus Christ. Amen.

Ref: *Science News*, 10/19/02, p. 246, S. Milius, "Spying on Plant Defenses."

Life from Blood

Genesis 9:4
"But flesh with the life thereof, which is the blood thereof, shall ye not eat."

The Bible teaches us that our physical life is in our blood. It also teaches us that our spiritual and eternal life is dependent upon the blood of Jesus Christ.

Your heart pumps blood at a speed of more than three feet per second. This means that any given red blood cell will make a full circulatory trip from your lungs and back in only about a minute. But your heart is not the only hard-working part of your circulatory system. Your red blood cells live only about 4 months. In that time, a red blood cell has made over 170,000 trips from your lungs to bring oxygen to every part of your body. That means your body must constantly replace red blood cells. So your body produces about 2 million new red blood cells every second. Your body does this most efficiently by recycling the iron from dead red blood cells into the new red blood cells. Iron, of course, gives the hemoglobin in red blood cells the ability to carry oxygen.

As we learn more about our circulatory systems, we see that physical life is a daily gift from God. Yet, it was the life-blood of our Savior, Jesus Christ, shed on the cross for us in His holy, innocent suffering and death that makes eternal life possible for us.

Prayer: Lord Jesus Christ, thank You for shedding Your life-blood on the cross so that I am forgiven and accepted by God. Amen.

Ref: *Science News*, 6/3/06, pp. 346-348, Ben Harder, "Blood, Iron, and Gray Hair."

Another Evolution Claim Goes Extinct

1 Corinthians 2:13a

"Which things also we speak, not in the words which man's wisdom teacheth, but which the Holy Ghost teacheth...."

Evolutionists regularly announce that they have scientifically proven that this creature evolved from that creature. Or they say that science proves that this creature or that one has been extinct for millions of years. Further, such claims are not to be questioned because they have been proven by science.

It's been well over a century since Darwin laid the foundation for these claims. Since that time, whole books have been written about how the alleged claims of scientific proof have, themselves, been proven wrong. Today, we add one more discovery to the list of unproven claims. Evolution claims that the Diatomydae, commonly known as the rat-squirrel, has been extinct for eleven million years. That is, until freshly caught rat-squirrels were found for sale at a meat market in Laos. The creatures have a rat-like face with a squirrel-like body and a not-very-bushy tail. They are smaller than the common squirrel. A careful analysis of the fossils and the skeletons of the modern specimens have convinced scientists that they are indeed the same creature. The rat-squirrels live deep in the forests of Laos seldom visited by Westerners.

Man's wisdom has given birth to the theory of evolution. God's wisdom, the heart of which is the Gospel of salvation in Jesus Christ, naturally contradicts man's wisdom where man is wrong. You can count on it.

Prayer: Father, I thank You for Your wisdom in Your Word. Help Your wisdom to dispel man's wisdom in my life. Amen.

Ref: *USA Today*, 3/9/06, Mark A. Klinger, "Rat-squirrel not extinct after all."

Hummingbird Wristwatches

Psalm 25:6
"Remember, O LORD, thy tender mercies and thy lovingkindnesses; for they have been ever of old."

When you remember something that happened and where and when it happened, you are using what scientists call episodic memory. Scientists have traditionally thought that such memory was unique to man.

Other scientists suspected that possibly some creatures may have episodic memory. For example, take the hummingbird with its fast metabolism. They need to eat often and remember where reliable sources of nutrition are to be found. At the same time, different flowers regenerate nectar at different rates. Researchers went to the natural habitat of the rufous hummingbird, equipped with some fake flowers and sugar water. The manmade flowers were constructed with reservoirs that could hold the sugar water. Half the flowers were refilled ten minutes after a bird would feed from it, while the other half were refilled twenty minutes after a feeding. Researchers found that the birds quickly learned which flowers were filled at which intervals. They soon returned to the flowers that were filled every ten minutes at ten-minute intervals while they waited twenty minutes in between visits to the other flowers. They noted that the birds did a good job of this even though they were keeping track of eight flowers.

It makes more sense to believe that episodic memory is a sophisticated ability that is the gift from a caring God to those creatures whom He knew would need it.

Prayer: Father, never let me forget Your love to me through Jesus Christ, Your Son. Amen.

Ref: *Science News*, 4/15/06, p. 237, "Hummingbirds can clock flower refills."

Doctor Lobster?

Leviticus 13:8
"And if the priest see that, behold, the scab spreadeth in the skin, then the priest shall pronounce him unclean: it is a leprosy."

The spiny lobster is a social creature. Lobsters like to congregate in groups in crevices and cooperate in defending their home against danger. When they migrate, they walk head to tail in single-file groups.

However, researchers have noted that certain lobster lairs contained only one lobster. They also noted that some of these loners did not appear healthy. Upon further study, they found that the lobsters that looked unwell were infected with a virus they named PaV1. That virus, they learned, is commonly spread by physical contact, although young lobsters can be infected through water contaminated with the virus. Further, underwater surveys revealed that even when the disease is not apparent, healthy lobsters avoid those infected with the virus. While 56 percent of the healthy lobsters were found sharing a lair, only 7 percent of the infected lobsters shared living space. In lab tests, 60 percent of the healthy lobsters avoided a hiding place it if had an infected lobster in it. Scientists don't know how the healthy lobsters can sense the virus, but it is obvious that they do and they avoid their sick comrades.

Before the advent of modern medicine, people knew to avoid others with obvious diseases like leprosy. It appears that God also gave the same ability to sense disease and avoid contact with it to the lowly lobster.

Prayer: Father, I thank You for the blessings of modern medicine. But I thank You more for the healing I have in Christ. Amen.

Ref: *Science News*, 5/27/06, pp. 325-326, S. Milius, "Lobster Hygiene."

Trying to Spin an Evolutionary History Out of Spider Silk

Job 8:13-14
"So are the paths of all that forget God; and the hypocrite's hope shall perish: Whose hope shall be cut off, and whose trust shall be a spider's web."

Scientists recently examined a well-preserved spider web encased in amber. It is the oldest example of a spider web in existence and was declared to be 110 million years old.

The researchers were eager to find out what the specimen might teach them about spider evolution. The web consisted of 26 strands of silk preserved in the amber while the pattern of the web appeared to be just like that of the modern orb-weaving spider. Three insects that were held by the web when it was encased in amber were also preserved. Interestingly, these three insects – a wasp, a fly and a mite – are the same three insects that are most often caught by modern orb spiders. Today's orb spiders place drops of glue along their web to capture their insects. The composition of the ancient glue and the modern glue were the same; however, it turned out that the ancient spider had applied the glue in a slightly different way from its modern cousin. From this small detail the researchers tried to spin an evolutionary tale about this spider. Mankind the world over uses different techniques to achieve the same purpose.

The fact remains that the ancient spider's web design and way of making a living were identical to that of modern spiders. There was certainly no evidence of evolution here.

Prayer: Lord, help me to more clearly see Your hand in Your creation and remember Your mercies to me every day. Amen.

Ref: *Science News*, 6/24/06, p. 390, S. Perkins, "Sticky Subjects."

Electric Singing and Arguing

Genesis 1:20a
"And God said, Let the waters bring forth abundantly the moving creature that hath life ...."

The brown ghost knifefish, popular in many aquariums, generates a weak electric signal that it uses for navigation and communication. The electric field they generate is too weak to stun prey. However, the electric organs that run along the sides of their bodies can pick up any changes in the field when the field encounters something with a conductivity that is different than water.

The communication aspects of the field are even more amazing. Male knifefish have been recorded singing to females by modulating their electric field. Researchers report that the males will sing like this for hours at night. However, when two knifefish who are hostile to one another encounter each other, they will raise the frequency of their electric field to jam their rival's signal. Researchers confirmed their conclusion that the knifefish were attempting to jam an enemy's signal by using a dummy knife fish. They rigged the dummy to generate signals that mimicked a knifefish. Then they placed two male knifefish in the tank with it. The two males were rivals to the dummy, and both male knifefish quickly raised their frequencies to jam the rival's signal.

Some people believe that mindless evolution gave the knifefish the ability to generate and control electric fields for communication as well as the ability to receive those signals. That credit clearly belongs to God!

Prayer: Father, I thank You that You have communicated Your love for me through the Gospel of Jesus Christ. Amen.

Ref: *Science News*, 11/19/05, pp. 324-325, S. Milius, "Tszzzzzt!"

You Can't Hear this Surprise

Psalm 5:3

"My voice shalt thou hear in the morning, O LORD; in the morning will I direct my prayer unto thee, and will look up."

The concave-eared torrent frog of China sings like a bird with a wide assortment of whistles and chirps. They live where streams and rivers splash down rocky mountainsides.

Researchers got a surprise when they were studying sonograms of the frog's singing that they had recorded on equipment used to study bats. The sonograms revealed strong signals above 20 kilohertz, and way above human hearing range. So scientists wondered, can the frogs hear such ultrasonic signals? To find out, they went to the frogs' habitat with equipment designed to record and play the full range of their songs. They then played the ultrasonic songs they had recorded. One of the native male frogs quickly responded. To verify that the frogs could actually hear the ultrasonic calls, researchers then placed electrodes into the portion of the frog's brain that processes hearing. Sure enough, the frog was hearing the ultrasonic calls. Further testing showed that the frogs can hear sounds as high-pitched as 34 kilohertz. They then realized that this makes perfect sense. The water splashing over the rocks in their habitat creates a lot of white noise, so the frogs need to communicate in sound frequencies well above that of the surrounding white noise.

This unique design reminds us that God cares for all of His creatures and has fully prepared each kind for survival.

Prayer: Thank You, Father, that You have promised to always hear the prayers of Your children in Christ. Amen.

Ref: *Science News*, 3/18/06, pp. 165-166, S. Milius, "Can You Hear Me Now?"

A Real Crime-Fighting Bat

Mark 4:22
"For there is nothing hid, which shall not be manifested; neither is any thing kept secret, but that it should come abroad."

Airport security is a major concern these days. There are many ways for those who don't have good intentions to hide things beneath their clothes. Now, thanks to a design they borrowed from our Creator God, scientists have come up with a way to make that virtually impossible,

The new security device is called Tadar and uses harmless high frequency waves to create images on a screen. The high frequency waves have a wavelength of only 3 millimeters. These waves reflect from anything that is blocking a person's natural radiation. This means that anything hidden under someone's clothing will be seen on the Tadar's screen. The screen itself provides ten 3-dimensional images per second. Tadar can see anything from a metal gun to plastic explosives since any object will obstruct some of the body's natural radiation. Tadar is also not invasive and can pick up objects hidden behind clothing up to 160 feet away. Tadar is named after the Brazilian bat, *Tadarida brasiliensis*, which uses the same high frequency pulses to find its prey.

The more sophisticated our technology becomes, the more obvious it becomes that the living things around us are not the product of chance. But while science can show us the hand of the Creator, only Scripture tells us of His love for us by sending His Son to save us.

Prayer: Father, I thank You that Your love for me is not hidden. It is shown to me in the death and resurrection of Jesus. Amen.

Ref: *Photonics Spectra*, 12/05, p. 172, "Bat Patrol."

Cooked Wasps

Psalm 82:3
"Defend the poor and fatherless: do justice to the afflicted and needy."

Domesticated honeybees in China are preyed upon by a native wasp. A single wasp can wipe out a nest of 6,000 bees before carrying off the larvae to feed its own young. The wasp does this by stationing itself at the entrance to the nest and killing the guards one by one as they come out to defend the hive.

However, the Chinese honeybees are not defenseless. If enough of them can get to a wasp, they will literally coat the wasp. Research shows that they are doing something even more effective than stinging it. They are cooking the wasp to death. Bees generate heat by shivering their flight muscles. Both European and Chinese honeybees use this strategy to heat their nest when it gets cold. Researchers found that a wasp, fully encased in honeybees, will be heated to 113 degrees F in five minutes, enough to kill the wasp. European and Asian honeybees can stand temperatures over 120 degrees. However, the Asian bees must muster half again as many bees to cook the wasp.

In God's foreknowledge, He knew that man's eventual sin would affect the entire creation. So He gave the creatures of His creation the ability to defend themselves. Likewise, He protects us from sin, death and the devil through the forgiveness of sins that is ours through Jesus Christ.

Prayer: Father, I thank You for Your protection from sin in Jesus Christ. Help me to protect the weak. Amen.

Ref: *Science News*, 9/24/05, p. 197, S. Milius, "Balls of Fire."

Photosynthesis in the Dark

Psalm 136:4
"To him who alone doeth great wonders: for his mercy endureth for ever."

A new bacterium that grows at depths of over 8,000 feet below the ocean's surface has been discovered. This discovery wouldn't normally be very noteworthy except for the fact that none of the sun's light reaches that depth, yet the bacterium makes its living through photosynthesis.

The emerald green organism was discovered off the Mexican coast in the Pacific Ocean. Named GSB1, the bacterium is what is classified as a green sulfur bacterium. These organisms thrive in a low oxygen, high sulfur environment. Those are the conditions found in deep-sea hydrothermal vents known as black smokers. These vents spew sulfur-rich, low oxygen hot water as hot as 750 degrees F. Just as a hot stove burner emits a small amount of light, water this hot also emits a small amount of visible light. Most of the light is infrared, which cannot be used for photosynthesis. The visible portion of the light is so dim that it cannot be seen except through night goggles. Yet the bacterium manages to perform photosynthesis in this very dim glow. This is the only known organism that performs photosynthesis without sunlight.

We are still learning about the wonders of God's unlimited creativity. However, His greatest wonder is His love, which led Him to send His only Son, Jesus Christ, to redeem us from sin, death and the devil.

Prayer: Father, I praise you for all Your wonders, especially the wonder of Your love and salvation. Amen.

Ref: *Science News*, 6/25/05, pp. 405-406, N. Moreira, "Grow in the Dark."

Plant Sniffs Out Prey

Psalm 104:14
"He causeth the grass to grow for the cattle, and herb for the service of man: that he may bring forth food out of the earth...."

The dodder is a very unusual plant and is known as one of the ten worst weeds found in the United States. A newly sprouted dodder seed does not bother to grow roots. Rather, it sprouts a tendril that grows out, looking for other plants. It has, at most, a week to find a plant from which to steal water and nutrients.

The dodder is a parasite and while it does not kill its victims, it will take enough water and nutrition to stunt their growth. The dodder actually costs California tomato growers $4,000,000 a year in losses. Researchers found that the species of dodder that causes most trouble to tomato plants actually "sniffs out" its victims. Scientists knew that plants emit pheromones or scents unique to each species. The researchers gave a sprouting dodder seed a choice of targets to grow toward, including a tomato plant. When the dodder seed sprouted, it immediately sent a tendril out to the tomato. In a more rigorous test, researchers connected possible targets in separate enclosures to the sprouting dodder with curved tubes. The dodder still found the tomato plant.

The dodder has no nervous system, and scientists marvel at what it can do. Rather, they should be marveling at what our Creator can do in providing for the needs of all living things.

Prayer: Father, I thank You for supplying our daily bread as well as our eternal salvation. In Jesus' Name. Amen.

Ref: *Science News*, 9/30/06, p. 214, S. Milius, "Scent Stalking."

Smart Mollusks

Job 21:22
"Shall any teach God knowledge? seeing he judgeth those that are high."

According to modern thinking, intelligence is a product of several factors. Of course, the most important requirement is that the creature must be high on the evolutionary tree. Intelligence is also related to life span, the longer the better, and the fact that they are social creatures.

However, don't tell this to a group of creatures who are considered very low on the evolutionary tree because they have very short life spans and are usually solitary. Various studies are showing that octopuses, cousin to the lowly clam, are among the most intelligent creatures on earth. Researchers have found that octopuses not only learn how to solve problems like mazes, but remember what they learn. They report that at one marine lab, some octopuses would sneak out of their tanks at night to eat fish in other tanks. But more indicative of intelligence is the fact that octopuses show personality. Different individuals may, for example, react to an unfamiliar item with curiosity, fear or even by attacking it. Another indication of intelligence is play. Octopuses will play with floating objects in their tanks in much the same way as a child will play with floating toys in the tub.

None of the traditional evolutionary explanations for intelligence apply to the octopus. Actually, none of those explanations apply to any creature since all received their intelligence from our Creator.

Prayer: Father, I thank You for intelligence. Help me to use it wisely to number my days on Earth. Amen.

Ref: *Discover*, 10/03, pp. 46-51, Eric Scigliano, "Through the Eye of an Octopus."

You Need a Healthy Laugh

Proverbs 17:22
"A merry heart doeth good like a medicine: but a broken spirit drieth the bones."

Laughing is good for you even if it does begin with the release of adrenaline and other stress hormones.

Whether you are tickled or reacting to a good joke, at least seven different centers in the brain react in various ways. Your response begins with the release of stress hormones. Your normal breathing rhythm gets interrupted, and various neurotransmitters, including dopamine, are released. And, yes, your brain also interprets the tickle so that you cannot tickle yourself since your brain knows when your own fingers are involved. Scientists also believe that as you begin laughing, your saliva glands begin to secrete extra immune compounds. Antibodies and virus-killing T-cells are also released in larger doses. Your heartbeats also increase, and your blood pressure goes up to support the muscle spasms that result from your laugh. Those muscle spasms are actually a good aerobic exercise. In fact, one minute of a good laugh is said to be as good as ten minutes of exercise on a rowing machine!

Besides promoting social bonds, laughing is indeed good for you in many ways. Tickling is a common way that parents bond with their young children. And wholesome humor can cheer the heart and raise the spirits. Moreover, while laughing appears to have no evolutionary advantage, it is easily explained as a gift of God to raise our spirits.

Prayer: Father, I thank You for the gift of laughter. Help me to use humor and laughing in a wholesome way. Amen.

Ref: *Discover*, 4/03, pp. 62-69, Steve Johnson, "Laughter."

What We Don't Know

Job 38:2-3

"Who is this that darkeneth counsel by words without knowledge? Gird up now thy loins like a man; for I will demand of thee, and answer thou me."

When we read biology textbooks or watch television programs about science and discovery we are led to believe that evolution is not a theory but a scientifically established fact. We are told with great confidence how life first arose on the ancient Earth or when each species first evolved and the precise evolutionary relationships between different creatures. And, of course, the impression is given that all of this is established beyond question.

But is that what scientists themselves are telling each other behind the closed walls of academia? In 2005, the scientific journal *Science* celebrated its 125th anniversary. As part of their celebration, they listed 125 questions that science has not answered. One of the questions was, "How and where did life on earth arise?" Apparently, scientists have not established the origin of life as a fact. Another question they said that science has not answered was, "What determines species diversity?" If this question has not been answered by science, how can science describe the history of the various species and their evolutionary relationships?

It would seem that the origin and evolution of life are not scientifically established facts despite how these are portrayed in textbooks and on television. These godless and fraudulent claims made for what is still the *theory* of evolution should not be allowed to deceive us and our children.

Prayer: Father, I thank You for Your revealed truth in Holy Scripture. Guide us so that none are misled by the world. Amen.

Ref: *World*, 7/23/05, p. 30, "Unanswered *Science* Questions."

A Potpourri of Blessings

Hebrews 6:7
"For the earth which drinketh in the rain that cometh oft upon it, and bringeth forth herbs meet for them by whom it is dressed, receiveth blessing from God...."

Many people like to have a nice perfume around the house. They brew a potpourri of mint, citronella, lavender and similar fragrant plants to make home smell more like home. But humans aren't the only creatures that appreciate a nice smell around their house.

During field studies, scientists have found that a small bird called the Corsican Blue Tit also likes to have a pleasant-smelling nest. This was an unexpected discovery, made quite accidentally when one researcher discovered various sprigs of aromatic plants in dozens of nests. When she starts to lay her eggs, the female bird will begin keeping her nest stocked with fresh, fragrant herbs until all the eggs hatch. The birds prefer yarrow, citronella, mint and lavender. When researchers secretly removed these herbs from the nests that they were observing, the parent birds were quick to replace the fragrant sprigs with others. It also turns out that these herbs also have disinfectant and anti-pest characteristics. They inhibit bacteria and fungi and act as mosquito repellents. Rather than simply beautifying their nests or adding a nice perfume, the birds are also protecting their offspring from diseases and pests. You might wonder, Who taught them to do this?

As the Bible says, herbs are a blessing from God. They are not just a blessing to man, but also to many of God's creatures.

Prayer: Lord, I thank You for all of the blessings You have given us. I especially thank You that You sent Your Son to save us. Amen.

Ref: *Discover*, 11/02, p. 13, Josie Glausiusz, "Eau D'Oiseau."

The Secrets of Hot Mineral Water

Genesis 7:11b
"... the same day were all the fountains of the great deep broken up, and the windows of heaven were opened."

How long does it take for large mineral formations to form? While evolutionists say millions of years, creationists assume that most of the rock formations we see formed relatively quickly as the waters of the Genesis flood receded.

In 1903, someone pounded an iron pipe into the ground in what is today Hot Springs State Park. The mineral-rich water beneath the ground immediately began flowing out of the pipe. As the warm mineral water evaporated, the minerals that were left behind deposited as travertine. Within just a few years, there was a mound of travertine as high as the pipe and tapering to the ground. Today, the water has stopped flowing. What remains today is a mound of minerals sheeted in pastel curtains over 20 feet high and more than 15 feet across.

The Bible's description of the fountains of the deep being broken up at the beginning of the Genesis flood suggests huge hot water geysers. Much of that water would undoubtedly have been like the mineral-rich waters of today's hot springs. This mineral water then mixed with the sediment created by the violence of the flood. As the sediment finally settled out and the waters dried up, the remaining minerals would help quickly bind the sediment together into the sedimentary rock layers we commonly see today. Those long evolutionary ages would be unnecessary.

Prayer: Father, I thank You that in Christ, you do not judge me as You judged those in Noah's day. Amen.

Ref: *Creation*, 9-11/05, p. 56, Tas Walker, "A Monstrous Mound of ... Minerals!"

The Latest on What Plants Are Saying

Psalm 33:20
"Our soul waiteth for the LORD: he is our help and our shield."

In past Creation Moments we have told how certain plants release aromatics known as pheromones when attacked. By this means they communicate to others of its species or even to animals. These discoveries led more researchers to enter this field, and a great deal is now known about what can only be called plant communication.

Researchers report that this plant communication is more widespread than thought. In fact, they suspect that it is almost universal among plants. What's more, plants not only communicate with their own species, but with other plants and even with animals. Some, like the wild tobacco, even know not to communicate when the intended recipient of the message is not around. It does not emit its anti-caterpillar scent until night time when nocturnal moths are liable to be around to lay eggs on them. Should the moths lay eggs on the plants, the plant will signal to an all-purpose insect ally to eat the eggs. That same ally will also eat other insect pests that harm the plant. Scientists say that not only are the plants' messages specific, it appears that an individual plant will vary its message based on its experience.

That plants even communicate with other species is a wonder that cannot be explained by chance mutations. That their messages are so specific bespeaks the intelligence of their Creator.

Prayer: Father, I thank You that I can call out to You when I need help, and You will help me because I am Yours in Christ. Amen.

Ref: *Discover*, 4/02, pp. 46-51, Sharman Apt Russel, "Talking Plants."

True Superglue

Psalm 9:1b
"I will praise thee, O LORD, with my whole heart; I will shew forth all thy marvellous works."

Try using superglue in wet conditions, and you'll find that the glue is not so super. Even epoxy doesn't work well in water. Scientists finally decided to turn to the lowly mussel to learn how to make better glues for use in wet environments.

Mussels manufacture their glue under water, yet the glue can withstand the force of a thousand pounds per square inch. Mussel glue will even stick to Teflon! The mussel begins by making the glue in two parts, each part made by a separate gland. One gland produces proteins that are like resin. The other gland makes the hardeners. When these are mixed, they harden into a strand in only a couple of minutes. The mussel will make many of these strands as it fastens itself to a rock. As more of these strands are made, they begin to cross-link with one another, greatly adding to the strength of the bond. The mussel makes between five and ten different kinds of protein strands, carefully limiting the cross-linking to produce the greatest strength. Without this mix, the bond would be brittle and easily break.

God's creation is marvelously designed. His designs are still teaching us how to do even simple things better. The theory of evolution depends upon random chance events that, even if believable, can teach us nothing.

Prayer: Father, I stand in awe of Your handiwork and rejoice in Your salvation. Amen.

Ref: *Discover*, 2/03, pp. 22-23, Alan Burdick, "Cement on the Half Shell."

The Biggest Flower You Wouldn't Want

Song of Solomon 2:12
"The flowers appear on the earth; the time of the singing of birds is come, and the voice of the turtle is heard in our land...."

The largest flower in the world is a bright red-orange color and, according to its DNA, is related to the poinsettia. That relationship might make you suspect that the world's largest flower would be beautiful. But you probably wouldn't want the flower, called the rafflesia, growing in your garden.

The largest of this species has flower buds the size of a basketball. When it opens, the flower is three feet across. Its petals not only look like big slabs of meat but the flower smells like rotting meat. The result is a rather ugly flower that you wouldn't want around. That bad smell attracts the carrion-eating insects that pollinate it. The flower looks so strange that when they were first discovered, scientists debated whether they were flowering plants or fungi. If this is not all strange enough, rafflesias have no true roots or leaves. They make their living as parasites growing on other plants. This makes them so difficult to grow that only four botanical gardens in the world have done it successfully.

The rafflesia's beauty lies not in its appearance, but in its amazing design features. Little about its design seems to be helpful for survival, as evidenced by how difficult it is to grow. This fact, of course, works against evolution's claim that the living things we see are the survivors of the fittest.

Prayer: Father, I praise Your unlimited creativity and the care You provide to all of Your creatures. Amen.

Ref: *Science News*, 1/13/07, p. 21, S. Milius, "Biggest Bloom."

Monkeys as Intelligent as College Students?

Colossians 4:6
"Let your speech be alway with grace, seasoned with salt, that ye may know how ye ought to answer every man."

Evolutionists claim that human intelligence began to develop when early man invented language. Genesis tells us that human language began when Adam named the animals. Names – that is, nouns – are the first requirement for language, but this must be preceded by intelligence. Creationists have always viewed both language and intelligence as gifts from God.

New research disproves the old evolutionary idea. Of course, we use language to test human intelligence using, say, a series of cards. Researchers at Columbia University did something similar with rhesus macaques. They sat the monkeys in front of computers with touch screens. The screens showed seven photographs that were not in sequential order. After learning how to place the photographs in order, the monkeys did just that for a banana pellet. This task involves both memory and logic. The monkeys quickly became good at ordering the photos. As they were shown new pictures, they showed that they could apply what they had learned to new problems. What's more, they learned the task as quickly as a control group made up of college students!

Since the monkeys in this experiment don't use language and they clearly possess memory and logic, language cannot be the source of our intelligence. A better explanation is that both language and intelligence are the gifts of God, given us by the Word Who created us.

Prayer: Father, thank You for the gifts of language and intelligence. Help me to always use these gifts to Your glory. Amen.

Ref: *Discover*, 6/03, p. 13, Jocelyn Selim, "The Smart, Speechless Types."

True Milk of Human Kindness

Jeremiah 32:22

"And hast given them this land, which thou didst swear to their fathers to give them, a land flowing with milk and honey...."

While many people recognize the virtues of feeding their infants human breast milk, science is still learning its amazing secrets. Although cow's milk contains many substances found in human milk, it does not contain certain very specific substances necessary to protect the infant.

Human milk not only helps protect the infant's digestive system by discouraging bad bacteria, it also introduces and encourages good bacteria. In fact, some of the good bacteria that protect the infant are found in no other place on Earth. Oligosaccharides in milk kill bad bacteria in a way in which the bad bacteria can never develop immunity. Lactoferrin in human milk can suppress inflammation. It also boosts the immune system and kills viruses, bad bacteria and fungi. Not only does the mother's milk pass mom's immunities on to the infant, the milk's oligosaccharides give infants immunity to germs the mother has never even encountered. The protein alphalactalbumin in an acid environment such as the digestive tract can even reduce warts and kill cancer cells. So far, alphalactalbumin has been shown to effectively kill forty different kinds of cancer cells. Use of this protein in preliminary clinical trials to treat bladder cancer has been promising.

While God has given us so many good things, we are still only discovering them. But the greatest of His gifts is salvation through His Son, Jesus Christ.

Prayer: Dear Father, thank You for all Your good gifts, especially the forgiveness of sins, eternal life and salvation. Amen.

Ref: *Science News*, 12/9/06, pp. 376-378, Julie J. Rehmeyer, "Milk Therapy."

The Sounds Smells Right

Psalm 4:1b

"Hear me when I call, O God of my righteousness: thou hast enlarged me when I was in distress; have mercy upon me, and hear my prayer."

Insects offer some novel designs. For example, they can have ears on their stomachs, wings or legs. Now, scientists at the University of Zurich in Switzerland have discovered an even more novel arrangement in the fruit fly.

Scientists have been aware for many years that fruit flies can respond to sound. Sound plays an important part in their mating rituals. However, scientists were unsure just how the fruit fly's hearing worked. They also knew that their antennae, known singularly as arista, had something to do with the way the fruit fly can hear sound. Because an arista is so small, only 300 microns long, scientists have until recently lacked the ability to take the fine measurements necessary to find out what is really going on. Now, all that has been overcome, and we learn that the base of the arista, which also senses smells, actually turns each arista toward the incoming sound. In short, the fruit fly actually rotates its nose so that it can hear better. Researchers have since found a similar arrangement in related flies. They suspect that such an arrangement will be found in several related species.

As amazing as this arrangement is, God's greatest wisdom is seen in His plan of salvation. Through His Son, Jesus Christ, He has gained the victory over sin, death and Satan for mankind.

Prayer: I praise You, heavenly Father, as I see Your wisdom all around me, especially in Your plan of salvation for me. Amen.

Ref: *Science News*, 6/23/01, p. 391, S. Milius, "Fruit Flies Hear by Spinning Their Noses."

Singing Mice?

Psalm 40:3
"And he hath put a new song in my mouth, even praise unto our God: many shall see it, and fear, and shall trust in the LORD."

Birds do it. Whales do it. Now, it appears that male mice do it. They all sing!

Scientists have long known that mice produce ultrasound. Their pitch is about two octaves above what we can hear. For example, when mouse pups lose track of mom, they begin to cry so that mom can find them. Researchers carried out investigations to see whether there is any structure to the sounds that adult mice make. They did this by recording the vocalizations of 45 male mice. Then they slowed down the recordings to study them. The researchers found distinct syllables at about ten syllables per second. In addition, their "voices" also rise and fall in pitch at varying rates. The researchers then found that certain syllables were repeated, creating phrasing sequences that sound very much like music. The researchers compare the mouse vocalizations to the songs sung by whales and birds. While other scientists recognize that the mouse sounds are not random, they question whether they should be called "song".

We know that music is a gift from God. It appears that God has been generous with His gift of music and just possibly has even extended this to the animal kingdom. However, only we humans have the privilege of praising Him with words and music for His gift of salvation through His Son, Jesus Christ.

Prayer: I praise You, Father, for the gift and beauty of music and for sharing it with so much of Your creation. Amen.

Ref: *Science News*, 11/5/05, p. 293, B. Harder "Beyond Falsetto."

A Most Amazing Escape Artist

Job 38:41
"Who provideth for the raven his food? when his young ones cry unto God, they wander for lack of meat."

A parasitic worm that matures on land but must breed under the water has some remarkable abilities to make this difficult trick possible.

The worm grows to maturity on dry land but must return to a body of water to find a mate and breed. It grows inside insects like crickets. The insects it infests are typically not aquatic, making this problem number one. When breeding time comes, the worm causes the insect to move in such an uncontrolled manner that it eventually ends up in the water. Once in the water, it takes the worm about 10 minutes to escape from the insect. However, an insect struggling on the surface of the water is very attractive to a hungry fish. This is problem number two. But if the worm can't wriggle free of the insect before it is eaten, the worm has more abilities to put into play. The worm inside an eaten insect continues to wriggle until it finally escapes through the fish's mouth or gills. Scientists studying the worm reported observing six escapes each from frogs and perch and more than 20 escapes from trout.

God has marvelously provided for this little worm. But then, this is easy for Him, considering He has provided us with escape from sin, death and Satan through the innocent death of His Son, Jesus Christ.

Prayer: Thank You for providing for all Your creatures, Father, and especially for providing me salvation in Jesus Christ. Amen.

Ref: *Science News*, 4/22/06, p. 252, "Worm Can Crawl Out of Predator."

The Lazarus Rat

1 Corinthians 8:2
"And if any man think that he knoweth any thing, he knoweth nothing yet as he ought to know."

According to evolutionists, the early family of mammals called Diatomyidae has been extinct for eleven million years. Of course, as creationists, we do not accept this dating. This Diatomyidae family included rat-like creatures with long skulls, a furry tail and rounded ears.

Then, in 1996, a wildlife-survey team bought some strange looking animals in a meat market in Laos. This led to the discovery of living Laotian rock rats. These animals were placed into a family that includes porcupines and guinea pigs. Others argued that it belonged to a new family. The debate sparked a more detailed look at its DNA and bone structure by researchers in five countries. The results ruled out any possibility that the rats were related to guinea pigs. But the rock rat's characteristic long skull, furred tail and round ears seemed to settle the matter. The Diatomyidae are not extinct, and the Laotian rock rat is indeed a member of this family. This discovery of thought-to-be extinct families happens frequently enough that such families are called Lazarus taxon or, more popularly, "living fossils."

So, when evolutionists proclaim that this or that creature or family has been extinct for millions of years, it takes only one living specimen to disprove it. Furthermore, many creatures do not appear in the recent fossil record, and this puts the entire interpretation into question.

Prayer: Lord, I yield all my wisdom to Your greater wisdom and ask for Your Holy Spirit to grant me heavenly wisdom. Amen.

Ref: *Science News*, 4/28/07, p. 260, S. Milius, "Living Fossil."

Lobsters Can Affect Our Thinking

Jeremiah 5:26
"For among my people are found wicked men: they lay wait, as he that setteth snares; they set a trap, they catch men."

With no backbone and not much of a brain, the lobster is usually depicted as pretty low on the evolutionary scale. It follows that lobsters are also intellectually pretty dim.

Populations of many sought-after species in North American fisheries have been dropping, as indicated by the numbers caught. The same appeared to be happening with lobsters. However, divers surveying lobster populations in lobster fisheries reported that there were plenty of lobsters. Why, then, were the catches going down? Zoologists curious about what was going on mounted video cameras on some of the lobster traps. The video showed that lobsters were entering the trap to eat the bait through the funnel-shaped opening, and when they were done they casually left through the same opening. The dimwitted lobsters were not supposed to be able to get out of the trap. Our so-called traps are, in reality, nothing more than lobster luncheonettes. Researchers concluded that the only lobsters that get caught are the lobsters who happen to be eating in the trap when it is pulled up.

The fact that lobsters are far more intelligent than worldly appearances would suggest means that we need to look at the world around us far differently than the people of the world. That's exactly what we are doing when we believe in creation as well as trust in Jesus Christ for the forgiveness of our sins.

Prayer: Father, deliver us from the traps of the devil – that we may rest in safety and peace under Your protective hand. Amen.

Ref: *Creation*, 3-5/09, pp. 38-39, David Catchpoole, "Lowly Lobster Surprise."

The Lonely, Bold Traveler

Psalm 107:8
*"Oh that men would praise the LORD for his goodness,
and for his wonderful works to the children of men!"*

Even life that exists where sunlight never reaches
nevertheless gets its nutrients as a result of photosynthesis.
Furthermore, no matter what the organism, it always lives in some
sort of community with other organisms.

Now a bacteria has been discovered that breaks both of
these rules. The organism, nicknamed "the bold traveler," was
discovered living in water-filled cracks in a South African gold
mine. It lives nearly two miles below the surface. And it shares its
habitat with no other species. Since there's no other life down
there, and they are totally cut off from the surface, scientists
wondered how they managed to get energy to carry on life. Further
study showed that the creatures are able to get energy directly from
the radioactive decay of the uranium that is found in the rock into
which the mine is cut. They are also able to extract carbon, which
is essential to life, directly from carbon dioxide. They can also
secure nitrogen, also essential for life, and which it extracts from
surrounding rocks. Scientists also say that the creature cannot
handle oxygen.

This discovery again illustrates the limitless creativity of
God. We rejoice as we see that He is not limited to creating life
that lives in what we call the "normal" way.

*Prayer: Father, we rejoice and marvel at the wonders
You have brought into being, the greatest of which is our
salvation. Amen.*

Ref: *New Scientist*, 10/9/08, Catherine Brahic, "Goldmine bug DNA may be key to alien
life," http://www.newscientist.com/article/dn14906-goldmine-bug-dna-may-be-key-to-
alien-life.html

Dinos on Ice?

Job 38:29

"Out of whose womb came the ice? and the hoary frost of heaven, who hath gendered it?"

The fact that dinosaur fossils are found in the Arctic suggests that there have been catastrophic changes on this Earth since those dinosaurs lived. Some of the changes, like the worldwide flood, are even described in the Bible.

More evidence of these cataclysmic changes are being found in Antarctica. Today, Antarctica is the coldest, driest place on Earth. Winds can rage at 200 miles per hour. Yet, under the ice, scientists are finding fossilized plants like ferns, pine trees and even ginkgoes. These finds provide evidence of a much warmer climate. But the fossilized remains of animals provide evidence of a considerably warmer climate. Fossils of three species of dinosaur have also been found. One has been named Cryolophosaurus or "cold-crested lizard," and was about 23 feet long. Another, Glacialisaurus, or "frozen lizard," was also about 23 feet long. A smaller dinosaur with spikes – named Antarctopelta or "Antarctic shield" – was about 13 feet long. These fossils were found in the same sedimentary flood layers as dinosaurs around the world. These fossils and the record of magnetization of various layers of rock provide evidence that Antarctica moved south to its present South Pole location during the year that it was covered with flood waters.

Even though God has allowed great cataclysms to strike the Earth, He has never left His own without His love and care.

Prayer: Father, in the face of dire predictions about catastrophe, teach me to take comfort in Your fatherly care. Amen.

Ref: *Answers*, 7-9/10, pp. 46-51, Buddy Davis, "Dinosaurs on Ice."

New Science Based on an Old Truth

Job 36:22
"Behold, God exalteth by his power: who teacheth like him?"

While the development of a new science is helping mankind, it says something that many scientists did not intend to say. The science is called biomimetics. As the name suggests, biomimetics is based on the idea that if we copy designs found in nature, we can often improve our own technology.

For example, a Japanese company developed special swimsuit material for the Beijing Olympics that provides less resistance in the water. Taking a cue from the swift marlin, the company developed material with imbedded polymers so that it mimics the marlin's skin's absorption of water. Schools of fish swim in a beautiful unison ballet without ever running into each other. Nissan Motor Company is studying fish schools to discover what it might do to build cars with better anti-collision equipment. Solar cells and light-emitting diodes certainly could be more efficient. Engineers learned that moths see so well in the dark because their eyes have special convex-concave design. That design means that the moth's eye surface reflects two to three-tenths of a percent of the light that hits it. Standard plastic film reflects four to five percent of the light hitting it, making the moth's eye much less reflective.

Whether biomimetics intends it or not, in looking to the creation to improve our designs, it recognizes the Creator as the Source of all knowledge.

> **Prayer: Father, the Source of all knowledge, we thank You for sharing Your knowledge with us. Help us to use it well. Amen.**

Ref: *The Nikkei Weekly*, 5/31/10, p. 17, "Preserving biodiversity benefits society, business, helps secure future."

In the Blink of an Eye

Psalm 6:6
"I am weary with my groaning; all the night make I my bed to swim; I water my couch with my tears."

The miracle takes place in the blink of an eye. Literally.

Every time you blink, you bathe the surface of your eye with a miraculous fluid called tears. Tears are not simply a salty water solution. They are made of water, but also have oils, electrolytes and sticky carbohydrates called mucins. In addition, they contain antibacterial and antiviral substances. One of these substances is called lysozyme. Any bacteria or virus that finds itself in tear fluid has a 95 percent chance of being dead within ten minutes. That blink of an eye keeps the surface of the eye properly moisturized so that our vision remains clear. Without this moisturization, your eyes would become red and painful, and, if untreated, you would probably go blind. Tear fluid also provides needed oxygen to the surface of your eyes.

But perhaps the most amazing property of tears is even more unexpected. Humans are the only creatures that cry emotional tears. Studies have shown that the ability to produce tears and cry actually helps us cope with emotional situations. There are some inherited diseases which make people unable to cry tears. Studies have shown that people with this disease cannot deal well with stress.

Tears are a blessing in many ways. But we also remember that God has promised to wipe away all our tears when we reach heaven.

> **Prayer: Father, I thank You for the gift of crying tears, and I thank You that You have promised to wipe away our tears in heaven. Amen.**

Ref: *Creation in the Crossfire*, 8/02, pp. 3-4, Jerry Bergman, "Design of tears: an example of irreducible complexity."

The Design of Speed and Precision

Psalm 8:3

"When I consider thy heavens, the work of thy fingers, the moon and the stars, which thou hast ordained...."

Studies show that it takes about a second to decide whether a person will do A or B. That's much too slow to make a successful typist or pianist. Good typists execute one key stroke every 60 thousands of a second. A pianist can play 30 notes with each hand about every 40 thousands of a second. How do they do it?

Then there is the precision of the microsurgeon who repairs structures in the body so small he must peer at them through a microscope. Part of the secret of this design is the muscle structure of each finger and the hand. The basic finger design begins with seven muscles. Your thumb has five additional muscles. And, believe it or not, your humble pinky finger has three more muscles than the basic design. The muscles don't work alone. The tendons of the hand and fingers add elastic force to the operation of the hand. Essential to making these elements work together with precision is your sense of touch. Your fingerprints add the ability to sense texture and forces with more precision. All of these elements combine with the brain which automatically thinks several keystrokes ahead of the typist's and pianist's keystrokes, resulting in the seemingly impossible abilities of the hand.

The human hand is a unique precision design that could only have come from God's hand.

Prayer: I rejoice, Father, in all that Your hands have made, including my hands, and in those Hands that were pierced for my salvation. Amen.

Ref: *Acts & Facts*, 10/09, pp. 10-11, Randy J. Guliuzza, "The Connecting Power of Hands."

The Fastest Flower in the Forest

Matthew 6:28

"And why take ye thought for raiment? Consider the lilies of the field, how they grow; they toil not, neither do they spin..."

The peace and serenity of North America's spruce forests is occasionally broken by little other than the rustle of a deer passing by. At least that's what most people think. In truth, there are things going on which would cause us profound wonder.

The bunchberry dogwood flower stands only about one-tenth of an inch tall. Scientists knew that the flowers opened explosively. The flowers do this to propel their pollen further. The scientists decided to find out precisely how fast the flowers really opened. So they decided to tape a flower opening with a high speed camera that is capable of taking 1,000 pictures a second. But the camera proved to be too slow. It was only with a camera that takes 10,000 pictures a second that they could clearly see what was going on. They saw that the petals opened, and in a separate action, the stamens unfold so fast that they catapult pollen into the air. All of this happens in four tenths of a thousandth of a second. That's more than a hundred times faster than a chameleon's tongue captures lunch. The stamens unfold so fast that they subject the pollen to 2,400 times the force of gravity.

There are no limits to the wonders God can conceive and create. His greatest wonder is His mercy which resulted in forgiveness and salvation.

Prayer: Father, Your wonders are generously spread about the creation. Thank You for the wonder they inspire. Amen.

Ref: *Creation*, 3-5/09, pp. 32-34, David Catchpoole, "Bunchberry Bang!"

Evolutionists Find Their Conclusions Flawed

Genesis 8:17

"Bring forth with thee every living thing that is with thee, of all flesh ... that they may breed abundantly in the earth..."

A surprising number of living things mimic other living things. We have done a number of programs on these wonders of God's creativity. However, evolutionary biologists discount such mimicry as any sort of wonder because in many cases the mimicry is imperfect. The biological term is "flawed mimicry."

Now evolutionary biologists admit that they may have to revisit their conclusions about flawed mimicry. Several species of orchid are known to mimic pollinators to attract their attention. An orchid called the *ophreys* orchid seeks to attract the males of several bee species by mimicking the scent of the female of the species. However, when scientists studied the exact composition of the pheromone mix used by the orchid, they found it wasn't quite the same as that used by the local female bees. So they labeled it flawed mimicry. However, as field scientists expanded their research, they made a surprising discovery. The orchids are able to change the pheromone mix of the scents they create to subtly change the scent they produce. In fact, the orchids were mimicking the scent of female bees some distance away. Why? Further research showed that male bees actually prefer so called out-of-town females to the local females.

What scientists thought was flawed mimicry is actually a fine-tuned design that can only be explained with intelligence.

Prayer: Lord, do not allow Your people to be misled by the flawed conclusions of false science when it contradicts Your Word. Amen.

Ref: http://www.sciencenews.org/view/generic/id/32628/title/Better_than_a_local_lady, Rachel Ehrenberg, "Better than a local lady."

253

Really the Universal Language

Luke 15:25
"Now his elder son was in the field: and as he came and drew nigh to the house, he heard musick and dancing."

It has often been said the music is the universal language. That now appears to be a scientific fact.

The Mafa farmers of Cameroon are almost completely insulated from Western culture, and that's fine with them. They don't know the Beatles from Beethoven. So scientists from the Max Planck Institute for Human Cognitive and Brain Sciences in Leipzig, Germany thought that they would be perfect for their study of music. Scientists played select pieces of Western music to Mafa volunteers. The volunteers, who had never heard the music before, were asked to identify what they thought the mood of the music was. Most of them identified as "sad" passages that were intended to be sad. Faster music was understood to be happy. And even passages intended to be understood as "fearful" were correctly understood by the volunteers. They also correctly interpreted the meaning of pieces written in major and minor keys. Likewise, Mafa music was played for Western volunteers. They correctly identified the mood being conveyed by the music. The Mafa people typically produce joyful flute music for their rituals.

Apparently, music really is the universal language. And music is natural to man. Genesis tells us that by the third generation of humans, musical instruments were already being fashioned.

Prayer: Thank You, Father, for the gift of music. Help me always to sing Your praises with joy in my heart. Amen.

Ref: *Science News*, 4/11/09, p.14. Bruce Bower, "Two Cultures Grasp Music's Universal Meaning."

Millions of Years Old DNA?

1 Timothy 6:20
"O Timothy, keep that which is committed to thy trust, avoiding profane and vain babblings, and oppositions of science falsely so called..."

While even many Christians feel obligated to accept millions of evolutionary years, evidence continues to build for a young creation. The evidence has mounted to the point that even many evolutionists feel they must find some explanation for it.

In a previous Creation Moments program, we talked about DNA and other cell material found unfossilized in what was otherwise a fossilized T. rex. Since then, a hadrosaur leg bone with intact blood cells has also been found. Then there is the mummified hadrosaur that was the subject of a television special. Even its internal organs were intact. According to evolutionists, we are supposed to believe that this mummy had not crumbled to dust in 77 million years. That claim is not credible, given our experience with the best preserved Egyptian mummies that are only a few thousand years old. Segments of DNA have also been found from Neanderthals, supposedly prehistoric mammals, plants and even bacteria. According to evolutionary dating, these samples range in age from 40,000 to 250 million years. Yet, we know that DNA is totally decayed in 10,000 years. Enough color pigment cells remain in a fossilized feather that you can still see the color pattern. Yet, it is supposedly more than 100 million years old.

While evolutionists have tried some explanations for this evidence, the simplest explanation is that they are young.

Prayer: Father, fill me with a greater hunger for Your Word so that, taught by You, I will not be misled by falsehood. Amen.

Ref: *Acts & Facts*, 6/09, p. 17, Brian Thomas, "Fossilized Biomaterials Must Be Young."

Chameleon Changes in Unexpected Way

Psalm 7:1b

"O LORD my God, in thee do I put my trust: save me from all them that persecute me, and deliver me..."

Evolutionary naturalists have predicted that a given creature should have pretty much the same strategy for dealing with any of the predators that seek it out. As our knowledge of the animal world grows, they are beginning to realize that they may have to reexamine their prediction.

Researchers have now established that a dwarf chameleon native to Africa does indeed use very different strategies depending on the predator. The two main predators the chameleon faces are snakes and birds. After observation in the wild, naturalists decided to test the chameleons' reactions to these predators under controlled conditions. They captured some chameleons and then tested their reactions to a fake snake or a stuffed bird. When the snake was placed where the chameleons could see it, the chameleons turned pale and hugged the branch they were on. When the bird was introduced, the chameleons color-matched their branch much more closely while hugging its underside. Further study led the researchers to see the wisdom of these strategies. The snake looks up from the ground and sees the chameleon against the bright sky. The birds look down and see the darker branch.

Obviously, the chameleons didn't figure this out by themselves. God gave them these strategies for their protection.

Prayer: Father, help me to trust more completely in Your protection, both in physical matters and in the spiritual. Amen.

Ref: http://www.sciencenews.org/view/generic/id/32396/titl/These_colors_dont_run, Susan Milius, "These Colors Don't Run."

The Buzz About Chance

Acts 1:26

*"And they gave forth their lots; and the lot fell upon
Matthias; and he was numbered with the eleven apostles."*

With the early morning dew on the leaves, a vegetable
garden may seem a very peaceful place. Actually, though, it's a
war zone.

If you know what they are, you don't want to see army
worms in your garden. But when they hear a wasp fly by, they stop
eating and sometimes even fall off the branch they are on. This is
probably because a number of wasps eat caterpillars. Researchers
realized that honeybees can produce the same result in caterpillars
since they sound like wasps. They decided to find out what was
really going on under controlled conditions. They set up two tents
with various types of plants. In one of the tents, they also placed a
beehive and then hung bottles of sugar water around the tent.
Researchers then placed beet army worms into both tents. In the
tent with no bees, the army worms munched away nonstop. But
much less damage was done in the tent with bees because the
worms stopped eating every time they heard a bee fly over.

The evolutionist researchers explained that this is simply a
"happy side of the effect of pollination." In other words, chance.
But the Bible teaches that there is no such thing as chance. God's
always in charge. This is why you find them casting lots in the
Bible to decide matters.

**Prayer: Father, I thank You that there is no such thing
as chance and that You are always in charge. Amen.**

Ref: http://www.sciencenews.org/view/generic/id/39514, 12/22/08, Susan Milius, "Buzzing
Bees Protect Plant Leaves."

Darwin and His Followers Draw the Wrong Conclusions

2 Peter 3:6
"Whereby the world that then was, being overflowed with water, perished..."

Charles Darwin once wrote of the fossil record, "No organism wholly soft can be preserved." That's because evolutionary orthodoxy says that fossils are buried and formed by slow, natural processes. In reality, there are many fossils of soft-bodied animals like jellyfish and squid. That is evidence, of course, of rapid, catastrophic burial at the time of the flood. Darwin rejected the flood and therefore got the science wrong.

It is not unusual to find deep sea creatures in the lowest levels of fossil-bearing rocks. This, too, would make sense in light of the flood. But it is clear that Darwin was wrong again. While living specimens of some of the fossilized squids have now been found, they also have all of the complete features of modern squids. They all have fully functional refracting-lens eyes and the well-known "jet propulsion" of modern squid. One fossilized squid, dated 150 million years old by evolutionists, was so perfectly preserved it looked like it could still have ink. Researchers even reconstituted real ink from its fossilized ink sac. The ink, which looks the same as modern squid ink, was even used to draw a picture of the fossil. There should have been no ink after all that time, so it looks like the Darwinists were wrong on the age, too.

In contrast, God's Word stands vindicated.

Prayer: Father, lead me into all truth, and preserve me and Your church from being misled by falsehoods. Amen.

Ref: *Acts & Facts*, 8/10, p. 18, Brian Thomas, "Tentacular Squid, Re-writing Squid Stories Before the Ink Dries."

Meet the Horror Frog!

Psalm 20:1b
*"The LORD hear thee in the day of trouble; the name of
the God of Jacob defend thee..."*

Did you know that there are salamanders that can grow spines? They do this by forcing their ribs to grow through their skin. But a frog nicknamed the "horror frog" is even stranger.

When it is threatened, the "horror frog" breaks bones in its foot and extends the ends of the broken bone through its hind foot pads. The result is a catlike claw. The "horror frog" is actually a family of eleven frog species, nine of which are able to perform this grisly feat. Most of these species are native to Cameroon. One end of the broken bone is attached to a special muscle that pushes the bone through the foot pads. Once the threat is past, the bone claw pulls back into the foot and the tissue heals. To add to the "horror frog" aspect, these frogs also are hairy. The hair actually turns out to be hair-like skin growth. As unappetizing as they sound, they are prized for roasting and eating.

Before death came into the world, the "horror frog" would probably not have any need for claws to defend itself. Yet, just as God knew that we would need a plan for our salvation, He also knew that creatures like this frog could benefit from a method of defending itself. So He gave this frog this creative method of defending itself.

Prayer: Father, protect me from all dangers in this life, both spiritual and physical, assuring me of Your presence. Amen.

Ref: http://www.newscientist.com/article/dn13991-horror-frog-breaks-own-bones-to-produce-claws.html?full=true&print=true, 5/28/08, Catherine Brahic, "'Horror frog' breaks own bones to produce claws."

Letting God Create Your Day, Volume 6 Index

Contact us to order:

- *Letting God Create Your Day* books as well as other books and DVDs about biblical creation.

- "Creation Moments" on CD
  (each containing 30 programs).

- Ministry information.

Creation Moments, Inc.
P. O. Box 839
Foley, MN 56329
1-800-422-4253
www.creationmoments.com